Praise for *When Loving You Means Losing Me*

"Through many years of personal and professional experience, Amy Lewis Bear helps us understand the dangers of losing oneself in a relationship. Among other essential insights, she illuminates twelve core truths and seven paradoxical cycles that culminate in abusive relationship dynamics. Then she walks us so brilliantly through the process of healing and ending self-neglect to help us reconnect with our true selves. This book, in combination with her first book, *From Charm to Harm*, helps us see clearly the intricate, often impossible-to-describe dynamics that permeate relationships and lead to loss of self. She beautifully partners with readers to help them take a hard look at the truth in their relationships through the unique insights gleaned from her own and her clients' stories. This is a masterfully written must-read that helps articulate the full extent of the damage and pain that, once acknowledged, can be healed. This book will help my clients and me in numerous ways. Thank you, Amy, for this helpful clinical guide."

—**Tara Arnold**, PhD, licensed clinical social worker; founder and clinical director of Deepen Wellness & Psychotherapy

"We find companions with similar life struggles in the most unexpected places. I'm very fortunate to have met Amy Lewis Bear and been afforded the honor of reading her personal journey, insight, and clinical awareness to identify what so many women and men experience. She has put into words the very story, feelings, confusion, and doubt that I also endured. Defense mechanisms I employed are clearly identified and understood; physical responses I felt were isolated issues are, in fact, not. The puzzle pieces that were scattered on the floor for the last twenty-eight years are knowingly and intentionally placed and connected seamlessly by this author, now showing me what I knew but couldn't see. So many loving and empathetic people need help finding their way through one-sided relationships. Amy Lewis Bear takes your hand and walks with you through your self-discovery, only because she can see it from the inside. Anyone who has loved and struggled to understand why their energy is consumed, their empathy depleted, and their heart fortified against lies will find this book on their nightstand, dog-eared, highlighted, and with pencil marks in the margins on their personal journey to finding themselves again."

—**Christina Chapman**, medical social worker
and case management educator

"Amy Lewis Bear successfully extends the literature exploring how abusive relationship dynamics emerge and how one can manage and recover from these dynamics. Her insightful work is filled with research examples, clinical vignettes, and review questions to illustrate and explore concepts from the Echo Complex, and represents a much-needed contribution to the field of psychotherapy that is rooted in established psychoanalytic theory and psychological trauma recovery research. This book will benefit psychotherapy practitioners working with clients who are experiencing relational abuse, as well as those with lived experience of relational abuse who are seeking a deeper understanding of their experiences."

—**Courtney L. Crooks**, PhD, clinical psychologist and
psychoanalytic/psychodynamic psychotherapist

"Amy Lewis Bear's work powerfully clarifies how abusive relationship dynamics form and, more importantly, how people can heal from them. Grounded in solid psychoanalytic theory and trauma research, this book is an essential resource for both therapists and survivors seeking real understanding and recovery."

—**John Gray**, PhD, bestselling relationship author of
Men Are from Mars, Women Are from Venus

"*When Loving You Means Losing Me* is an eye-opening, heart-awakening guide for anyone who has slowly disappeared inside a relationship. With tenderness and insight, Amy Lewis Bear invites the reader to pause, listen beneath the surface, and recognize the subtle ways we trade our needs, desires, and values—our very sense of self—for connection. Through illuminating examples and soul-stirring reflection questions, the book helps us understand how we got here and reminds us that reclaiming ourselves is not only possible but necessary. Ultimately, the book leaves us with the empowering truth that our most vital relationship is the one we have with ourselves."

—**GG Renee Hill**, author of *Story Work: Field Notes on Self-Discovery and Reclaiming Your Narrative*

"Wow. This book puts words to what so many women feel but struggle to explain: the slow, quiet loss of self that can happen in love. Amy Lewis Bear masterfully reveals how emotional disconnection erodes confidence, identity, and voice, while guiding readers back to clarity, self-trust, and wholeness. *When Loving You Means Losing Me* is not just eye-opening; it's freeing. Every woman who has ever questioned herself in a relationship needs this book."

—**Rainie Howard**, bestselling author of *The Love Habit: Daily Self-Care Practices for a Happier Life and Healthier Relationships* and *Addicted to Pain: Renew Your Mind and Heal Your Spirit from a Toxic Relationship in 30 Days*

"Amy Lewis Bear shares her story and deftly weaves it in with the stories of her therapy clients to illuminate how relationships often accepted as 'normal' can erode one's sense of self. She offers her insights and meaningful steps toward reclaiming one's true identity. This is an all-too-necessary guide for our times."

—**Gus Kaufman**, PhD, cofounder of Men Stopping Violence

"Amy Lewis Bear offers a profoundly insightful and compassionate exploration of relational self-loss in *When Loving You Means Losing Me*. Through the lens of the Echo Complex, she brings clarity to dynamics that are often minimized, misunderstood, or misattributed, helping readers reclaim their inner authority, voice, and sense of self. This book is both a healing companion for readers and a vital clinical resource for mental health professionals."

—**Pamela Madsen**, licensed professional counselor, educator, clinical supervisor, and owner and clinical director of Sea Change Psychotherapy

"Amy Lewis Bear gives readers permission to dig deep and be vulnerable by honoring all of their parts, because she bravely does the same. *When Loving You Means Losing Me* tenderly captures how self-loss can happen in relationships and offers a hopeful, grounded road map back home to yourself. This book is both a mirror and a guide for anyone ready to reclaim their voice, boundaries, and sense of wholeness."

—**Leah Marone**, licensed clinical social worker and author of *Serial Fixer: Break Free from the Habit of Solving Other People's Problems*

"This enlightening, insightful, and deeply honest book illuminates the subtle dynamics that erode our sense of self in emotionally distant relationships. Blending professional wisdom with personal experience, the author offers clear truths, relatable stories, and practical tools that help readers recognize emotional distancing patterns, reclaim identity, and rebuild inner strength. It's a powerful guide for anyone who has ever lost themselves in love and is ready to break harmful cycles and reclaim their voice, inner clarity, and worth."

—**Lauren Taylor**, licensed clinical social worker and founder of Inner Balance Counseling

AMY LEWIS BEAR

When Loving You Means Losing Me

HOW TO ESCAPE THE ECHO COMPLEX AND RECLAIM YOUR SENSE OF SELF

BROADLEAF BOOKS
Minneapolis

WHEN LOVING YOU MEANS LOSING ME
How to Escape the Echo Complex and Reclaim Your Sense of Self

32 31 30 29 28 27 26 1 2 3 4 5 6 7 8 9

Library of Congress Control Number: 2026932157 (print)

Cover image: © Getty Images/ Tree drawing By johnwoodcock
Cover design: Broadleaf Books

Print ISBN: 979-8-3419-0074-5
eBook ISBN: 979-8-3419-0075-2

Printed in India

Safety Warning

If your partner is physically violent, or if you fear that they may become so, make safety for you and your children, if you have them, a top priority. Emotional abuse can escalate into physical violence, and reading this book may put you at greater risk if your partner is emotionally or physically abusive. If you are in any way concerned about your safety, please consider the following safety precautions:

Use caution when accessing this book. If you're reading digitally, consider using incognito or private browsing mode and clearing your browsing history afterward. Delete any downloads or eBooks from your device if you're concerned they may be discovered.

Keep physical copies in a secure location your partner doesn't have access to, such as at work, a friend's home, or tucked away in a personal item.

Do not confront your partner based on anything you read here. The knowledge you gather here should be used for safety and clarity, not to attempt to change your partner or engage them in conflict.

Have a safety plan. If you don't already have one, find one online or contact a domestic violence hotline or shelter to create one. Don't wait for a crisis to ask for help.

Where to Get Help:

United States:
National Domestic Violence Hotline: 1-800-799-SAFE (7233) or text "START" to 88788
[https://www.thehotline.org]

Canada:
Talk to someone 24/7: 1-866-863-0511
[https://www.sheltersafe.ca]

United Kingdom:
National Domestic Abuse Helpline: 0808 2000 247
[https://www.refuge.org.uk]

Australia:
1-800-RESPECT (1-800-737-7328)
[https://www.1800respect.org.au]

If you are outside these countries, search online for a local domestic violence helpline or shelter. Use a safe device if possible.

You don't have to be alone. Help is out there to keep you and your loved ones safe.

To Jay, whose integrity, generosity, and wholehearted
presence have shaped our lives in memorable ways.

CONTENTS

INTRODUCTION

On the day I married him, my first husband shoved a piece of wedding cake in my face. There I stood with a sticky mess around my mouth and down the front of my mother's wedding dress in the midst of white tables and bouquets of flowers and a Russian Balalaika band ready to entertain friends and family, some reacting with astonishment and others with nervous laughter. Forcing a silly grin to hide my humiliation, I knew his act was no joke. It seemed to say: *Don't get too close or I'll punish you.* But although the message he conveyed was literally in my face, I didn't get it. I spent the remainder of the day wondering why he had done that and who was to blame, him or me.

In the two years leading up to our wedding, I had experienced what felt like an undercurrent of resentment toward me expressed in his inconsiderate behavior. He often showed up late and made excuses, disapproved of things I said or did, and provoked bruising arguments over what seemed like insignificant things. Whenever I voiced my concern and questioned him about the reasons for his behavior, he dismissed my feelings. *It's no big deal. Get over it. Let's go to dinner.*

The stress in our relationship after we married grew more significant, influencing not only us, but also me. Unable to fully trust him or my own words and actions while in his presence, I began to feel emotionally unsafe with him. As I searched for meaning in the incomprehensible behavior of the man I loved, and who I thought loved me, I found myself striving, again and again, to reconcile with him after misunderstandings, arguments, and conflicts. My misguided attempts did at times seem to restore calm, at least temporarily. However, they also led to losing myself in the relationship. By that, I mean my thoughts, feelings, and actions were no longer those of the woman I had been before I met him. Rather, they became a reflection—or echo—of his confrontational behavior. Before I met him, I took pride in being an independent woman with good instincts and the ability to make sensible decisions. Now, I made many of my choices based on what I thought would avoid conflict, keep the peace, and what I believed he wanted. It got to the point where I hardly knew myself anymore. Still, for a decade, I clung to the illusion that ours was a devoted partnership without fully understanding what that required.

Years later, I looked back and realized that all my attempts to resolve the discord had been futile. Why? Because I had seen my relationship through a skewed lens. I misinterpreted his behavior, unaware of why my responses to it didn't work. My efforts to improve his behavior, such as giving up my right to make decisions, disregarding my need for emotional support and transparency, and explaining away his attacks on my self-worth, only made things worse. Both of us, in fact, misunderstood the real source of our turmoil. Given that lack of awareness, it was inevitable that fear, mistrust, and disconnection would ultimately lead to the end of our marriage.

In time, I remarried and had a very different marriage experience. I also became a therapist and found myself sitting across from others who wrestled with confusion, pain, and self-doubt in their relationships, just like I had in my first marriage. Many of them—targeted by their partner's rage, cruelty, and physical violence—had it worse than I did. But we all had one thing in common. We had let go of ourselves to hold on to our relationship.

I've now been a therapist for nearly twenty years, and over the course of my career, one truth stands out: Relationship troubles are shaped by a variety of unseen forces that can chip away at a person's sense of self. This loss of self often happens in relationships where there are other challenges, such as codependence, addiction, personality disorders, neurodivergence, cultural influences, and intimate partner violence (IPV), including emotional abuse. But those issues are not the focus of this book. Instead, this book is about the gradual loss of self that occurs in one partner as a reaction to the other's fear of emotional intimacy and the harsh and hidden ways they create emotional distance.

The good news is that finally seeing previously unseen forces that cause loss of self can help us be true to ourselves. We can stay grounded in our personal values, update ways of thinking that keep us stuck in misunderstanding, and reclaim our independence. In these pages, I will share with you the healing wisdom and insights I've gathered from a dual perspective as both a survivor and a healer. This perspective gives me a unique viewpoint on being in a relationship with a partner who fears intimacy and uses distancing behavior to avoid it. So, I use the word '*we*,' including myself, because I've been there too. Client stories and vignettes, with names and some details changed to protect confidentiality, will bring these insights to life by showing what happens in relationships in which one partner becomes an echo of the other. Introspective questions and exercises will help you discover new perspectives on relationship conflict and loss of self, and, most importantly, what you can do about it.

This book is for you if you've ever felt like you've given up parts of yourself in love, whether your relationship is new, long-term, or has ended, and whether you're in an opposite-sex or same-sex relationship. It will provide you with the knowledge you need to recognize what drives the loss of a sense of self, reclaim your identity, and determine whether there are possibilities for improvement in your relationship. This book is also intended for those who have a loved one who has lost themselves, or is at risk of losing themselves, in a relationship. Psychologists, psychotherapists, and other mental health professionals may find the book useful to better understand the Echo complex and provide a helpful resource for clients and patients. And this book is essential for young people entering intimate partnerships. Having these insights and learning from the experiences of others will help them make better choices and avoid losing their sense of self.

In part 1, I introduce the Echo complex: the gradual loss of self that results from misguided reactions to a partner's subtle and harsh ways of creating emotional distance. Understanding this complex is essential to recognizing and naming its harmful symptoms and effects on one's sense of self. Knowing this promotes healing and the reclaiming of selfhood. I also share my own story of how I lost myself and found my way back.

In this section, you'll also examine twelve core truths, such as why a partner's demeaning treatment often reflects their feelings about themselves rather than how they feel about you. We'll explore seven paradoxical cycles that arise when relationships turn out to be very different from what we expected, such as the glass wall paradox and the silent scream paradox. We'll delve into two echo mindsets that contribute to the loss of self and learn how to identify them, such as making assumptions biased toward existing beliefs, desires, and expectations, even when evidence suggests otherwise.

In part 2, we will delve into the heart of healing to reconnect with our true selves. This involves learning to recognize and respond to the signals our minds and bodies send when we feel threatened by our partner's refusal to see, hear, and understand us. By slowing down and paying attention, we realize that our bodies and emotions guide us, reminding us of what matters, what we need, and when we neglect ourselves. Trusting these inner signals helps us stay rooted in our values and aligned with our deeper truths.

In this section of the book, I invite you to join my therapy sessions with Sharon, Derek, and Sarah, where you'll witness pivotal moments as each of them begins to transform from an echo of their partner's actions to finding their voice in their relationships. In these examples, Sharon learns to stop trying to be the "good wife," Derek gets assertive with his domineering partner, and Sarah finds the strength to be the adult in her relationship.

At the end of most chapters, I've provided a list of key points along with questions and exercises to help you reflect on your relationship and better understand what you're feeling and why. Throughout the chapters, you'll find insights and guidelines that will help you feel grounded, more like yourself, and learn how to approach your partner from a position of strength when they avoid emotional intimacy with hurtful distancing behavior. I recommend having a safe place to keep a journal to record answers to the questions and writing exercises.

In the final chapter, I'll provide you with practical tools to help you build a sense of peace and safety, creating an inner sanctuary. These include ways to care for yourself with compassion, to release self-blame, and to understand that your partner and your relationship do not define your value. We'll also explore how to set personal boundaries without feeling guilty, how to love someone without taking responsibility for their actions, and whether there's a possibility to build emotional closeness with your partner, if and when that feels right for you.

As you read this book, you might feel a flicker of apprehension, maybe even fear. Looking inside the dynamics of your relationship with unflinching honesty can feel daunting. But truth, even when it shakes us, is the key that unlocks the door to freedom and growth. I know this because facing the truth about my first marriage changed everything. It cleared the way for the deep love and fulfilling life I have today. I've watched countless clients take that same brave step, transforming their lives in ways they once thought impossible.

Whether you're at risk of losing yourself in your relationship or recognize that a loss of self is already happening, this book is your invitation to see the unseen, to name what's been holding you back, and to step into the fullness of who you are, because losing yourself should never be the price of loving someone.

So settle in, take some deep breaths, and let's take this journey together.

Part I

Getting Lost in Intimate Relationships

CHAPTER ONE

The Echo Complex

PICTURE A WOMAN sitting in bed in the soft light of early morning, staring at her reflection in the dresser mirror across the room. The woman in the mirror appears faded, indistinct, as if parts of her are missing. The thought strikes her that her image reflects how she feels about herself—like a washed-out version of who she used to be. Forcing a dry swallow, she runs her fingers through her hair and wrestles with her confusion. How could who she is now be so different from the woman she was when she first met the man sleeping beside her? How is it possible to believe he loves her when she feels so wrong about their relationship?

At first, he told her he had been searching for her for a long time. He proudly introduced her to his friends and colleagues. They celebrated three months together with a trip to the Bahamas. She felt special.

Now, she feels small, like a shameful child who has misbehaved and longs to be forgiven.

He used to be receptive to her opinions and ideas and seemed impressed with the way she got around in the world. He asked her lots of questions and said he wanted to know everything about her. She felt acknowledged and understood.

Now, she feels unseen, like a prop brought onstage when needed and stored away in a prop closet when not.

Before she met him, she excelled at work, enjoyed hiking in the mountains with friends, and found purpose in organizing charity events. Now she leaves the house less often. When she's home and available for him, there's less chance he will accuse her of doing things she wouldn't dream of, like cheating.

She revisits her memories, trying to understand what went wrong. Although initially flattered by his insistence that they spend all their time together, she soon felt uncomfortable and pulled back on being available. But he objected, so she changed her plans to please him. She questions why she tolerated his demands on her time. He pushed her to move in, but when she said it felt too soon, he ghosted her. She feared losing him, so she agreed. Now, she struggles to make sense of his disrespectful behavior and why she ignored her concerns.

She recalls a time when they were out with friends and he called her stupid. His comment felt hostile, unlike how people in love usually treat each other. When she later expressed her embarrassment, he rolled his eyes and told her she was being too sensitive. On another occasion, she sought comfort and reassurance from her partner after a coworker claimed credit for her ideas. However, he doubted whether she really had the right to own them. A new question occurs to her: *Has he ever truly been a source of emotional support for me?*

She had swallowed many hurt feelings to hold onto hope for their future together. Why hadn't she realized that if he thought it was okay to demean her, it would happen again? She feels weighed down by the shame of all those painful feelings. Why would a man who claims to love her make her feel like she can't do anything right?

His behavior is often a mystery to her. Many times, she has asked him to tell her what's wrong when he sits in silence with a sour face for no clear reason. But he bars her attempts to draw him out by blaming her for some slight, unknown to her, or telling her to leave him alone. She has long wanted to know why he gets angry at trivial things, like the argument that broke out when she reminded him to take out the trash. Later, he stormed out of the house and returned late with a flimsy excuse for where he had been. She hadn't wanted to believe he'd cheated on her, so she'd cast aside her suspicions when he said he loved her the next day. But if he truly loved her, why did she feel bad about herself in their relationship?

She had tried countless times to get him to share his innermost thoughts when he seemed sad, worried, or alone, and calmly explain the reasons for his withdrawal or aggression toward her, but to no avail. She recalls a night during dinner out when she took his hand, looked into his eyes, and started what she hoped would be a heartfelt talk. But he yanked his hand away, told her they wouldn't have any problems if she weren't so selfish, and said she was the one who needed to change. She thought, *Change? Change what? Just tell me what it is, and I'll change. Anything to fix our relationship. Surely, there's something we or I could do to be happy in love again*. But he turned away, and she dropped the conversation like an egg splattering on the floor. Soon one egg turned into three, then ten, then dozens, and many more. Putting aside her needs and feelings, and measuring her words and actions to avoid conflict, became routine.

To cope with her hurt and frustration, she'd twisted the truth into all sorts of configurations in her mind, hoping he would eventually see the error of his ways. *We're seventy-five percent good, twenty-five percent bad. That's not so terrible*, she'd thought. *We have fun together and share friends. He seems to need me. Every relationship has its problems*. But her justifications were fleeting. After making them, she always relapsed into worry and confusion.

She had tried to tell a friend about the trouble she was having. But it was difficult to explain her relationship when she didn't understand it herself, when her shame made her feel like she was less than she needed to be for him. So she misrepresented his behavior and the depth of her distress. "He gets moody and angry at times," she told her friend. "And he's hard to talk to. But I put up with it because I really care about him. Plus, he's not always like that. I know he loves me in his own way." She'd left out the parts where he ridicules her when she dares to want affection and a listening ear. Where he expects her to drop everything when he needs something, calls her ugly names, and breaks promises. But her misery became impossible to conceal. Friends grew worried as her texts dwindled and the number of declined invitations piled up. At work, she no longer feels inspired. She has stopped taking pride in dressing well, has stopped trying to succeed at her job, has stopped trying, period.

As she sits gazing at her reflection, her mind spins with questions about why her life and relationship are so different from what she expected. *Is there something missing in me? Am I not smart enough, sexy enough, or interesting enough? Have I bought into the idea that it was my job to make him happy, believing that if I did, he would love me? Haven't I realized that spending most of my time tending to his needs and feelings meant neglecting my own?*

In the shadowed room, she looks down at her partner sleeping soundly. Her life revolves around him, and she's frightened by the prospect of leaving. But she has tried everything she knows, given all she's got to save the relationship, and there is no sign that things will change. She feels trapped in a relationship with a man who claims to love her but doesn't act like he does.

She realizes that she's been so consumed with saving her relationship that she couldn't see who she's become. Rising quietly from the bed, she walks to her dresser and looks into the mirror one more time.

How a Loss of Self Happens

Romantic relationships can be confusing, especially when someone says they love you but their actions tell a different story. Their words might sound right: "I love you," "I want you," "I couldn't make it without you." At times, you feel loved; at others, you feel overlooked and unimportant. They pull you close physically, but you don't feel fully seen, heard, and understood. And instead of mutual give-and-take, you feel like you do most of the giving.

You try to bridge the gap by tucking away your needs, quieting your feelings, and softening your edges, hoping that if you can just be easier to love, things will finally feel right. You convince yourself that maybe this is what love is supposed to be—messy, complicated, and sometimes an uneasy fit. But underneath, you feel a dull ache. You realize you're not fully present in the relationship because you feel a need to edit yourself to keep the peace.

This is how so many people begin to lose themselves in love, not all at once, but piece by piece. It feels like you're fighting for the relationship, but in reality, you're losing yourself in it. And that's the heartbreak no one talks about: being in a relationship where the very act of trying to be loved becomes the reason you stop being who you are.

Does any of the following ring true for you? When with others, you appear content, but on the inside, you're weighed down with worry that you can't shake off. It's as if you're living in an alternative reality where being in love means surrendering rather than savoring the best parts of yourself. Having a relationship with mutual understanding, trust, open communication, and the right balance of give and take seems to be too much to ask.

You're left feeling unsure how to respond to your partner's hurtful behavior. *Should I protest and fight back? Is it best to keep my hurt feelings inside and try to be the person my partner wants me to be? Am I to blame? Am I not giving enough? Am I being too sensitive? Too demanding, unappreciative, or too hard to please? If it's not just me, how can I fix my partner?* Continuing to ask yourself these questions without understanding the deeper reasons behind them will only pull you further into confusion. You'll keep trying to find the right way to respond, reshaping yourself to fit what you think your partner needs, until you lose sight of the best parts of who you are.

That's because you're asking yourself the wrong questions. Instead of focusing on what might be wrong with you or how you can "fix" your partner, ask why your partner doesn't "see" you. Ask why you're in a relationship with someone who won't share their inner thoughts and feelings and doesn't want to hear or appreciate yours. Ask why you're compromising yourself to enable this dynamic. Ask why your partner expects you to cater to their demands without considering how it affects you, and who doesn't value the importance of you maintaining a strong sense of self in the relationship. Because that's what could be happening here.

Having a strong sense of self requires being authentic, which is the core of healthy functioning. Some of the greatest minds in psychology over the past eight decades—such as Karen Horney, Carl Rogers, Irvin D. Yalom, Rollo May, and more recent psychologists like Marianne

Lammers—have shown that authenticity is not optional. It's vital. Being authentic allows us to live by our personal values, resist conformity or neurotic adaptation, and lead meaningful, connected lives. If you're not basing your questions on the truth about your relationship and finding the right answers, you're at risk of losing your authenticity.

When you start to realize how much of yourself you're giving up in your relationship, you begin to see a deeper pattern emerging. This is what I call the Echo complex. It happens when you feel unable to safely express your needs, feelings, and your true self. To avoid rejection or conflict, you adapt to your partner's demands, criticism, or emotionally distant behavior rather than openly expressing yourself. Or maybe you do express yourself, but your partner won't hear you.

In this state, your identity becomes muted, as if you're an echo of your partner rather than fully being yourself. While this defense might seem protective in the moment, over time it weakens your sense of self and, in some cases, your ability to form a deeper emotional connection with your partner.

The turning point happens when you realize you've developed the Echo complex. Whether or not you feel like you are losing your sense of self, you *are* holding back some of the best parts of who you are in the relationship. And if you can't be yourself, who are you? Seeing your relationship, your partner, and yourself from this perspective raises a new question: *Do I want to embrace my true self and live authentically in my relationship, or will I continue to be an echo of my partner?*

The Echo Complex, Explained

As with other psychological complexes, the Echo complex is not found in the *Diagnostic and Statistical Manual of Mental Disorders* (DSM-5). Rather, it is a reactive coping pattern that occurs in intimate relationships. It involves the erosion of a sense of self that arises from maladaptive thoughts, emotions, and behaviors developed in response to chronic conflict. When you experience the Echo complex, you often feel uncertain about whether you are to blame for the problems in your relationship. You say and do things that go against your personal values. Sometimes, you go along with your partner even when you don't want to. You may lash out in ways that contradict your true nature while attempting to defend yourself. You feel ashamed and struggle to feel good about yourself. You may tell others (and yourself) that the trouble you're encountering is a communication problem or the regular ups and downs of a relationship. You may see your partner as moody or stubborn, or as someone with anger issues.

But what's likely happening here is that your partner won't let you into their inner emotional life because they fear being vulnerable. So they keep you at an emotional distance with controlling behavior. And when we share our lives with a partner who avoids emotional intimacy with hurtful behavior, whether that behavior is withdrawal or aggression, it is vital to understand that serious harm is occurring. Psychologist Marti Tamm Loring, in her seminal 1994 book, *Emotional Abuse*, stated that one partner's intentional interference with emotional connection in an intimate relationship and the other partner's struggle to attach is an emotionally abusive dynamic. This dynamic is not a normal relationship conflict.

So don't underestimate the severity of what's happening when your partner intentionally withholds emotional connection, and you try to bridge that gap by compromising yourself. Understand that your hurt feelings come from your partner's lack of emotional transparency and your struggle to be truly seen and understood. When you recognize how they treat you for what it is, you'll have a much better chance of addressing it. Of course, you cannot change another person's behavior. You can, however, change your response to it. Which brings us back to the Echo complex. I refer to this condition as a complex for significant reasons that I'll explain.

Early in the twentieth century, renowned psychoanalysts Sigmund Freud and Carl Jung recognized that harmful psychological experiences can be identified and treated when they are named as complexes. A complex is a structure within the unconscious mind that links together emotions, memories, and perceptions arising from threats to the stability of the self. They saw complexes as deeply rooted in personal history and at the core of primary drives and conflicts. Although complexes are mostly unconscious, if we are unaware that we are experiencing one, it can take control of us. On the other hand, when we become aware of its influence, it begins to weaken and lose its power to affect us.

In their work, Freud and Jung utilized the importance of ancient myths to illustrate the universal nature of complexes. One myth that conveys the loss of self in relationships is the story of Narcissus and Echo. In Ovid's tale of the two wood nymphs, Narcissus spurns Echo's love and falls in love with his reflection in a pond. Echo, cursed to repeat only the last few words spoken to her rather than speak in her own voice, echoes his words of farewell until she wastes away. It's a story that symbolizes how one partner becomes an echo of the other partner's preoccupation with themselves.

Like many ancient myths, the tale symbolizes the human condition. Teacher and scholar Charnell Peters, who studies race and relationships, found in her research that loss of self in relationships can happen to anyone. I've also found this to be true in my experience treating clients for loss of self regardless of their race, gender identity, sexual orientation, ethnicity, religion or spirituality, nationality, age, ability, or socioeconomic status. All of them are looking for love and emotional connection.

Emotional Connection Is Love

On their second anniversary, Cassie sat across from Dirk in a quiet corner of an Italian restaurant, bathed in the soft glow of candlelight. The night should have been a lovely acknowledgment of their time together. But instead, Cassie felt a deep sense of loneliness that was getting harder to bear. After their server took their order, she took a sip of wine and tried one more time to talk with him. "I want to be with you, Dirk, and I believe we can build a happy life together," she said. "But I feel like you don't see me anymore. The way you treat me sometimes makes me feel like you don't even want to be with me." Dirk's jaw tightened. He set down his glass and glared at her. "What are you talking about? You're overreacting. We're fine. You just expect too much."

The sting of his words silenced her. Cassie wanted to explain that she wasn't blaming him. She only wanted him to share his inner thoughts and feelings with her. But Dirk wasn't comfortable with displays of tender feelings, his own or hers. As a child, he had learned to bury his emotions, believing they were a weakness to be ashamed of. When Cassie tried to feel closer to him, he saw her feelings as a weakness, too. She looked away, not knowing what else to say. She didn't want to turn their anniversary into a painful memory, so she took another sip of wine and let it go, for now.

The need for emotional connection is a powerful human instinct. We look for it in all our close relationships: family members, friends, and most of all, our intimate relationships. A caring, supportive partner who is tuned in to us, to our feelings, and to what matters to us, provides us with a sense of safety and well-being. This genuine connection requires open and honest communication, as well as a willingness for both parties to be vulnerable with one another. Psychologist Sue Johnson, the founder of emotionally focused couples therapy (EFT), one of the most effective therapeutic interventions for couples, says genuine intimacy and friendship can only develop between lovers within the safety of trust and acceptance. Many psychological theories, including relational-cultural theory, state that people need emotional connection and growth-fostering relationships based on trust, understanding, and acceptance to flourish. Without empathy, there can be no emotional intimacy.

When we can count on our romantic partners to provide a secure emotional base, we have the space to grow into the best version of ourselves. In her research, Carnegie Mellon University social psychologist Brooke C. Feeney found that close relationships promote thriving across the lifespan. Having the secure base of an intimate relationship, an individual can gain confidence, feel more positive and develop the courage to pursue their dreams, goals, and desires without jeopardizing their relationships. As we grow and learn more about ourselves in this freedom, we can live a better quality of life.

Think of a secure emotional connection as something like a mountaineer's base camp. For climbers, a base camp is more than just a pit stop. It's a lifeline. It's where they find rest, nourishment, and encouragement from their team. It's a place to regroup, acclimate to challenges, and gather the strength needed for the next ascent. Just as mountaineers wouldn't attempt to summit a treacherous peak without the security of their base camp, those of us in intimate partnerships also need a solid emotional foundation in our relationships—a space to feel safe, supported, and free to push beyond our limits, knowing we have a trusted place to return to. Here's what it looks like to have a base camp, or secure emotional connection, in your relationship:

Belonging—You and your partner feel a genuine sense of mutual understanding and being understood.

Acceptance—You both accept each other the way you are, quirks and all. Both partners also encourage each other's self-acceptance.

Support—Your relationship has a level of trust and safety that allows you and your partner to be vulnerable and reveal yourself to each other. You don't keep feelings from each other that cause emotional distance.

Encouragement—You and your partner encourage and support each other in reaching your full potential as individuals.

Courtesy—You and your partner feel mutual respect and treat each other with kindness.

Attentiveness—The two of you are fully present when you're together, which cultivates a deep sense of connection and closeness.

Make allowances—During disagreements, you and your partner both respect each other's right to their own viewpoint.

Patience—You and your partner navigate through each other's imperfections with compassion.

The emotional connection, or secure base camp, in our intimate relationships is a place where we can find comfort and security, knowing that we have a partner who truly sees and cares for us by listening with genuine interest and without judgment, by offering comfort and assurance when we're struggling, and by respecting our boundaries and differences. From a strong "we" emerges two secure "I's." Each person is free to go after their calling, purpose, and goals in life. Base camp provides a foundation for both parties to pursue their rightful life's journey, fueled by self-respect and the support of a loving partner.

Twelve Behaviors That Create Emotional Distance

1. Talking over your words and not listening to what you have to say.
2. Dismissing and invalidating your needs and emotions.
3. Accusing you of overreacting when you express a feeling.
4. Demonstrating a pattern of isolating behaviors, such as anger, stonewalling, and excessive absence or absence without explanation.
5. Expecting you to know what they want without telling you.
6. Refusing to share vulnerable feelings, such as fears, insecurities, or emotional pain.
7. Displaying a pattern of blame, accusation, harsh criticism, or unreasonable demands.
8. Avoiding an honest and open conversation about your relationship.
9. Disclosing in public something you shared with them in confidence.
10. Putting you down, but claiming they were joking.
11. Questioning or criticizing your skills, capabilities, intelligence, or achievements.
12. Contradicting what you say, starting unnecessary arguments, and always having to be right.

Seeing Beyond First Impressions

Finding a partner who can provide us with an emotional base camp is not easy. It takes some sleuthing beyond the excitement of a new relationship to uncover what lurks in the shadows of our initial perceptions. At the outset of a new relationship, we may not be able to detect if our partners have unresolved issues that hinder the trust, empathy, and vulnerability necessary for emotional connection. Sometimes we are drawn to such partners because we haven't faced our own unresolved issues, which can lead us to people who aren't emotionally available.

Later, after we've taken a blind dive into the relationship, driven by the inexorable pull of sexual chemistry and the seductive dreams of a future together, we may become puzzled and distressed when our love interest rebuffs our attempts to connect on a deeper emotional level, especially if they previously seemed to welcome them. If we aren't aware of the quick judgments we've made about our partners and the misconceptions we've come to believe about our relationship, we may find ourselves in a relationship that lacks the qualities we thought were there.

In this situation, it can feel as though the ground beneath us is shifting and crumbling as we struggle to establish an emotional connection. We feel self-doubt and distress instead of confidence and contentment. Sue Johnson explains in her book *Hold Me Tight* why the lack of emotional connection has such a powerful effect on our lives:

> Love is the best survival mechanism there is, and to feel suddenly cut off from a partner, disconnected, is terrifying. We need to reconnect and express our needs in a way that prompts our partner to respond. This longing for emotional connection with those nearest to us is the emotional priority, overshadowing even the drive for food or sex.

Occasional disconnection is not necessarily a problem. It's normal for couples to experience periods of disconnection due to life's changes and challenges, like the arrival of children, a loved one's illness or death, financial concerns, or difficulties at work. When both partners can openly discuss and resolve the disconnection with mutual trust and respect, it can reestablish the connection and even strengthen the relationship.

However, an emotional connection cannot exist when we cannot express our needs and feelings without fear of reprisal. That's because our needs and feelings comprise who we are as individuals. Psychiatrist Jean Baker Miller and clinical psychologist Irene Pierce Stiver, two of the founders of relationship-cultural theory, found in their research that when we conform to be accepted by our partners, our emotional health deteriorates, and it can lead to a loss of self.

Influences of the Past on Vulnerability

It's hard not to take our partners' treatment of us personally, but understand that their actions can reveal a lot more about them than they do about us. They mistreat us not because they don't accept who *we* are, but because they don't accept who *they* are. They're shaped by early experiences where needing love and understanding came at a cost—hurt, rejection, shame, and intimidation.

Psychologist and Turkish scholar Seydi Ahmet Satici led a team of researchers who found that childhood psychological neglect and maltreatment often causes lasting shame and distorts family communication patterns. These issues can predispose individuals to shame-driven defensive behaviors in adulthood. Polish-Swiss psychologist Alice Miller, in her classic book *The Drama of the Gifted Child*, emphasized that toxic shame, a deep-seated belief that one is fundamentally flawed and unworthy, can result in a lack of self-compassion, difficulty forming healthy relationships, and a tendency to repeat dysfunctional patterns. She explained that toxic shame develops during childhood in environments of abuse, including emotional neglect, inflicted by one or both parents. Processing such mistreatment is difficult for a child because they have an evolutionary drive to repress feelings of anger, blame, and betrayal so they can continue to receive their parents' acceptance and protection. Adults are often likely to repress these childhood memories, which a stressful life event, such as feeling vulnerable, may trigger. In his influential book, *Healing the Shame That Binds You*, American psychologist John Bradshaw argues that toxic shame can lead to dysfunctional family systems, characterized by a lack of intimacy, poor communication, and manipulative behavior. Those with toxic shame learn to associate vulnerability with danger, causing them to alienate themselves from it. As adults, they keep their guard up, convinced that sharing their inner emotional life will make them appear weak or defective. Their behavior, driven by shame, disregards their humanity, and since they don't respect their own, they're not likely to respect ours.

The paradox here is that our emotionally withholding partners need love even as their fear of it pushes away those who love them. Instead of being open to intimate conversations, they use power and control to keep us emotionally distant. They dismiss our feelings, needs, and opinions. They make irrational demands and groundless accusations. They criticize what we say and do. They may alternate between angry outbursts and stone-cold silence.

Of course, occasional transgressions may occur in any relationship, but it is the respectful resolution of them that allows couples to move past the conflict. Unfortunately, not all partners are willing and able to do this. Our partners' behavior tells us what is true for them. When our partners consistently treat us with contempt, it suggests they're unlikely to be genuinely interested in resolving problems, despite their claims. Resolving conflict requires being vulnerable and taking responsibility for wrongdoing. Their apologies may be genuine in the moment when they want to feel close, but if they repeat the behavior, it becomes clear that apologies alone, without action, are just empty words.

And so we learn to concede to their demands to protect ourselves from their defenses against vulnerability and preserve the relationship. However, this comes with a high cost. Our partners' defenses against vulnerability put us under stress, leading us to doubt our judgment, lose confidence, act in ways we wouldn't normally, and remain in a state of discontent.

The Seven Stages of Developing an Echo Complex

Little by little, it's possible to lose yourself in a relationship without fully realizing it. Over the years, I've observed how this unfolds, starting with subtle signs that become more noticeable. I've identified seven basic stages of how this happens. I share this not to alarm you but to help you notice when you might be falling into these patterns. My hope is that by recognizing them, you'll feel more able to protect your identity and well-being. These insights are drawn from this book and other experiences in my therapy practice. I've seen my clients go through some or all of these stages, as well as the stages of reclaiming selfhood (Refer to page 222 for the seven stages of reclaiming selfhood).

Keep in mind that everyone has their own experiences and outcomes in relationships. The stages aren't necessarily linear. Someone in a relationship who is at risk of developing the Echo complex might fluctuate between stages or remain stuck in one stage. As you read this book, you will find a more in-depth explanation of each stage.

1. A False Sense of Connection
   Believing in an emotional connection with someone before trust and genuine emotional intimacy has been firmly established. The need to believe overrides early signs of trouble.
2. Doubt and Disharmony
   Questioning a partner's actions and the disparity between personal feelings and the partner's feelings about their behavior. Sticking to existing beliefs about the partner and relationship, even when evidence suggests otherwise. Echo behavior often starts at this stage.
3. Misinterpretation
   Misinterpreting or downplaying a partner's harmful actions to fit existing beliefs. Upholding false perceptions while questioning or disregarding personal intuition and emotions.
4. Resistance and Compliance
   Alternating between pushing back and going along with a partner's distancing behavior to avoid conflict and keep up the illusion of a strong relationship. Compliance might not align with personal needs, values, or expectations.
5. Prioritizing the Relationship over Personal Identity
   Valuing a relationship over a sense of self. Making an unspoken agreement with a partner to give up needs, desires, and goals in order to maintain the relationship.

6. Resignation and Conforming
   Adjusting beliefs, values, and personality traits to appease a partner. Some aspects of identity may remain, such as parenting or career.
7. Loss of Self
   Having the feeling of living inside someone else's story. Their needs, moods, and judgments dominate, while personal identity feels erased, invisible, or unsafe to express.

Aggression as a Defense Against Intimacy

Jackson and Wyatt had been together for almost three years in a relationship that seemed stable from the outside. But what those outside the relationship couldn't see was that Jackson kept a lock on his tender emotions. He could discuss work frustrations or anger about random things that bothered him, but when Wyatt tried to explore Jackson's more vulnerable feelings—fears, hopes, the places where he hurt—Jackson closed up. He felt exposing his raw emotions would only end in disappointment. Wyatt, who prized openness and emotional intimacy, felt shut out of Jackson's inner world.

One evening, Wyatt confided in Jackson how alone he felt in their relationship. He needed to know what Jackson held in his heart, so they could feel they were truly sharing life rather than just living side by side. But instead of being open to Wyatt's loving words, Jackson folded his arms across his body, as if to say, *That door is closed.* The more Wyatt tried to explain his desire for closeness, the more Jackson's tone of voice became more abrupt, leading to blame, accusations, and hard feelings. Wyatt felt shaken, both by the aggression in Jackson's defense and by the dawning awareness that Jackson might not be capable of the emotional closeness Wyatt longed for.

Jackson and Wyatt show that what starts as a quiet holding back of vulnerable emotions can turn into a more aggressive form of defense. We often see these defenses as our fault for wanting too much from our relationship because that's what our partner tells us. We may hesitate to share our feelings, not only about our partners but also regarding other difficult life situations where we need emotional support, because we worry that our partners might withdraw emotionally. This can lead to a frustrating and painful sense of disconnection in the relationship.

Using Sex to Simulate Emotional Intimacy

Even though our withholding partners can become aggressive in defending their vulnerability, their desire for connection may lead them to seek emotional intimacy in ways that create the appearance of closeness without truly achieving it.

For some, sex can be a way to feel connected without feeling vulnerable. It offers a fleeting sense of bonding without the emotional risks that genuine intimacy requires. The dopamine rush from sex can also serve as a temporary escape from feelings of emptiness or loneliness. In some cases, sex can be about exerting power and control rather than being the meaningful experience that loving partners seek.

When one partner is emotionally distant during sex, it can make the experience feel disconnected for the other person or cause them to feel used, especially if they were pressured into it by their partner but weren't feeling up to it because of hurt and resentment. For the partner who pressured them, instead of acknowledging their part in causing the disconnection, they might blame the other for refusing sex. They often fail to see that their partner's hesitancy isn't about rejecting them sexually but about feeling emotionally unsafe with them.

The opposite problem can also happen. Sometimes, the emotionally distant partner refuses sex when the partner seeking intimacy wants it. When someone struggles with toxic shame and an intense fear of emotional intimacy, they might withhold sex as a way to protect their vulnerability. Because vulnerability triggers shame, they avoid sexual intimacy to keep those painful feelings at bay. Withholding can also serve as a way to gain control in a relationship. In this way, the refusal isn't just avoidance but also a defense, keeping them safe from shame while making their partner feel "small" and unwanted.

When this happens, the partner avoiding intimacy might seek emotional and sexual validation outside the relationship, where flirtation, affairs, or pornography feels safer to them. Casual or anonymous sex seems less intimidating than the genuine connection needed for a committed relationship.

Choosing the Relationship over Ourselves

When our partner's behavior conditions us to read their moods first and then react, over time, we become muddled about what actually occurred. As we struggle to understand why our partners dismiss us, we often give in to their demands to gain approval, whether in small or large ways.

Personal identity slowly diminishes as the relationship takes precedence, beginning with small concessions that grow into more significant ones. We might let our partners choose the movies we watch, the places we eat, or the clothes we wear. Over time, we make larger concessions, such as giving up work that we love or other interests and hobbies, or we tolerate neglect and verbal abuse. We might isolate from friends or relatives or act in ways that would have been unthinkable just a short time ago. Making personal choices is our right, and giving them up takes an emotional toll on us. We begin to feel anxious and depressed, and we may develop physical ailments caused by our body's reaction to stress. Common responses to stress include anxiety, headaches and migraines, muscle tension, digestive issues, sleep disturbances, fatigue, and low energy. Our passions and activities may lose their appeal. Our feelings of guilt, shame, and resentment accumulate and eventually block our ability to be free and spontaneous.

Charnell Peters and her doctoral student Aimee J. Burns highlight the importance of recognizing how a partner's hurtful behavior can affect us. In their extensive research, Peters and Burns explain how tactics such as coercion, intimidation, or manipulation, can significantly distort a person's sense of self and their relationships. They introduce the concept of "identity veiling," in which the identity formed through the relationship overshadows a person's original identity. They argue that recognizing and naming their partner's offensive behavior is a critical first step toward recovery. Without it, individuals may remain trapped within the "veiled" identity constructed by their partner's manipulative behavior.

When Family and Friends Are Concerned

We aren't the only ones questioning the changes in us. Family or close friends may tell us they've noticed a difference in us, that we seem glum and not like ourselves, or say they don't see us as much anymore. They might mention incidents they've witnessed of our partners being controlling, selfish, or disrespectful. The observations of others can be hard for us to accept if we've coped by minimizing or denying the seriousness of our partner's behavior and its impact on us. Psychologist and researcher Federico Lauria explains why someone might subconsciously deny or downplay the severity of their partner's controlling behavior. Accepting those harsh truths can feel emotionally overwhelming if they see themselves as ill-equipped to handle it, so they regulate their emotional pain by denying or minimizing it. (More about defense mechanisms in chapter 6). Confiding in others can be intimidating, and we may worry that doing so will only expose what we would rather keep private. But in fact, getting support from those we trust is a step toward healing.

Personal Awareness and the Echo Complex

Those of us in a relationship with an emotionally avoidant partner might start believing that we are the reason they aren't there for us. And yes, we play a significant role in the challenges we face. But the problem is not that we're flawed or unlovable. Rather, we fail to understand the magnitude of what we're up against.

One of the primary causes of loss of self is when an intimacy-seeking partner attempts to connect with their avoidant partner through openness and vulnerability, wanting the same openness in return. However, these attempts to connect can trigger a shame spiral in an avoidant partner, leading to their anger and defensiveness. When the avoidant partner senses that the intimacy-seeking partner is getting too close, they withdraw because the intimacy-seeking partner is expressing feelings, needs, or desires that the avoidant partner has pushed away, often due to deep-seated shame. In his research on toxic shame, Bradshaw acknowledged that by denying our basic human needs, we create a false self, and with a false self, true intimacy becomes impossible. Shame-based individuals constantly feel the need to prove that their perspectives and actions are correct. They live in a defensive stance and cannot accept mistakes. They are more focused on defending themselves than on considering the needs and feelings of others.

Unaware that they are triggering shame in their partner, the intimacy-seeking partner tries even harder, putting more energy, care, and persistence into breaking through their partner's barrier. But because this approach keeps colliding with avoidance, it only feeds the cycle. Over time, the seeker's pursuit can start to feel less like a genuine expression of their own needs and more like an echo of the avoidant partner's defenses.

Genuine Versus Superficial Connection

To break free from these unhealthy patterns, we need to figure out why we're in a relationship with someone who's emotionally unavailable. Did we sense a lack of connection at the beginning but ignore it? Were we drawn to an emotionally unavailable partner because it felt familiar, or were we too afraid to be vulnerable with our own emotions? Do we truly understand what ingredients are needed for a real emotional connection with a partner? (The post-chapter exercises and detailed questions will help you consider your answers to those questions.)

Sometimes, the issue is that we haven't yet learned to distinguish between the illusion of emotional closeness and real emotional intimacy. Not realizing that our feelings of love can mask the truth of our situation, we might believe we have a genuine emotional connection with our partner when, in fact, we only have a superficial bond.

In some relationships, what appears to be emotional closeness is actually a connection that seems warm on the surface but lacks the depth and safety of genuine intimacy. This illusion often relies on shared routines, affectionate gestures, sexual encounters, or moments of intense emotion that mimic real closeness. However, these moments tend to be situational and inconsistent, preventing the true vulnerability that emotional intimacy requires. In this pattern, personal truths are withheld, difficult conversations are avoided, and harmony is maintained by concealing deeper fears, insecurities, or needs. The closeness exists, but it is conditional and fragile, easily broken by conflict or unmet expectations.

True emotional intimacy, on the other hand, is based on a mutual willingness to be fully seen and accepted, not only in moments of passion or comfort, but also in the everyday and challenging parts of life. It requires vulnerability without fear of being exploited, trust that holds through conflict, and a commitment to facing rather than avoiding discomfort. Communication in such relationships goes beyond surface-level harmony, enabling honest exchanges of feelings, needs, and truths. Here, affection naturally flows from being known and loved for who one truly is. Unlike illusions, genuine intimacy deepens over time, cultivating a steady sense of safety, connection, and mutual care.

A lack of understanding of genuine intimacy can prevent us from seeing what is missing from our relationship: trust. Trust is a crucial part of emotional intimacy, and we can't afford to ignore its absence. When we misread our partner's actions to fit our own desired narrative, we might miss signs that they're not trustworthy. But by letting go of self-deception, we can ask ourselves: *If trust is a core value for me, why am I in a relationship with someone I don't fully trust?* This clearer perspective better equips us to confront relationship issues head-on.

Empowered to Break the Pattern

When we realize we might be contributing to a harmful cycle in our relationship, we can shift our focus and energy toward understanding and changing our behavior, breaking that cycle, and exploring potential opportunities for growth. This book will help you begin that process. With the support of trusted friends and family, a professional therapist can help you gain deeper insight into yourself and the choices you've made. They can guide you through the next steps of personal growth and healing.

It's essential for us to accept that if our partners are unwilling to take responsibility for their hurtful behaviors, there is little we can do to change them. All our tears, wishes, pleading, and coaxing, as well as what we sacrifice, will not force our partners to open up to a deeper connection when they are guarded against it. It's on them to face past losses and traumas that still cause pain and distress in their lives and in the lives of those who love them.

Change in your relationship begins with you. You can start by taking a look at how much of yourself you're giving away in your relationship. Nothing good comes of failing to face reality. Knowing where you are, on the other hand, will help you determine where you want to go.

Do You Show Symptoms of Having the Echo Complex?

The questions below will help you understand the thoughts, emotions, and behaviors that one partner develops in response to the other partner's defenses against emotional intimacy. These reactive effects can be subtle. But while you may see some of the upsetting interactions with your partner as being normal or not unsafe, it's important to know that these effects accumulate over time and can lead to the erosion of a sense of self.

Thoughts

1. Do discussions with your partner about your needs and feelings often leave you feeling misunderstood? Do you ever wonder if your partner would understand you better if only you expressed yourself more clearly?
2. Do you spend a lot of time trying to figure out how to get your partner to listen and offer supportive, validating comments?
3. Do you dwell on what you want to say to your partner, but never say it? Or do you express your thoughts, but feel they come out all wrong?
4. Do you feel confused about why your partner reacts with indifference, talks over you, mocks you, or gets angry when you try to have a conversation that involves sharing deeper feelings?
5. Do you often try to understand whether or not you triggered your partner's anger or disrespectful behavior? Do you feel confused about how to respond to a cutting remark or breach of trust that they dismiss as a harmless joke?
6. Do you take responsibility for conflict in your relationship, even for things that are not your fault, to avoid confrontation?
7. Is it sometimes hard to know when you genuinely agree with your partner and when you agree to avoid their backlash?
8. Are you feeling a loss of motivation and energy for things that once inspired you? Do you spend a significant amount of energy trying to mend your relationship?
9. Do you sometimes overlook your partner's troubling behavior because you're unsure how to address it? Does it occur so often that you've stopped trying to get them to change it?
10. Even if you're hurt and resentful, does your partner's kind behavior make you think you should let go of your feelings without expressing or resolving them first?

Emotions

1. Do you filter what you say to your partner out of fear of criticism or anger? Do you remain silent or go along with them to avoid confrontation or punishment?
2. Do you sometimes feel numb or detached during a stressful interaction with your partner?
3. Do you feel inadequate in some way when with your partner? Has your self-esteem dropped since you started your relationship?
4. Do you feel unhappy with how you respond to your partner's treatment? Do you sometimes feel ashamed for not standing up for your beliefs and feelings? After a conflict, do you ever dwell on what you should have said or done?
5. Do you view your partner's acts of kindness as a form of emotional intimacy even as you feel emotionally distant from them?
6. Do you often wonder why someone who professes to love you acts in a way that harms you or makes you feel bad about yourself?
7. Do you still hold on to hope that your partner will change, despite having seen no lasting evidence of change?
8. Do you often experience feelings of sadness, frustration, and hopelessness due to the turmoil in your life? Does the impact of your relationship with your partner affect your other relationships, including those with friends and family or colleagues at work?
9. Do you feel emotionally unsafe during sex with your partner because of the way they treat you when you're not having sex? Do you engage in sex to appease your partner even though you feel angry and resentful?
10. Have you experienced fatigue, anxiety, depression, or physical issues like headaches or digestive problems since your relationship began?

Behaviors

1. Is it difficult to find the right words to express yourself when talking with your partner about your needs and feelings, or their behavior?
2. Do you feel so frustrated by your partner's lack of respect for your needs and feelings that you react with anger and frustration, saying and doing things that don't reflect who you are in other relationships and areas of life?
3. Do you let your partner make decisions in your relationship, even those that should be yours to make?
4. Do you present yourself as being okay with your partner's unreasonable demands and contemptuous actions because you know that if you don't go along with them, the same behavior will only escalate?
5. Do you doubt your judgment? Have you conceded to your partner so often that you no longer trust your intuition? Do you engage in disturbing actions or behaviors that you would never have engaged in prior to your relationship?
6. Has the quality and frequency of your visits with family and friends decreased? Do you often prefer to isolate to avoid their questions and concerns?
7. Do you deny, make excuses, and downplay your partner's disrespectful behavior around your family and friends? Or do you frequently complain to others about how your partner treats you, yet continue to tolerate that behavior?
8. Do you keep up the appearance of a happy couple when you're out with friends and at public events? Do you sometimes feel detached, as if you're watching yourself in a movie?
9. Have you engaged in unhealthy behaviors, such as substance abuse, overeating, or overspending, to avoid your anxiety and painful feelings?

10. Do you deny, make excuses, or downplay the issues in your relationship with your children? Are you hesitant to ask them how they feel about the family problem and how it's affecting them?

Your answers to these questions can help you identify harmful patterns that have become so familiar that you expect or accept them, even though they upset you. Here's what your score might indicate:

1–5 Yes Answers: There are issues in your relationship that will take a greater toll on your emotional health if you do not address them. You may already feel the effects of isolation, self-doubt, or anxiety, even if those conditions don't yet dominate your daily life. This is a critical moment that calls for serious reflection and action to address the issues affecting your vitality and sense of self before they set a precedent in your relationship.

6–10 Yes Answers: You're on your way to giving up parts of yourself in your relationship. The signs of emotional disconnection, self-neglect, and inner conflict are becoming increasingly hard to ignore. You may feel that you must manage your partner's emotions by silencing your own. You may have started withdrawing from friends and family, making excuses for your partner's behavior. You may feel less confident in your intuition and judgment.

10 or More Yes Answers: Your sense of self is significantly diminished, and without intervention, you will continue to feel isolated, detached, and emotionally drained. You might cope in unhealthy ways to get through the day or avoid noticing how your children and loved ones are impacted. You may experience a profound sense of emptiness, finding it difficult to trust your intuition and make your own decisions.

Regardless of where you are on this scale, once you recognize how your partner creates emotional distance—whether overt or subtle—and how this has affected your thoughts, feelings, and actions, you will be better prepared to begin reclaiming yourself. Acceptance is an awakening.

Address your concerns now. Use the insights and guidelines in this book to regain a position of strength in your relationship. If I had understood the underlying forces in my relationship and my role in them earlier in life, I might have been able to keep from losing myself in my first marriage. In the next chapter, I share the story of how I got lost and found my way back.

Key Points

1. The Echo complex happens when one partner develops maladaptive thoughts, feelings, and behaviors in reaction to the harsh and hidden ways the other partner avoids emotional intimacy.
2. Just as it can be hard to tell if an echo is a real voice, when we experience the Echo complex, it's difficult to distinguish which of our thoughts and actions are truly ours and which ones are ways of coping with our partner's distancing behavior.
3. Loss of self occurs when we fail to recognize and address harmful patterns in our relationships.
4. Human beings are biologically and psychologically wired to seek close, meaningful bonds with others as a survival instinct. This is rooted in both evolutionary biology and attachment science.
5. Intimacy-withholding partners also crave emotional closeness, but their fear of vulnerability causes them to avoid it.
6. Our attempts to connect with our partner through care, tenderness, and vulnerability can trigger their fear of

these emotions, leading them to shut us out of their inner emotional life.

7. Intentionally disrupting emotional connection in an intimate relationship is an emotionally abusive dynamic.
8. There is little we can do to change our partner's fear of emotional intimacy. They must choose to accept responsibility for their avoidance behavior and the reasons driving it before they can heal.
9. Addressing the symptoms of the Echo complex instead of allowing them to persist can help break the pattern of losing oneself in a relationship.
10. A base camp relationship cultivates trust, safety, support, and emotional transparency, allowing both partners to experience personal growth.

Self-Reflection: How Your Relationship Affects You

Go through the description of a base camp on page 18 and compare it with your relationship. Identify the elements of a base camp that are present in your relationship and those that are absent. Then answer these questions:

1. At the beginning of your relationship, did you feel that you had all the necessary elements of a base camp? If not, what elements were missing?
2. How did you react when you realized that some qualities were lacking in your relationship? Did you discuss with your partner what you needed? How did your partner respond?
3. Can you recall an early incident in your relationship when you compromised your values to please your partner? How did it make you feel? Have you continued to compromise yourself, and if so, in what ways?
4. Has your relationship changed how you feel about yourself? If so, how do you feel about yourself now compared to before your relationship?
5. Has your self-image changed how you interact with your partner? How has it influenced your relationships with family, friends, and colleagues?

CHAPTER TWO

My Story

HAVE YOU EVER fallen deeply in love with someone, only to feel like a lesser version of yourself in the relationship? That's what happened to me, and the devastating impact of that experience drove me to become a therapist so I could help others in similar circumstances. I well understood their pain and frustration, having lived it myself. I got how easy it is to choose love over trust, belief over truth, and desire over self-respect. I, too, once sought refuge in hope, in my dream of a secure and loving relationship, even though that dream stayed beyond my reach. But I eventually realized that by uncovering the deeper reasons for the unrest and understanding its effects, I could finally find my way back to myself.

This is the story of how I developed the Echo complex during my first marriage and how I found myself again, eventually finding happiness in a new relationship. I have changed some details for confidentiality, including the real name of my first husband, whom I will call "Todd."

A Hopeful Start

In the beginning, I felt a rush of excitement every time I saw Todd. He came into my life as if straight out of my imagination: a six-foot-four Adonis with sun-kissed hair and a rakish smile; an entrepreneur and adventurous spirit with a sharp wit that made me laugh. During our time together, we had a lot of fun. We went on long drives through the mountains, where we got out and rolled around in piles of brilliant autumn leaves. We went boating on Lake Lanier and dined at trendy restaurants. I was sure I had found my soulmate. I had never been so happy in a relationship.

After we got married, we continued to look like the ideal couple—at least to the outside observer. We lived in a modern home nestled in Atlanta's forested hills, traveled to Europe, and went to dazzling parties that were also attended by Atlanta Braves baseball players, city leaders, and media celebrities. It was the 1980s, and downtown Atlanta was going through a time of rapid growth. I had a promising job in public relations at the Westin Peachtree Plaza hotel, then the world's tallest hotel, and was a member of Intown, Inc., a group of young business executives. Todd owned a growing commercial construction company that generated handsome profits.

But life on the inside of our marriage was far different. Beneath our shiny image, the man who claimed to love me whittled away at my self-esteem with ridicule, deception, blame, and humiliation. Even while we were still dating, his behavior began to deviate from everything I thought I knew about him. However, my quickly formed impressions and what I wanted to believe about him led me to dismiss the red flags, even as they grew more obvious. And so I found myself in a marriage I didn't understand or know how to handle.

Ignoring Early Warning Signs

The change started early on. After two months of dating, we were out one night enjoying drinks and conversation with other people at a crowded nightclub when he slammed his glass on the bar and jumped up from his stool. He told me to feel free to go home with the man sitting next to me. Then he rushed out to the parking lot.

Shaken and embarrassed by his outburst, I followed. I had barely made it into the car when he punched the gas and spun the car around into the street. I tried to explain that my conversation with the man had been cordial and meant nothing. But he wouldn't listen and insisted I take responsibility for the incident. I thought he overreacted, but I wanted to resolve the interaction, so I apologized for upsetting him.

In the days that followed, I convinced myself that he cared about me so much that he feared losing me to another guy. Whether out of ignorance or willfulness, I continued to believe he was a kind, caring, and understanding person, even though the erratic episodes persisted, often following his accusations that I had slighted him in some way. I questioned my judgment. *Who is responsible for these conflicts, him or me?*

I ignored the nagging feeling that something wasn't right, even as my roommate told me in no uncertain terms, "He's trouble." But I thought she didn't know him as well as I did. For one thing, he'd treated his parents with respect when we visited them at their seaside condo. He brought his mother a gift and took us all to dinner. I had the impression that he came from a nice family. My mother always told me that it was important.

When we had been together for less than half a year, Todd suggested we move in together. Although I had concerns about his behavior and making a big commitment so soon, my faith in our relationship outweighed my hesitation. I had been raised in a traditional family where you get married first and then live together. My desire to keep our living arrangements a secret from my parents led me to consider marriage sooner rather than later.

But rushing into the commitment had not been a good idea. Todd's moodiness gave way to long periods of grumpy silence. This happened at home and while traveling. I recall one time on a road trip when we were driving to another state to visit his parents, and he remained quiet for the entire seven-hour trip. When I asked him what was bothering him, he told me, "You know what you did." But I had no idea. I felt frustrated as I waited for him to come out of his dark mood.

Getting in Deeper

Still, I refused to give up on us. Todd was under a lot of pressure as the head of a growing company, and he felt responsible for his employees' lives and well-being. He treated them well, and they loved him for it. I told myself I could be a supportive partner, and that in time, things would improve.

On Christmas Eve at his parents' home with his mother, father, and grandmother, he handed me a black velvet box displaying a ring with a two-carat diamond that had been in his family for generations. I found it strange that he gave me the ring in front of his family without any remarks—no "Will you marry me," or "I want to spend my life with you." I thought, *Does he think I would say 'no' if we were alone?* Members of his family may have agreed with me, but they just smiled with delight as though his proposal had not been out of the ordinary. I felt such relief that he had finally committed to me that I enthusiastically agreed and felt confident our engagement meant the start of a better relationship.

We got married at a quaint log cabin church near Atlanta on an idyllic summer day. As we posed for photographs in the churchyard near flowering trees, Todd made silly faces and hurried the session. His discomfort resurfaced at the reception on the top floor of the Westin Peachtree Plaza when a Russian Balalaika band in full costume paused their music, and the crowd gathered around the five-tiered wedding cake made by the hotel's executive chef. I suspected that going through with the tradition of feeding each other a bite of cake might not end well, but there was no avoiding it: all eyes were on us. I cut the first piece of cake and gently placed a bite into Todd's mouth. When it was his turn, he smashed the piece of cake onto my mouth before I could open it. I hid my humiliation by pretending I thought it was funny.

On our wedding night, instead of feeling exhilarated that this would be the beginning of a close and loving relationship, I felt sad. I had reached my objective of getting married—now what? Would I have to endure more of his misbehavior with occasional periods of calm and acts of kindness? Although he lay beside me, I felt we were a thousand miles apart. But I didn't want to start an argument on our wedding night, so I attributed his behavior to feeling awkward around the abundance of flowers and bow-tied ribbons, and everyone making a big deal over us. I buried my feelings and hoped for the best.

A honeymoon tour of Europe distracted me from my sorrow, but only briefly. It seemed as though he looked for opportunities to disagree with me. I had the directions to our hotel in Paris mapped out. He had a quicker way to get there. I wanted to dine at a traditional French restaurant with white tablecloths and servers dressed in long black aprons. He had a hankering for some Asian food. I wanted to take a bus tour of Paris to see its most famous attractions. He said bus tours were boring. My disappointment and irritation with his constant defiance sparked an argument. There we were on our honeymoon in one of the most romantic cities in the world, locked in conflict. I thought, *I don't understand why trying to make such simple and pleasant decisions could lead to arguments. Why can't we just enjoy ourselves and get along?*

Losing Myself

Once home, the novelty of being married kept things calm for a while. We bought and furnished a house and invited friends over for dinner. But soon his uncaring behavior resumed. He rarely made direct insults. Instead, he delivered calculated jabs disguised to conceal his true intent of belittling me, comments that you can almost convince yourself don't matter. One night with friends, after watching a horror film with a deeply moving theme about the destruction of wildlife caused by urban sprawl, I mentioned how heartbreaking it was that so many animals are killed by thoughtless people. He turned toward me, eyes wide with disbelief. "How could you watch the movie and miss the entire point of it?" Although his words seemed casual, they hit like a slap. My comment wasn't wrong. He only wanted to humiliate me and make me doubt myself. Later, when I brought up his disrespectful remark, he smirked and dismissed my feelings. And just like that, his hurtful comment was buried under my supposed overreaction. That's how it worked: a slow, steady erosion of my confidence until I couldn't tell if his aggression was real, or if I had imagined it.

Todd also began to discourage me from seeing my close friends, whom he often referred to as "airheads." Sometimes, he'd give me an ominous look and say to me about one of them, "She's not your friend," implying that she had made sexual overtures to him. Once, when a beloved childhood friend was in town for one evening, he insisted that instead of spending time with her, I accompany him to dinner with one of his clients.

Our personal views were another point of contention. Regardless of the issue or topic, he tended to take the opposite viewpoint. He always had to be right. When he had too much to drink, he interrogated me like a hostile attorney. My efforts to defend myself against his accusations often led to a heated argument, sometimes while we were dining out. One evening, the owner and chef of a favorite restaurant, an affable Swiss man we had befriended, offered to place our table on the terrace so we could enjoy what he described as our usual routine of "dining and fighting."

Another time, for our first anniversary, our best friends, a married couple who had witnessed our arguments, gave us two ball caps designed to represent the dynamics in our relationship. One hat had a fist attached to the visor, looking like a plush toy, as if it were ready to punch someone. The other hat had two stuffed arms, with one hand grabbing the bicep of the other, bent at the elbow (the sign for "screw you"). I put on the hat with the two stuffed arms and laughed to conceal my embarrassment. The presents were meant as a joke, but they revealed an uncomfortable truth about our verbal sparring.

Behaviors Escalate

In those days, I often felt on guard, waiting for the next incident. I refrained from speaking freely to avoid Todd's caustic responses. I carried his criticism in my mind even when he wasn't around. At work, when I wanted to speak up in meetings and express my ideas, I heard his voice in my head calling me a "space cadet." I feared my colleagues' judgment and criticism, even though they had given me no reason to feel that way.

Once, during a business trip with Todd, I kept apologizing to his client for any inconvenience they experienced, such as the long elevator wait or slow restaurant service. Finally, the client asked me why I felt the need to apologize for things I couldn't control. Taken aback, I realized my self-esteem had reached a new low. The next incident only confirmed it.

One morning after Todd got home late at night, I went into his closet to get his dry cleaning and found pink angora-wool fuzz all over the jacket he had worn the night before. I'd caught him off guard without time to make a solid excuse, and all he managed to say was that he didn't know how that happened. Deeply hurt and angry, I didn't speak to him for days. I kept imagining him and a woman in a pink angora-wool sweater, together in a nightclub, a car, or wherever he had been. I went out searching for an apartment to get relief from my anguish.

But soon after, he drew me back in. The sharp edges of his hostility seemed to soften overnight. He started coming home on time, greeting me with a warm hug instead of a cold shoulder. He brought me a jade sculpture of an egret and a long, flowing dress, the kind I loved to wear on hot days. He asked about my day and really listened. His mood seemed lighter, and he suggested fun activities, like taking a drive to the Blue Ridge Mountains or planning a trip. These gestures made me want to believe he'd realized the error of his ways. The tension between us eased, and my plan to move out began to fade. But I kept a watchful eye on him, fearing more of his callous behavior.

A Glimpse Behind His Defenses

Todd's continuing acts of caring helped me stay in denial about the fault line in our marriage. He personally installed the wood floor I wanted in our dining room. He brought me an expensive Swiss watch he bought on a business trip to Europe. I reasoned that these acts were his way of telling me *I'm sorry that I hurt you*, although he never said the words. I have blue eyes, and one afternoon in the car, while listening to Elton John's song "Blue Eyes," Todd reached over and took my hand. Another time, stressed to the breaking point, I got into bed in the middle of the day and pulled the covers over me. He came into the room and asked what was wrong. When I said, "I feel so alone," he lay down and, saying nothing, put his arms around me. When his beloved grandmother's health was failing, I saw tears in his eyes as he spoke of her. All these gestures proved to me that he could show tenderness, but they also made me wonder why it happened so rarely.

During these times, I sensed that he did need me, but something held him back from letting himself feel and express his love, and from trusting someone to love him in return. Did that something have anything to do with the childhood story he'd told me about his father busting his lip at the family dinner table when he held his fork the wrong way? Could it have anything to do with his mother ordering him to "steel up" when he got sad? Or with the angry disputes he got into with one of his three brothers that sometimes came to blows? I now understand that it did. But at the time, I only had a vague notion of the connection between his upbringing and the way he treated me.

I continued to see signs of his ability to care for others. I saw how much he loved his two Gordon Setters and the beautiful paintings and sculptures of animals he collected with such passion. How much he adored sailing, snorkeling, and sunbathing on the beach. But I remained puzzled that he could embrace his love for other things but not for me. It didn't occur to me that those were things that provided an emotional connection without the risk of feeling vulnerable, things that wouldn't hurt him.

I sensed that Todd had an inner emotional life that he fiercely guarded, but he wouldn't let me in. I so wanted to experience the tenderness, warmth, and appreciation he showed for other things he loved. I needed to find answers to the questions circulating in my head. *How can you claim to love me yet treat me with such contempt? Why do you seem happy with me sometimes and at other times cast me aside as if I don't matter to you? Why can't you love me and let me love you?* I wanted him to acknowledge his cold-hearted behavior, to explain his fear, shame, past losses, and regrets, whatever had been driving him to keep me at an emotional distance. I wanted his promise to change. But he continued to block my attempts to penetrate his defenses by picking fights and blaming me.

The Illusion of Getting Better

Four years into our marriage, Todd told me he was going on a boating trip with a friend and needed "time to think" about our relationship, as if he were deciding whether to stay in it. His words left me reeling. Part of me was convinced I must have driven him away, and part of me was seething over the turmoil he'd put me through. For two long weeks, there was nothing, no contact, just silence. When he returned, he looked into my eyes and said he loved me, that I was the only one he wanted to be with. The rare tenderness in his voice and the way he held me felt like a breakthrough. Not long after, I got pregnant.

One night when I was six months along, I went to dinner with Todd and a boyhood friend of his who was visiting from out of town. During our meal, to make his friend laugh, Todd embarrassed me by describing a farcical attempt to have sex with a pregnant woman. The next morning, I squeezed my large belly behind the steering wheel and escaped to my parents' home four hours away. One week later, he called to tell me to come home. I knew I couldn't stay at my parents' house and that I'd eventually have to face the situation at home, so I returned. As usual, he said nothing about what had happened, but he had finished installing beautiful granite countertops in the kitchen. I told him that if his disrespect continued, I would leave him and take our baby. He stayed on good behavior for the remainder of my pregnancy.

After the birth of our son, Todd got irritated by the amount of time I spent with the baby and refused to be involved with his care. "That's your job," he said. As our son grew out of infancy, Todd seemed more like a jealous older brother than a father. He made comments like, "You coddle him too much." Once, when I had to go on a business trip and his mother came to stay with our child, he told friends that I treated our son like a toy: I brought him down from the shelf when I wanted to play with him and put him back when I didn't. We frequently argued over how to raise our child.

One afternoon, when we were at an outdoor shopping center, Todd pulled me behind a wall so we would be hidden from our toddler, who promptly started to cry. I pulled away and reappeared immediately. As I comforted my child, I thought, *How could a father take pleasure in frightening his baby son?* After that incident, I kept a close watch on Todd to prevent him from mistreating our child.

The following year, we relocated to Florida to take advantage of Todd's business opportunities. The sweeping landscape with its radiant sunshine, ocean views, and towering palm trees brought a welcome change of scenery and gave me hope for a fresh start. We moved into a spacious home on a golf course. He bought a sailboat and docked it in the Florida Keys.

One evening, we attended Todd's father's seventieth birthday party at a yacht club. Todd disappeared for close to an hour, and I found him in a dark corner of a deserted banquet room with a work colleague's twenty-three-year-old daughter on his lap. Devastated, I had a friend take me home. When Todd got home, he said they were "just talking," and he scolded me for losing my temper.

By then, I had become familiar with the routine. For a few days, I would simmer in hurt and resentment, longing for reconciliation but fearing another rash of empty excuses and blame. He would be on his best behavior. Then things would settle down for a while. But this time was different. This time, I lost hope that he would ever be capable of loving me, that our relationship could work. The only thing that kept me going now was my beautiful son and my delight in being a mother.

The Turning Point

Although at the time I didn't understand the fundamental reasons for my troubled marriage, I knew that I didn't want to live in a situation where I couldn't trust my judgment, express myself, be spontaneous, and see friends. Where my emotions had been rubbed raw. I began to imagine a new life away from him. An inner voice that had primarily grown critical changed its tone, reminding me of my ambition, my desire to meet people, learn things, and have new experiences. The chaos and confusion I was living in became even clearer when the next incident happened. I realized it was no longer just about me.

One evening, I came home late from work in order to complete a project due the next day. Todd, who had often accused me of lying to him, although his accusations had no basis in fact, yelled at me, insisting I tell him who I had been with. He grabbed my arms and shook me in front of our toddler son, who cried and ran into another room to hide. I knew then that I had to leave my marriage, not only to protect myself but also to protect my child. When I told Todd I wanted a divorce, he replied that it was too late, that we had a child now, and had to stay together. His tone was unemotional, but I sensed he was holding back shock and dismay, as if a long-held fear that I would eventually leave him had become a reality.

After I told him I had made up my mind, we lived separate lives in the same house for a couple of months, and then I moved out with our son. During that time, he was civil to me when he wasn't on his sailboat in the Keys. But I suspected it was because he had started a new relationship and wanted to make it seem like he was blameless for the breakup of our marriage.

In the period that followed, I didn't know if I'd ever want to trust someone again. After loving someone who used that love to hurt me and make me feel small, the idea of opening myself to a new relationship felt risky. I still guarded my heart, knowing how easy it would be to fall for the wrong person. But beneath the fear and caution, I longed for something safe, mutual, and real. I wanted to find love again.

Finding Love Again

I eventually returned to Atlanta with my son, where I focused on my public relations career and being a mother. Five years later, a casual friend who'd hosted a birthday tea for my son's godmother asked me if I would be interested in going on a blind date with her boss, Jay. She told me she had known him for years and that he was a nice man, so I agreed.

After Jay and I spoke on the phone, we arranged to meet for lunch. I felt at ease right away with his engaging manner. However, after I accidentally knocked over a glass of water that spilled on him, I braced myself for a gruff response. Todd had often used my blunders as an excuse to degrade me. But Jay just laughed and said he was relieved that I was the one who'd spilled the water, since he tended to be the clumsy one. After lunch, we didn't want to part ways, so we took a walk for an hour in the parking lot. Though my attraction to him was intense, I promised myself I wouldn't make snap judgments this time. I had been down that road before and would take my time getting to know him while keeping an eye out for indicators of his true character.

As we spent more time together, I wanted to trust Jay, but when he made attempts at emotional intimacy by asking probing questions about my first marriage, I told him, "That's over now. I'm fine and don't need to talk about it." In truth, the unresolved trauma and pain of my first marriage kept me from the deep emotional connection Jay and I both wanted.

I didn't realize how guarded I had been until one autumn afternoon, six months into dating Jay. We were in his hometown for his high school reunion, and he decided to show me the places where he grew up. As we drove down quiet streets shaded by ancient live oaks draped in Spanish moss, Jay began sharing pieces of his past, stories tinged with both joy and heartache. The families of both of his parents had originally immigrated from Europe to this small Southern town to escape oppression, and they had built successful businesses. His father owned an ice cream factory and parlor, where Jay's friends gathered. Although his parents provided well for his basic needs, there was little attunement to his feelings and interests. This emotional absence shaped a childhood marked by loneliness, self-doubt, and insecurity. They often took trips to gamble in another town, leaving him in the care of a nanny, whom he thought was his "mommy." At school, being Jewish meant always feeling different. He told me how he and another Jewish child were asked to step out of the classroom during Christian prayers and skip Christmas festivities, and that Jews were banned from the town's social clubs.

His voice softened as he remembered his childhood and the difficult emotions he experienced. Then he turned to me. "What was your childhood like?" I gave him the polished, edited version. "Oh, it was like a storybook," I said lightly. "We traveled through Europe, visited castles, beaches, and lived in a château with a French family. Everything was great." I stopped there as he pulled the car over to the side of the road, his frustration spilling out. "There's more to that story. . .There always is," he said. "We've been together for months now, and I don't feel like you're letting me in. Tell me the real story. You don't have to hide from me."

He was right. The truth was far from a fairy tale. My childhood had been a series of uprooted starts. I attended ten schools before graduating from high school. My parents loved me, but I couldn't confide in them. There was a lot to say about the challenges I went through as a kid, but I didn't feel comfortable sharing them with Jay.

In that moment, I realized that if I continued to hide my true self, I would never find the love I wanted. It was the very thing standing in my way. So I worked on opening myself again, and it deepened our relationship.

After two years, we got married at a country club surrounded by friends and family. My relationship with Jay was very different from the one I'd had with Todd. But I had some unfinished business from my first marriage, which caused me to fall into low-grade depression. Concerned for me, Jay recommended a psychotherapist who guided me in releasing the pent-up anger, sadness, shame, and guilt I had been unable to reconcile. She helped me understand the deeper reasons for the trouble in my first marriage and helped me reclaim my sense of self.

Reclaiming Myself

It took time to fully understand what had happened in my first marriage. My husband wasn't just distant or difficult. He used control and manipulation to keep me at an emotional distance. That wasn't because of a flaw in me that needed fixing. Once I understood this clearly, some of the shame and confusion I had been carrying began to loosen its grip.

Healing didn't follow a straight path. Reclaiming myself was a layered and sometimes difficult process. It involved sorting through all the parts of myself that had been shaped by someone else's needs, expectations, and demands. I had to untangle who I had become to survive in a relationship where the real me had gradually faded away. Each layer of this work unearthed painful memories and patterns I had fallen into, along with the false beliefs I held on to and that Todd had instilled in me. To let go of these things, I had to accept the truth that I married a man who couldn't love me back, despite his desire or intentions. The therapist also helped me better understand how my background and old ways of thinking and behavior had made me vulnerable to partnering with an emotionally unavailable man and contributed to the harmful dynamics in my first marriage.

How My Background Influenced Loss of Self

When I was growing up, my parents provided a loving home for my older brother, my younger sister, and me. However, their 'keep your emotions to yourself' style of communication discouraged us from expressing the full range of our feelings. My mom, who had been raised by an overbearing mother, often left our house in a huff when she got angry and said nothing when she returned. My dad, raised on a farm during the Great Depression, had learned to endure hardship without showing his feelings. Their unwillingness to express emotions sent me the message, "Your feelings aren't important. Keep them to yourself."

So I did.

Stuffing down my feelings became a way to cope with being raised in a military family that moved to a new place every year in the U.S. and overseas. A shy girl, I had to find ways to fit in at the never-ending succession of schools I attended. I recall the humiliation I felt during third grade in Hanau, Germany, in the cafeteria of a new school when I sat at an empty table and burst into tears. Girls I didn't know at the next table saw me and brought their trays over to sit with me. I still get teary when I think of their kindness.

Years later, when I was thirteen and we had moved to Huntsville, Alabama, to be near an Army base, I skipped church one day and shoplifted three tubes of lipstick from a nearby drugstore. I had learned to steal from a friend in the town where we'd last lived. However, my sleight of hand wasn't as skilled as hers, and I got caught. The store manager called two police officers, who asked a few questions and handed me over to my father. Terrified that I would be thrown in jail and ashamed of what I had done, I desperately wanted to talk about what had happened and be forgiven. But my father remained silent. So, I stayed quiet too.

Another time, my mother suspected I had changed my grades on my report card and called my teacher. My guilt and fear convinced me I would be kicked out of tenth grade, and I wanted to talk with my mother about it. However, although my mother glared at me in disgust, neither of my parents took the time to discuss with me why I felt the need to change my grades, nor did they help me learn from my mistake. I often reflect on those times and others as my attempts to break the unwritten rule in our family: ignore problems, and they'll go away. As a kid, I wanted to understand why it never seemed to work for me.

I want to emphasize here that I don't blame my parents. They raised me as they were raised, and I believe they tried their best to be good parents. I understood later that it was up to me to break the harmful pattern of suppressing my emotions.

As a young adult, I kept up my pattern of hiding my feelings and judging my self-worth based on whether others accepted me. And that's what led me into the relationship with my first husband, who fiercely guarded his vulnerability by attacking mine. That dynamic, combined with my desire to be accepted by him, put me at risk of losing myself in the relationship.

As I finally began to identify and break free from old, limiting thought patterns that had caused me to lose my sense of self, my newfound insights sparked a desire to help others facing similar challenges in their relationships. I enrolled in the graduate program for professional counseling at Georgia State University. After working in the behavioral health unit at an inner-city hospital to achieve my professional license, I opened a private practice specializing in treatment for emotional abuse and loss of self.

A Brighter Future

Jay and I have now been married for more than twenty-five years. I am grateful every day to have him as my life partner. With him, I've learned how fulfilling a relationship can be when it has a base camp. We share our deepest confidences and laugh at our flaws and foibles. We delight in each other's company and look forward to discussing our daily experiences. I have a partner who encourages me to be the best version of myself, someone who truly loves me and reciprocates my love. Together, we created an environment where we can both reveal ourselves without fear of rejection and live full and meaningful lives.

Our marriage has also been a healthy environment for my son, who has matured into a wise and vibrant young man. He, his lovely wife, seven-year-old son, and five-year-old daughter bring great joy into our lives.

Throughout my years as a therapist, I've heard countless stories like mine, and some more tragic. The details vary, but they all include similar dynamics that lead to a loss of self in a relationship. Many of my clients used the insights they gained from therapy and their experiences to build better lives. I hope that as you read this book, you will find the healing wisdom in your own story.

Self-Reflection: Your Story

Reflecting on difficult experiences offers a unique opportunity to gain healing insight. Studies have shown that sharing stories and finding meaning in them is an effective way to recover from emotional distress. In psychotherapy, narrative therapy is an intervention that focuses on the stories people tell about their lives, helping them to interpret their narratives in a more empowering and positive way.

If you're not currently working with a therapist, you can begin to explore the deeper meaning of your experience and move toward recovery by keeping a journal. I invite you to begin telling your story using the following format. If you have left your relationship, include where you are now. Take as much time as you need to consider the questions thoughtfully. You can do this exercise all at once, or in stages, depending on what works best for you.

1. How did you meet your partner? Describe some early experiences you had with them that drew you into the relationship.
2. Were there early warning signs that there would be trouble ahead? If so, how did you react to these warning signs? If not, did you have any false beliefs or impressions of your partner?
3. Did you minimize or make excuses for any of your partner's behaviors that concerned you?
   Were you reluctant to enter a committed relationship with your partner? If so, what were your concerns?
4. How did your partner make you feel about yourself? Describe some experiences in which you felt inadequate in your relationship as a result of your partner's demands and expectations.
5. How did you respond to your partner's behavior toward you that made you feel deficient in some way?
6. Did you feel like you couldn't be completely yourself around your partner, or that doing so might threaten your relationship?
7. Do you have insight into how your childhood and family background may have influenced your relationship choices?
8. How would you describe your relationship now, and the way you feel about yourself in your relationship? If you're no longer in the relationship, describe how you left and how the relationship experience has affected you.
9. Describe some key insights regarding what you've learned about yourself, your partner, and your relationship so far. Describe three goals you have for yourself regarding your relationship.

Once you've finished reading this book, I'll ask you to rewrite your story using the insights you've gained. By comparing your before-and-after stories, you'll gain a deeper understanding of the key factors in your relationship that led to losing yourself, and start to find ways to break free from hurtful patterns and reclaim your true self.

CHAPTER THREE

Twelve Healing Truths About Self-Loss in Relationships

IF I COULD go back to those moments in my first marriage—those heated, confusing exchanges when I reacted before I took time to think—I'd gently take my younger self by the shoulders and say, "Pause. Breathe. Get curious. What's really going on here?"

Back then, I didn't know how to stop and look beneath the surface. I hadn't yet realized that my partner needed to keep me at an emotional distance and that my instinctive, often clueless reactions only reinforced his defenses. If I'd understood that truth sooner, I might have made different choices. Maybe the marriage still wouldn't have lasted, but I could have walked away feeling more whole, less broken by confusion and self-doubt.

Over the years, I've come to realize that avoiding the loss of self in a relationship begins with acknowledging the truth. When uncovered, truth doesn't just explain what went wrong; it opens the door to change and healing. In this chapter, I have outlined twelve essential truths about a partner's distancing behavior. Knowing these truths will help prevent falling back into old habits or self-doubt. We can get a clearer view of the situation and make choices that help us move from acting impulsively to responding thoughtfully, all while protecting our self-worth.

Some of these truths may bring comfort, while others are difficult to accept. That's because they confront the stories we've told ourselves to excuse our partner's unacceptable behavior, stories that hold us back from responding in healthier ways. They matter because they can help us navigate conflicts in ways that safeguard our well-being.

Twelve Truths About Self-Loss

1. Living with unresolved emotions caused by a lack of connection with a partner is emotionally unsafe.
2. Giving up parts of ourselves in an attempt to control our partner's behavior will never lead to an emotional connection.
3. Our partner's distancing behavior can arise from their feelings about themselves, rather than from their feelings about us.
4. Stirring up trouble in a relationship is a common way to avoid emotional intimacy.
5. Raw emotion and acting out of character in response to our partner's offensive treatment is not "drama."
6. It's not always obvious when emotional abuse is happening.
7. Thinking we can fix or change our partner wrongly shifts their responsibility onto us.
8. Emotional mistreatment by an intimate partner can lead the other partner to self-sabotage.
9. Giving too much in an intimate partnership can become a form of self-neglect disguised as devotion.
10. When we tolerate our partner's distancing behavior, we perpetuate a cycle of that behavior and our reaction to it.
11. We're not betraying our partners when we have relationships with family and friends we can confide in. We're betraying ourselves when we don't.
12. When we accept the truth in our relationship, we can take action to create change.

Let's take a closer look at these truths and why they're essential for preserving a strong sense of self in an intimate relationship. Losing ourselves doesn't happen all at once. The self is worn down when we ignore our needs, excuse hurtful behavior, or take on problems that aren't ours to solve. These truths reveal the patterns that keep us in unsafe dynamics and show why sacrificing parts of ourselves never creates real closeness. They help us stop confusing self-sacrifice with connection, see when a partner's behavior is about them, and take steps to restore the most important relationship: the one we have with ourselves.

Truth #1
Living with unresolved emotions caused by a lack of connection with a partner is emotionally unsafe.

When clients walk into my office with slumped shoulders and eyes filled with sadness, it's often because they feel emotionally unsafe in their relationships. They long to share their feelings with the person who should be their closest supporter. But when they express their disappointment and frustration, their partners don't seem to understand or care. Instead, they assign blame, as if having these feelings is a flaw or something to be ashamed of.

The impact of their partner's dismissal runs deep. They say, "I feel like I'm going crazy," "Maybe I'm expecting too much," and "I just can't do anything right." My clients have learned to withhold their real feelings and speak in ways that feel inauthentic because opening up to a partner who won't listen makes them feel worse.

But within the safety of our work together, my clients start to understand something life-changing: emotional transparency isn't a luxury. It's vital. It's the lifeblood of deep connection and genuine love. When they finally realize that the breakdown in the relationship wasn't because they were "too much" or "too needy," but because their partner could not or would not meet them in a place of emotional honesty, their shame begins to loosen its grip. They realize that the trouble was not their fault.

One of the primary functions of an intimate relationship is to make the people in it feel safe. When we have a partner who exerts power and control over us, it can feel like trauma, a frightening and destabilizing state. Often, we don't even notice this is happening. We're so intent on reestablishing an emotional connection with our partners that we don't realize how much of ourselves we're giving up. We feel emotionally unsafe because our partner's withdrawal and control cause us to seek their approval, fearing we might lose their affection. This fear can lead us to neglect our own needs and identity, undermining our sense of stability in the relationship. There is emotional neglect and often abuse when this happens in a relationship.

Science confirms what so many have felt in the deepest parts of themselves: When our emotional safety is threatened, it changes us. It affects the way we think, the way we see ourselves, and the way we show up in the world. These are not small shifts. They influence our sense of self-worth and our capacity for deep connection.

While much of the research conducted on the effects of emotional disconnection and abuse has focused on how women are affected, I have observed in my practice with diverse clients that the emotional consequences show striking similarities across cultures, genders, sexual orientations, and life circumstances. There's no way to know the true numbers. One study suggested that there is a greater level of reporting by women than by men experiencing emotional abuse by their partners. Still, we can learn a great deal from the research. Here is a sampling of the research on emotional disconnection and abuse and its effect on people and their relationships:

- Attachment trauma, which happens when there are disruptions in the bond between a child and their primary caregiver, creates profound stress and undermines a person's ability to manage that distress. Example: As a little boy, Miguel learned quickly that crying or showing sadness made his father scold him for being a "baby," saying that boys don't cry. He taught himself to hide his feelings, but as an adult, this left him paralyzed in relationships, unable to trust that anyone would comfort him if he reached out. Instead of expressing his feelings to his partner, he got angry at himself for being "weak."

- The most devastating consequence of psychological abuse is a sense of disconnection and isolation, which often leads to psychological struggles. Example: After years of subtle put-downs and cold silences from her partner, Grace stopped talking to her closest friends. She didn't want to explain why she was so unhappy, and she found herself sitting alone most nights. She shut down emotionally to avoid the pain of caring about someone.
- Women in emotionally abusive relationships often experience emotional loneliness, despair, guilt, confusion, fear, diminished self-esteem, a loss of identity, and anger. Example: Josie often woke up in the morning with a troubled mix of feelings about the way her partner treated her. She had tried everything from venting her frustration and anger to tolerating her partner's criticism and temper tantrums. But whatever she did seemed to make the situation worse. She felt shame and anger at herself for being defective, that she was not enough and didn't deserve to be loved.
- Some women in abusive relationships report feeling they've lost their core selves. Example: Before meeting her partner, Helen was outgoing and creative. But after years of adjusting to his moods, opinions, and demands, she no longer painted, laughed freely, or even voiced her preferences. When she looked at herself in an earlier photograph, she felt deeply sad that she was no longer the vibrant person she had been.
- Over time, the constant need to adapt to and accommodate an abusive partner leads to physical and emotional illness and a complete breakdown of one's sense of self. Example: For months, Rocky ignored his headaches, indigestion, and daily fatigue, chalking them up to stress. But the truth was, years of hiding his true self in his relationship with a domineering and emotionally distant partner had drained his

> body as much as his spirit, leaving him feeling like a hollow shell of the person he once was.

Let's be clear: Feeling that it's not safe to be ourselves and experiencing a lack of emotional connection in an intimate relationship isn't just painful; it's traumatic. And this lack of safety should be taken seriously. Not only does the stress of emotional abandonment lead to losing parts of ourselves, it also produces biological effects that can lead to physical illness. Recognizing our partners' barriers to emotional closeness and their impact on us puts us in a stronger position to preserve and restore our well-being.

Truth #2

Giving up parts of ourselves in an attempt to control our partner's behavior will never lead to an emotional connection.

I can't count how many times I've sat across from a client who says something like, "I just didn't want to upset him," or "I figured it wasn't worth the fight," or even, "I acted like I was fine, but I was really falling apart inside." At first, these choices may seem insignificant, but they fail to acknowledge our needs and feelings—the very things that establish an emotional connection between partners.

What's happening here is that, in an attempt to maintain peace or feel safer in a controlling relationship, we shrink ourselves to cope with what seems too difficult to overcome. Ironically, by tailoring our emotions for our partner's benefit—whether to avoid conflict, gain approval, or attract care—we engage in a passive-aggressive strategy that is also a form of control.

We may start by withholding complaints or pretending to be okay with things we deeply resent. Over time, we may go even further, moving beyond avoidance to feigning emotions. This could be faking agreement, satisfaction, or even distress, when doing so serves our goal of managing our partner's behavior. We might, for example, overstate our vulnerability to gain a softer response or downplay our need to avoid a confrontation. This inauthentic expression becomes a way to control how our partner sees and interacts with us. The question here is: *Am I reacting in a way that feels true, or because I'm trying to get a certain response from my partner?*

When we avoid facing reality to feel safer, we react in ways that feel untrue. This further erodes the connection because our authentic selves are no longer present in the relationship; only a curated version of ourselves remains. Our behavior is no longer a reflection of truth, but of defense.

When this happens, both partners become trapped in roles that reinforce each other. This creates a relational echo chamber where neither partner connects from a place of vulnerability or integrity. As a result, we remain unseen and misunderstood by our partners.

Both partners must be honest, including being transparent about their fears, disappointments, and desires. Two people can't relate to each other if neither one is fully present. When this happens, the relationship remains more about managing perceptions than about building a connection.

Truth #3
Our partner's distancing behavior can arise from their feelings about themselves, rather than from their feelings about us.

This is a truth that's often overlooked because it's difficult to notice. When our partners pull away emotionally, it's easy to assume there's something wrong with us. But here's the truth: their distancing behavior often relates more to what's going on inside of them than it does to us. There could be several reasons they push us away. As we've seen, they might fear being vulnerable or harbor deep shame. They might have trouble forming deep bonds or struggle with their gender or sexuality. They may be involved with someone else, or have a personality disorder like narcissism, in which they lack empathy. Whatever the reason, it's not always about something we've done.

Still, many of us automatically assume the opposite. We think, *If they're pushing me away, it must be my fault.* That's such a painful and unfair conclusion to draw, but it's also a common one.

I've seen how quickly my therapy clients blame themselves when their partner withdraws or becomes angry, cold, or critical. "Maybe I hurt them in some way," they wonder. "Maybe I pushed too hard." They try to rewind the conversation and figure out what they did wrong, hoping that if they can just identify the misstep, they can fix it and restore the connection.

However, what may be happening here is that our partner can't handle an inner conflict, so they see us as the problem. When they experience unwanted thoughts, feelings, or motives, they attribute them to us. This is called projection.

Projection is a defense mechanism that protects the ego from experiencing the distress and anxiety caused by undesirable aspects of oneself. Instead of confronting and managing uncomfortable feelings or traits—such as shortcomings, undesirable qualities, or emotions like shame, guilt, or insecurity—those who project unconsciously see them in others. By assigning their own negative traits to other people, they can attempt to maintain a positive self-image. Also, it seems easier to blame others than to take responsibility for one's own feelings or actions.

Let's say a person is tempted to get involved with someone outside their relationship, or they are already involved with that person. They may accuse their partner of being unfaithful, projecting their own issues onto them. Someone who feels insecure about their intelligence might accuse others of being stupid or of making foolish mistakes, rather than confronting their feelings of inadequacy.

This shame-dumping can lead to serious misunderstandings. The partner on the receiving end feels attacked, confused about why they are being criticized. Meanwhile, the partner doing the projecting remains unaware that they are not truly seeing their partner. Recognizing that this is occurring can shift our perspective from *Why am I being treated this way?* to *What's going on with my partner?*

Having empathy for a partner who struggles with their emotions doesn't mean excusing bad behavior. The important questions here are: *Is my partner willing to acknowledge their inner struggles and work on them?* and *Are we both capable of having an open conversation that leads to mutual understanding?*

Realizing that this is what happens helps us approach relationship issues more honestly. We can set new boundaries, and if we feel it's safe to do so, hold our partners accountable for hurtful behavior, and make space for growth in the relationship.

Truth #4
Stirring up trouble in a relationship is a common way to avoid emotional intimacy.

Here's another truth that's hard to spot, leading many people to blame themselves for trouble that their partner has cooked up. I've had clients ask, "Why does it always feel like something's off?" or "Why does my partner start fights right when we're finally connecting?" It's another one of those moments when the person on the receiving end starts scanning themselves for answers: *What did I say? What did I miss? Did I do something to provoke this?*

But here's what's important to understand: Not all relationship conflict stems from real issues. There's the kind of trouble that arises from miscommunication or unmet needs in a partnership, and then there's the kind that seems to come out of nowhere, just when things were beginning to settle down. Knowing the difference between conflict with a good reason and conflict to avoid emotional intimacy is essential.

For those able to do so, emotional intimacy enables real connection, understanding, and a love that's true. For those who aren't capable or willing, the vulnerability required to reveal their inner emotional life can lead someone to create a smokescreen of drama to avoid emotional closeness.

When one partner consistently stirs up conflict, it often reflects their struggle for self-preservation. Their unresolved issues make emotional intimacy feel like stepping into a trap. Rather than risk the pain of vulnerability or give up their need for control, they build a barricade of anger, criticism, or blame. They may feel undeserving of their partner's love and feel their partner will reject them if they reveal their true selves. They see attempts to get closer to them as threats they need to defend against.

For others, troublemaking may become a strategy to gain attention. If their childhood experiences of love—the times they felt seen or valued—were generally tied to moments of crisis, they may believe that conflict equals connection. By instigating chaos, they provoke a response, be it anger or concern, which gives them a fleeting sense of being acknowledged. However, one partner's anger can trigger anger and resentment in the other, and this disconnection can weaken trust and respect.

The tragedy of creating problems as a defense against emotional intimacy is that it often leads to what our partners fear most: the deterioration of the relationship. What's meant to be protective ends up isolating them emotionally, rather than giving them the comfort of being truly seen and loved.

Instead of taking the blame for a partner who stirs up trouble, recognize that it reveals more about their fears than it does our flaws. Creating trouble has no place in a loving relationship.

Truth #5
Raw emotion and acting out of character in response to our partner's offensive treatment is not "drama."

I remember a moment during my first marriage when I was so exasperated with my husband that I grabbed a lamp and threw it at him. I had reached such a high level of frustration due to the emotional torment he caused that I behaved in ways that were uncharacteristic of me. Since then, I've realized that my actions are not uncommon in relationships filled with frustration and despair.

Nonviolent ways of expressing emotions in a relationship are important for the well-being of both partners. But when we reach our limit of emotional endurance, we might yell, say things we don't mean, or make threats. We may even engage in physical violence, which is never acceptable, regardless of the circumstances.

When we express these raw, unfiltered emotions, our partners might label us as "drama queens" or accuse us of overreacting. They refuse to recognize not only our feelings but also their own behavior and its effects on us. By downplaying the seriousness of their actions and invalidating our reactions, they shift the focus from themselves to us. This is gaslighting, a form of psychological manipulation where someone distorts, denies, or twists reality to make another person question their perceptions, memories, or sanity. When this happens, we respond as anyone would in deep emotional pain. Expressing visceral emotion is not a sign of weakness or neediness. It's a testament to our innate desire to feel seen, heard, and cared for. These feelings are not wrong or excessive. They are essential to loving relationships. So, let's not be too hard on ourselves for how we've reacted to our partner's distancing behavior. Instead, let's recognize the validity of our emotions and the circumstances that led us to our breaking point.

Truth #6
It is not always obvious when emotional abuse is happening.

Some of the most painful forms of mistreatment are those we can't easily see. Many of my clients come to therapy burdened by anxiety, depression, or a deep sense of inadequacy, yet they don't describe their partners as abusive, even when this is the case. They're emotionally drained and not fully aware of why they're having such a hard time in their relationships.

That's because emotional abuse hides in plain sight. It doesn't always look the way we expect it to. It might not happen with shouting or threats. Rather, it may appear as a joke that cuts too deep, a "concern" that feels more like criticism, an unreasonable demand that we feel obligated to meet, or affection that's given and then withdrawn like a reward. Because it's so subtle, it can be difficult to recognize the true purpose of the behavior.

The intent of hidden emotional mistreatment is to exert power and control over someone by undermining their emotional stability. Unlike overt abuse—such as yelling, name-calling, or public humiliation—hidden abuse operates by gradually eroding the victim's self-esteem and sense of reality without leaving clear evidence.

One study by clinical social workers and family therapy scholars Kerrie James and Laurie MacKinnon from the University of New South Wales in Sydney, Australia, likened nonphysical abuse to an iceberg, where the visible tip is evident on the surface, but the substantial body lies submerged and undetectable. The researchers' findings indicated that, eventually, participants came to believe the emotional abuse was justified. They concealed their situation from others out of fear of being blamed and ultimately became clinically depressed. Additionally, they grew more dependent and attached to their emotionally abusive partner.

It's also not uncommon for people in this kind of relationship to dismiss disrespectful behavior as an expression of traditional or conservative gender roles or cultural influences. Research shows that women with male partners often attribute their partners' abusive actions to typical male behavior, rather than recognizing these actions as abuse. Other studies found that those experiencing emotional abuse often respond with denial and question their worth. In one study of women in abusive relationships, many participants reported that they initially ignored their growing dissatisfaction with their partners and blamed themselves for not being good enough.

That's disheartening research, revealing a reality hard to accept. And yet, I frequently encounter this reality in my therapy practice. The truth is that people in harmful relationships often resist the idea that their partners are abusive. Personal factors, such as commitment to the relationship, hopes for improvement, financial concerns, children, and fear of being alone, can cloud one's judgment. Individuals in such partnerships may dread losing the relationship, leading them to accept the status quo even when there's potential for change. When we finally recognize emotional abuse hidden behind its mask of normalcy, however, we become better equipped to protect ourselves against what we couldn't see clearly before.

Truth #7
Thinking we can fix or change our partner wrongly shifts their responsibility onto us.

Here's another typical relationship issue where we take responsibility for something that isn't ours to handle. I've often seen this pattern: someone who is deeply committed to their partner, giving their all to the relationship and trying their best to make it work, only to have their partner swing between seeming to care and being emotionally distant, controlling, and hurtful.

It's distressing to see because the person trying to "fix" their partner is often generous, loyal, and full of love. Yet, they feel dejected, not because they are doing something wrong, but because they've taken on a burden that wasn't theirs to carry: the responsibility to "make" the relationship work when their partner isn't meeting them halfway.

Knowing the difference between our responsibilities in a relationship and those of our partner is essential to maintaining a strong sense of self. Without that clarity, we might give more than we should, all the while believing we're just one step away from earning our partner's love.

It's not our responsibility when our partners regularly shut down, blow up, and keep us at arm's length. It's up to them to lower their defenses and do their part in fostering a more loving and connected relationship. It's easy to lose sight of that truth, however, when we're pouring our hearts into the relationship. We might tell ourselves, *if I'm patient and loving enough, they'll change.* And at times, they may even show us glimpses of the person we believe they could be. However, unless those moments lead to substantial change that's consistent and lasting, we're banking on hope, and hope is a hollow investment unless our partners take action to achieve what we're hoping for.

The cultural messages we receive don't make the challenge of an emotionally distant partner any easier. Movies, books, and stories tell us that if we're loving and patient enough, we can help someone heal from their pain and make the relationship whole. It's a beautiful idea, but it sets us up for heartbreak. Believing this might lead us to measure our worth by how much we can endure.

Sometimes, our partners push away emotional closeness without even realizing that they are afraid of it. That's another reason why it's essential that we express our feelings and explain how their behavior impacts us. Doing so can create opportunities for them to improve their behavior.

Letting go of the hope that we can change another person isn't a failure. It's a sign of maturity. From that grounded place, we are better prepared to face challenges in the relationship or, if necessary, make the brave decision to walk away. And if we choose to leave and learn from the experience, we are more likely to find love with a partner who doesn't need to be "fixed."

Truth #8
Emotional mistreatment by an intimate partner can lead the other partner to self-sabotage.

When clients show up feeling anxious, emotionally drained, and unsure of their role in their relationship's troubles, I ask if they feel like they've lost parts of themselves. "Yes!" comes the resounding answer. And sometimes, they're just realizing it. Each story behind losing oneself is unique, but one common theme repeats. They have been subjected to a subtle form of psychological control by their partners that's easy to overlook but can lead to self-sabotage over time.

What's most painful is how this kind of emotional mistreatment can quietly cause someone to turn against themselves. They are in a situation where they can't see the risks of reshaping themselves to meet a partner's unreasonable demands. Partners who use harsh tactics to avoid emotional closeness often blur the lines between care and criticism, love and power. It's confusing. Their harsh critique might be delivered in a soft voice with the words, "I'm only telling you this because I care." And because we want to see the good in someone we love, we don't always see their statement as a control tactic. We start to think, *Maybe it is my fault*, *Maybe I do need to try harder, Maybe I should be more patient and agreeable with them.* We call it self-improvement. But what's actually happening is self-sabotage.

This pattern can play out in the smallest, everyday moments. We defend choices that shouldn't need defense: why we wore what we wore, who we texted, and which way we drove home. We may think we're avoiding conflict, but really, we're living under surveillance. The more we explain ourselves, the more power we hand over.

We don't bring up needs, hurts, or disagreements because we're afraid of being labeled dramatic, needy, or ungrateful. We tell ourselves we're being strong. But often, this kind of silence is fear in disguise. What appears to be emotional steadiness is actually emotional suppression. And what feels like loyalty might be learned helplessness.

It's also common to misinterpret our partner's behavior by making excuses for it: *They didn't mean it. They're just stressed.* But every time we explain away behavior that hurts, we invalidate our own experience. We quiet the inner voice that says, *This isn't okay.*

So how do we begin to break this cycle? We start by staying present with ourselves. In moments of confusion or conflict, pause and ask: *Why do I feel the need to stay silent or explain myself right now? What am I afraid will happen if I don't? Why do I often feel bad about myself when my partner confronts me? Are my reactions a problem, or is their behavior causing harm?* Answering these questions is an act of self-preservation.

Self-protection isn't about complying out of fear. It's about acting with self-respect. It's the part of us that says: *I have the right to feel safe, respected, and whole. I don't need to earn that through silence or sacrifice.* The truth is, we never have to justify our feelings or defend our worth, not to anyone.

Truth #9

Giving too much in an intimate partnership can become a form of self-neglect disguised as devotion.

A young woman sat across from me, eyes tired, voice hoarse. "I do everything I can," she said. "I plan our weekends, I stay quiet when he snaps, I listen when he's upset, but somehow, I'm always falling short." I asked what she needed in the relationship. She hesitated, then realized, "I haven't thought about that in a long time." Her love was genuine. But it had become one-sided, less a relationship, more a form of self-neglect.

When one partner is constantly accommodating while the other takes without giving anything in return, it's not a partnership. It's a performance. When emotional support, patience, and care are met with entitlement or indifference, someone ends up carrying the load for both. Over time, the burden becomes overwhelming. We start to feel like an echo: Our reactions mirror what we believe our partner wants us to say and do.

This pattern often triggers self-doubt: *I must not be doing enough or might be doing things wrong. Maybe I'm the problem here.* However, this isn't a failure of our love. It's the cost of overfunctioning in a relationship that lacks reciprocity. And while overgiving might maintain peace in the short term, it enables unhealthy behaviors and keeps both partners in a dysfunctional cycle. The one who gives too much loses themselves, while the one who takes too much avoids accepting responsibility for their behavior.

The turning point happens when we stop asking, *How can I fix this?* and start asking, *What do I need to feel like an equal?* Those questions shift the focus back to our needs, our worth, our right to be met halfway. They help us set a boundary that encourages connection instead of compliance.

True partnership requires both individuals to show up and take responsibility. When this balance is lost, it signals a need to reevaluate our partnership, rather than increasing our efforts. Being loved means being seen and supported for who we are as a whole person, not just the parts our partner wants from us.

Truth #10
When we tolerate our partner's distancing behavior, we perpetuate a cycle of that behavior and our reaction to it.

When we repeatedly excuse or downplay sarcasm, stonewalling, dismissiveness, rage, and other distancing behaviors, we're not just coping with those behaviors, we're allowing them to continue. Consider the following example. (In this sketch, the woman is the emotionally withholding partner. As already noted, both men and women can demonstrate emotionally distancing behaviors, and both can experience a loss of self.)

Let's say a man is sharing a moment with his female partner that feels real and connected. Then, seemingly out of nowhere, she cuts the moment short with a biting comment. Maybe it's one that conveys cynicism or suspicion. Just like that, the emotional warmth vanishes, leaving her partner hurt and confused. He tries to speak up by saying, "Why would you say that?" But instead of owning her spiteful behavior, she rolls her eyes and dismisses him. What began as closeness ends in distance. Like many times before, he wonders what went wrong. Perhaps you've experienced something similar. I know I have.

This is often the point where echo behavior comes in, prompted by feelings of shame for wanting to feel close to our partners. In a moment like this, a partner seeking intimacy might think, *What did I do to make my partner push me away?* They might then spend the next two days with that experience swirling around in their minds, trying to figure out how to prevent it from happening again. But when one partner attempts to offload their unprocessed emotions onto the other, that person should ask, *Why is my partner ruining what could be a beautiful moment of closeness between us?*

Individuals trapped in this dynamic must seize every opportunity to hold their partners accountable for their dismissive treatment. If not in the moment, then at some point when they've had time to steady themselves and consider the best way to address the unacceptable behavior. (More on appropriate responses to dismissive behavior in part 2.)

Truth #11
We're not betraying our partners when we have relationships with family and friends we can confide in. We're betraying ourselves when we don't.

Sasha hadn't heard much from Gabriele in weeks, just a few vague texts and one missed call. So when Gabriele showed up at her door one evening with puffy eyes, dressed in sweatpants and a T-shirt, as if she hadn't planned to go out, Sasha didn't ask questions. She simply stepped aside and pulled her into a hug.

She invited Gabriele to make herself comfortable on the living room couch and returned with two cups of hot tea and a soft throw blanket. Then she sat beside her. "Whenever you're ready," she said gently. At first, Gabriele hesitated. She'd kept so much to herself about what was happening in her relationship. But then her words spilled out: "He blames me for everything. Even when he hurts me, he says it's my fault. He twists things. I started recording our arguments because I can't tell what's real anymore. And sometimes . . . I actually believe him." Gabriele looked down, covering her face with her hands. "I feel like I'm losing my mind." Sasha reached over and rested a hand on her shoulder. "You're not crazy," she said. "You're thoughtful and kind, and none of this is your fault."

Gabriele let her friend's soothing words sink in. Sasha didn't give advice or try to fix anything. She simply stayed close and listened. For the first time in a long while, Gabriele felt the tension flow out of her body. She looked at her friend and exhaled a ragged breath, like surfacing after being underwater too long.

What would we all do without close relationships outside our partnership? We need our loved ones, and they need us, not only for care, enjoyment, trust, and shared experiences, but also for emotional support and validation.

No one ever has the right to cut us off from those connections. However, this often happens when our partner feels threatened by our relationships. They might not attempt to cut us off directly. Instead, they discourage us from spending time with others or sow doubts about someone through deceptive comments, such as questioning their intentions. Sometimes, the people we're being distanced from have noticed signs of disrespect or manipulation in our relationships and are concerned about our well-being. They want to help us, but we don't let them because our partners have convinced us that what they said is true. For example, in an attempt to isolate us from others, our partner might claim that no one understands us as well as they do, or that others are simply jealous of our relationship. They may accuse others of lying or not really caring about us.

Our partner's efforts to isolate us can be significant. If we withdraw from close relationships that matter to us, we lose the honest reflection of truth that those who care for us provide. This is another symptom of echo behavior.

Another reason we may distance ourselves from supportive people is that we feel ashamed of our relationship and cannot explain why we stay in it. On rare occasions when we open up, it's usually about what our partner did, how they treated us, and their anger. But that's only one side of the equation. What's even more critical than voicing our complaints and concerns about our partner is recognizing the severe effects of their behavior and letting our loved ones help us.

Keep in mind that when we keep secrets from our loved ones about harm in our relationships, we're willfully breaking the emotional connection with them, just as our partners have with us. The people who love us want to know what's happening in our lives, good and bad. We're not a burden to them. When we open up, we give them the opportunity to show us how much they care.

Admitting that we're hurting takes courage. We thrive when we have the support, perspective, and resources of others to help us navigate life's challenges. Having community and connections with people who genuinely care about us is never wrong.

Truth #12
When we accept the truth in our relationship, we can take action to create change.

Who enters a relationship knowing that their sense of self will be reshaped by their partner's need to keep them at an emotional distance? No one! At first, we believed we had the trust and understanding that love requires. When things didn't unfold the way we expected, we made excuses for our partner's put-downs, irrational demands, unjustified anger, and silent treatment. We carried the burden of unresolved issues and unspoken feelings. We prioritized the relationship over our personal values and lost parts of ourselves in the relationship. Those are likely some of the experiences that led you to pick up this book.

We can, however, say goodbye to that path and get on a new one. How? By accepting the truth. By no longer making excuses for our partner's choice to prioritize distance over connection. By no longer attributing their behavior to being moody or controlling, having anger issues, or enduring a difficult childhood. By taking pride in our precious selves and refusing to be less than we truly are.

Changing course takes a lot of energy. And we can get that energy by turning our anger into action. Not rage or aggression, but a deep, simmering realization: *Enough!* That kind of anger is potent. When the truth hits, anger often fuels the courage to draw a line in the sand and to stop shrinking or second-guessing ourselves.

Our partners keep us at an emotional distance *because they can*. When there are no consequences, nothing changes (more on what these consequences should be in an upcoming chapter). Many of my clients reach a turning point when they speak up, assert their needs, and hold their partners accountable for their actions. This act of standing up for the truth shifts the relationship dynamic, and it's impressive to witness. Research by Marianne Lammers and her colleagues supports what I've observed: for women recovering from partner abuse, recognizing the injustice, feeling the anger it sparks, and acknowledging its harmful impact was a critical step toward their recovery.

And here's the thing: Some partners do start to change. It takes time and effort to shift a mindset that considers avoiding emotional intimacy with hurtful treatment acceptable, but even small changes in behavior can be meaningful. If our partners refuse to improve their behavior, we can still take steps toward healing and rebuilding our sense of self independently of our relationships.

After going through the Echo complex, clarity is the first gift we give ourselves. These twelve truths offer some of that clarity. They expose misbeliefs that cause us to doubt ourselves, excuse mistreatment, and give away parts of who we are in the hope of restoring connection. They remind us that safety can't exist where there's emotional distance, that compromising ourselves never creates closeness, and that our partner's behavior often reveals more about their inner world than about our worth. They uncover the harsh truth that emotional abuse isn't always obvious, that "fixing" a partner shifts responsibility away from where it should be, and that what we call self-protection may actually be self-sabotage. They show that true partnership can't exist when one person does all the giving, and that tolerating emotional distance only strengthens the cycle that weakens us.

Taken together, these truths can give us the confidence to pause, understand relationship dynamics for what they truly are, and respond in ways that uphold our dignity. They remind us that our worth is nonnegotiable, that we can reclaim lost parts of ourselves, and that we always have the opportunity to live our lives with courage and honesty.

Seeing the truth is a turning point, but even when we understand the patterns of emotional distance and the toll they take, we can still find ourselves getting pulled into dynamics that defy logic. Next, we'll explore the paradoxical cycles in emotionally distant relationships that widen the emotional gap between us and our partners.

Self-Reflection: Seeing Truth

1. Do you feel emotionally unsafe in your relationship? If so, describe what makes you feel unsafe.
2. Do you feel the need to hide parts of yourself in your relationship to affect your partner's behavior in some way? If so, which parts of yourself are you hiding? How has this impacted you? What makes you feel seen, safe, and supported?
3. Do you feel that your partner causes trouble by getting angry at you over trivial incidents? When this occurs, do you confront them about their behavior, or do you avoid conflict by backing down? What is the outcome of your reaction?
4. Does your partner often behave in ways that upset you, yet you don't view this behavior as emotionally abusive? If so, describe your partner's actions and your reactions to them. How does your partner's treatment of you affect the way you see yourself?
5. Have you distanced yourself from friends, family, or your community since entering your relationship? If so, provide some reasons for your isolation. How does feeling isolated influence your self-image? If you don't feel isolated, how have your relationships with friends and family changed since you've been with your partner?

CHAPTER FOUR

Seven Paradoxes of the Echo Complex

EVERYONE LONGS FOR safety and intimacy in their relationships, but not everyone finds it there. Some of us who desire closeness feel distant. We want safety, but sense threat. We seek reassurance yet remain unsure. When these feelings arise, they might be a sign that we're caught in a paradoxical cycle in our relationship that undermines who we are and what we want. Recognizing the paradox helps us understand what to do about it.

In my therapy practice over the years, I have observed seven distinct paradoxical cycles in relationships. In each cycle, partners may want closeness, but their words and actions cause more distance. Once caught in these patterns, partners may reinforce the very dynamics that are keeping them apart.

The twelve truths discussed in the last chapter reveal what is often hard to see in a relationship with an emotionally avoidant partner: clarity. Knowing those truths helps keep us grounded in times of conflict. They remind us of what is real when self-doubt clouds our judgment or when we question ourselves. We can see our partner's actions for what they are and why our feelings are justified.

While the twelve truths help us find our footing, the seven paradoxes reveal cycles in our relationships that hinder emotional closeness and may keep us in a relationship that will never give us what we need and want. Recognizing these harmful cycles helps us determine what feels right, whether that's working toward a closer, safer bond with our partners or honestly evaluating the relationship and exploring other options.

These are the Seven Paradoxes of The Echo Complex:

1. *The Echo Paradox*: In our effort to build a deep emotional connection with our partners, we give up parts of ourselves, which only fuels the cycle of disconnection.
2. *The Prophecy Paradox*: Acting in ways we believe will help us avoid our partner's rejection actually leads to the rejection we fear.
3. *The Lonely Love Paradox*: We stay in a relationship because we want to be loved, even though we often feel unloved.
4. *The Boundaries Paradox*: In seeking emotional connection, we fail to maintain personal boundaries that foster that connection.
5. *The Silent Scream Paradox*: We suppress painful emotions and unwanted thoughts even though expressing and resolving them can lead to healing.
6. *The Glass Wall Paradox*: One partner's fear of being vulnerable causes them to remain physically close but emotionally distant, making the other partner feel like there's a pane of glass between them: seen but never truly understood.
7. *The Trial by Fire Paradox*: Someone's deep-seated fear of rejection drives them to keep testing their partner's love, which results in the very rejection they're trying to avoid.

The first five paradoxes involve traps we fall into through misguided thinking: We want our partners to fully see us, but we hide parts of ourselves. We are in a love relationship, but feel lonely and unloved. We loosen our boundaries to get closer to our partners, yet firm boundaries promote closeness. We hold in painful feelings when expressing them could set us free. The last two paradoxes relate to the behavior of an emotionally avoidant partner: in fearing rejection, they create the very circumstances that lead to it.

Now, let's take a closer look at these cycles, using real-life examples to make them more relatable, and what needs to happen to overcome them.

The Paradoxes

1. *The Echo Paradox*: In our effort to build a deep emotional connection with our partners, we give up parts of ourselves, which only fuels the cycle of disconnection.

We already understand that sacrificing parts of ourselves won't bring us closer to our partners, but let's look at this truth from a different perspective that highlights its paradoxical nature.

Most people enter a relationship expecting acceptance instead of rejection. They open their hearts and risk being vulnerable to build an emotional connection. However, when they have a partner who believes their own acceptance depends on maintaining emotional distance, the partner seeking intimacy shifts their goal. Instead of wanting to be fully seen and accepted as they are, they focus on adapting themselves to become the person they think their partner wants them to be. Here is how that happens.

Seeing a partner's emotional distance as a sign that they don't accept us for who we are can lead us to believe that we've fallen short of the person with whom our partners fell in love. We might wonder, *Now that they know me better and see my flaws, they're disappointed. I'm not the person they thought I was. I need to be more like what they expected of me.*

The irony here is that our partner seeks acceptance by creating emotional distance, while we seek acceptance by changing ourselves. This dynamic will never fulfill either partner's goal. Instead, it blocks the development of an emotional base camp in the relationship and, if it persists, puts the intimacy-seeking partner at risk of developing the Echo complex.

That's what happens to Ina and Jackson, who meet at a mutual friend's party and are immediately attracted to each other. During their first few months together, they share common interests and have bonding conversations. However, as they grow closer, Jackson begins to criticize Ina over trivial things and dismisses her feelings when she pushes back. He denies his insensitive actions when she confronts him. He doesn't recognize them as hurtful because his fragile self-image is buried beneath layers of defenses he justifies in his mind. He doesn't experience his behavior as "I feel small" moments. Instead, he feels anger, contempt, and a need to assert superiority, as if she deserves his criticism.

As you can see, there's a clear disconnect happening here. In Jackson's mind, he can hide his fragile ego by making Ina feel inferior. Meanwhile, Ina believes that if she can change herself to fit Jackson's idea of an ideal partner, he will return to the loving person she thinks he can be. So she measures her words and keeps her feelings to herself to avoid conflict. She sometimes agrees with his opinions, even when she disagrees. She gives up regular visits with her friends and complies with his demand to always be available to him.

Ina doesn't realize that changing who she is to become what she thinks Jackson wants her to be won't improve how he treats her. It might even make things worse by teaching him that it's okay to withhold emotional support as a way to manipulate her. Regardless of what she does to win his affection, he will maintain an emotional barrier, and she will keep trying to build a connection by holding herself back. Only when Ina recognizes that her efforts are not only futile but also harmful will she be ready to break the paradoxical cycle that is drawing her into the Echo complex.

2. *The Prophecy Paradox*: Acting in ways we think will help us avoid our partner's rejection actually leads to the rejection we fear.

We usually start relationships hoping to be with someone who can understand how we feel, what we need, and who we can turn to for comfort and support. Yet sometimes, despite our best intentions, we end up with someone who is emotionally distant. How does this happen?

Often, the answer is found in the stories we carry about ourselves, stories written long before we knew how to question them. Early experiences with parents, caregivers, siblings, or even peers can shape our beliefs about love and connection. Maybe we learned that love must be earned by taking care of someone or making them happy. Or we came to believe that asking for what we need might drive people away.

Without realizing it, we're drawn to partners who fit these outdated beliefs, even when those relationships ultimately hurt us. It's as if the past pulls us back to what's familiar, not necessarily what's healthy. When we seek love and acceptance without truly understanding what influences our decisions, we might find ourselves going in circles, repeating patterns that hold us back from achieving the relationship we desire. And without that awareness, what we fear most—lack of acceptance, controlling behavior, emotional distance—often becomes the very thing we experience.

Consider Simone, a woman whose domineering father conditioned her to depend on others for her sense of self-worth. Her dad taught her that to earn his approval, she had to set aside her own needs and desires. Whenever she crossed him, he became angry and distant.

Now grown, Simone begins a relationship with Jaden, who initially seems quite different from her father. He helps her find a job, cooks dinner for her, and they go on fun weekend trips together. What a pleasant change—and a relief!

However, as their relationship develops, Jaden gets annoyed whenever she doesn't do what he wants. But instead of trying to reason with him, her old habits cause her to respond to his demands the same way she did to her father's. She tries hard to please him, even when he doesn't consider how his controlling behavior affects her. She doesn't realize that complying with his demands has set a pattern similar to the one she had with her father.

Even though Jaden's behavior upsets Simone, she minimizes his controlling actions, some of which seem normal to her. Even when he slams doors, breaks things, and stonewalls her for hours, she doesn't recognize the root of their issues or her part in them. She keeps trying to be the person she believes he wants her to be, but the more she tries to win him over, the more she remains stuck in the situation that harms her.

Simone has unintentionally recreated the situation she always feared: being rejected by someone she loves. Her conditioned response of suppressing her needs and feelings to avoid confrontation has brought her back to the same circumstances she had as a child. When Simone claims her power as an adult and realizes she doesn't have to tolerate her partner's mistreatment, she can begin to realize the senselessness of her echo behavior and start working on claiming her independence.

3. *The Lonely Love Paradox*: We stay in a relationship because we want to be loved, even though we often feel unloved.

It's upsetting and confusing when our partner claims to love us, but their actions say otherwise. Sometimes, they show affection with kind gestures and words that make us feel seen and appreciated. At other times, they treat us with contempt and a troubling lack of empathy. Feeling loved one moment and unloved the next creates a deep unease in our relationship, leaving us to wonder: *If they truly love me, then why do they hurt me?*

When this happens, we are caught in a tug-of-war between two opposing stories: one that confirms our importance to our partner and another that denies it. In this paradoxical state, we struggle to reconcile our partner's caring behavior with their cold-hearted treatment. Not knowing what's true, we overanalyze our partner's words and actions in search of clues on how to change our behavior to avoid getting hurt again. This hypervigilance can lead us to question our self-worth.

Enid and Carmine demonstrate the lonely love paradox. During Enid's fifteen-year marriage to Carmine, he alternates between acts of kindness, like surprising her with flowers, and alarming behavior, such as exploding into anger over nothing. He tells her how much he loves her, but when she shares her opinion, he says, "That's the dumbest thing I've ever heard," and calls her "clueless." Sometimes he tells her, "You're lucky I stay with you. I could do better." Occasionally, he raises his hand as if to slap her or makes false threats to beat her up. His pattern of switching between being the caring, loving partner and the dismissive, critical adversary creates a cycle that shames Enid and keeps her on edge.

In Enid's efforts to reconcile Carmine's harmful actions with his acts of kindness, she convinces herself that he doesn't mean it or that's just his nature. However, she still feels hurt and disconnected from him. She doesn't realize that his anger and demeaning comments are control tactics meant to keep her at an emotional distance.

For his part, Carmine believes he loves Enid and views his behavior as a temporary glitch that can be fixed with declarations of love or another bouquet. After all, it's how his father treated his mother. In his mind, love is about grand gestures rather than consistent acts of kindness, respect, and emotional support that sustain a relationship. His idea of love lacks the depth and reliability needed for a caring connection.

The paradox of being loved yet feeling unloved is wearing down Enid's sense of self. She is losing sight of her values and beliefs, and her physical health has declined. Her blood pressure has gone up, and her doctor urges her to take steps to bring down her stress level. She is torn between her need for Carmine's love and the fact that she has become someone she does not want to be. Carmine is fine with their relationship because it suits him. He has a partner with whom he can maintain the appearance of emotional intimacy while avoiding the real thing, which he finds threatening. If Enid is going to break the cycle and escape the Echo complex, she will need to set boundaries against Carmine's abusive behavior and work on reclaiming her true self.

4. *The Boundaries Paradox*: In seeking emotional connection, we fail to maintain personal boundaries that foster that connection.

Boundaries are essential in relationships, but they're often misunderstood. People sometimes confuse boundaries with defenses, but they are not the same. Defenses are walls built to keep others out. Boundaries are guardrails that help us stay whole while still being open to connection.

Think of boundaries as lines that help you maintain your sense of self. Without them, you risk losing sight of who you are within the relationship. It's like mixing two paint colors in the same jar. The colors don't retain their distinct character. Boundaries, however, enable you to maintain your own identity while also respecting your partner's. They say, "I respect you as a unique person with your own needs, values, and desires, and I ask you to respect mine, too."

Here's the paradox: When you're with an emotionally distant partner, especially one who avoids closeness through withdrawal, blame, or criticism, it can feel risky to set boundaries. You might fear that insisting on trust, honesty, respect, and emotional transparency will only drive them further away. But the opposite usually happens. When you don't hold those boundaries, you feel less secure in your sense of self, while your partner's behavior doesn't change because nothing is being challenged.

Boundaries foster intimacy by promoting authenticity. They communicate, "This is who I am, this is what I need, and I'm willing to hear the same from you." If your partner responds with the respect and openness you're asking for, the relationship becomes stronger. If they can't or won't, then you can at least see the truth about what you're dealing with, and this knowledge empowers you to decide what's best for you. Either way, setting personal boundaries is not the enemy of intimacy. They are the doorway to it.

Let's consider the example of Nicole and Darryl, who have more defenses than boundaries in their relationship. They have been married for five years without having children, and their income provides a comfortable lifestyle. They live in a luxury high-rise condominium and enjoy fine dining and travel. Although they spend a lot of time together, Nicole longs for emotional intimacy with Darryl. However, when she expresses her frustration about his snide remarks in response to her efforts to get him to open up or listen to her, he defends himself with gaslighting—a form of emotional manipulation that makes someone doubt their own perceptions.

When Nicole complains to Darryl about how he treats her, he says, "I have no idea what you're talking about." He tells her to quit being an "emotional infant" and demands that she leave him alone, saying he doesn't like her "trying to get inside my head all the time." Sometimes, he tells her to leave the relationship if she has a problem with it.

Darryl denies his harmful behavior and sees nothing wrong in how he treats Nicole. He believes he simply doesn't do feelings, even though he managed to convince Nicole that he was open to sharing his feelings early in their relationship when he was trying to win her over. He left home at sixteen and made his way in life by drawing on the lessons he learned from growing up with a single mother of five children and an absent father. His overwhelmed and exhausted mother couldn't nurture her children's emotional needs. Instead, she shamed them for needing her love and attention. Darryl learned that being vulnerable could lead to rejection and shame. In his current state of mind, he's incapable of the emotional intimacy Nicole desires. He believes she should be happy in their relationship because he doesn't cheat on her, and she doesn't have to worry about financial security.

Nicole spends a lot of time feeling distressed about their relationship, trying different ways to reach him. Darryl violates her boundaries of emotional transparency, but she believes spending more time together will help him open up, or at least she tells herself it will. However, her repeated efforts to have sincere conversations trigger the shame he felt as a child for having feelings, causing him to quickly shut her out. Sometimes he says he wants her to be happy with him and that he would do anything she asks. He agrees to go to counseling but backs out at the last minute.

As Nicole struggles to connect with Darryl, she feels anxious around him, never knowing when he will turn hostile, like when he told her he didn't want to be seen with her because he disliked her new hairstyle. This ongoing tension and uncertainty affect Nicole's mental health. She questions her worth and doubts her perceptions. Sometimes she breaks out in hives when she's around him. She longs to be heard, appreciated, and loved by Darryl. She doesn't realize that he will continue to cross her boundaries, using defenses to turn moments of potential connection into emotional standoffs.

When Nicole begins to enforce her boundaries of trust, respect, and emotional transparency, she will realize that Darryl will likely never provide her with the intimacy she longs for in their relationship. She can choose to accept less than she desires or move on in search of a partner who respects her boundaries, rather than feeling threatened by them.

5. *The Silent Scream Paradox*: We suppress painful emotions and unwanted thoughts even though expressing and resolving them can lead to healing.

The silent scream paradox can affect both partners: the one seeking emotional closeness and the one trying to avoid it. When we're distressed by relationship and personal issues but choose to hide our pain, it can feel like a silent scream.

Trying to stuff down upsetting emotions and unwanted thoughts doesn't make them go away. Whenever we remain silent or get aggressive in an attempt to hide or suppress them, they remain active in our minds and bodies, demanding more attention. Carrying the burden of these unexpressed feelings can cause anxiety, depression, unexplained body aches, or more serious health problems. Why? Because we lose touch with who we are if we don't address the part of ourselves that makes us human. Throughout psychological theory, there is a consensus that avoiding negative emotions is a major cause of mental suffering. Only by facing our painful emotions can we move toward healing.

This paradox plays out in the relationship between Kat and Myra. Kat grew up with an emotionally abusive father and a submissive mother who didn't protect her from her father's rages. She's terrified of opening herself up to the painful vulnerability she experienced as a child. Although she longs for a deeper emotional connection with Myra, Kat's fears hinder her from reaching out to her.

Meanwhile, Myra has her own issues in the relationship. She never addressed the emotional neglect from her parents, who often left her with a strict and unsympathetic nanny while they traveled. Her parents' frequent absence and disregard for her feelings led her to believe they didn't matter. She craves Kat's affection and reassurance, but her need to feel close to Kat triggers the painful emotions from her childhood, preventing her from asking for what she needs. The deep shame and anxiety both Kat and Myra carry prevent them from expressing their torment caused by emotional distance in their relationship.

Whenever Myra musters the courage to express her affection, Kat's instinct is to create emotional distance. During these moments, Kat uses jokes, teasing, or sarcasm to break the emotional tension by saying, "Oh, please. Spare me the drama!" or "Stop being so sappy." Or she shifts the conversation to something impersonal. Kat loves Myra and doesn't understand why she sometimes feels so uneasy with her.

Living in a silent scream paradox takes its toll on both of them. Myra suffers from back pain and has trouble sleeping, while Kat often feels tired and unmotivated. Despite their mutual desire for a closer bond, each of them retreats to their respective corners of the relationship. They remain caught in a paradoxical cycle that keeps them living side by side but separated by unspoken feelings neither one is willing to voice.

6. *The Glass Wall Paradox*: One partner's fear of being vulnerable causes them to remain physically close but emotionally distant, making the other partner feel like there's a pane of glass between them: seen but never truly understood.

When the fear of emotions that bring a person closer to their partner gets in the way of emotional closeness, they might be compelled to stay physically close but emotionally distant. They convince themselves, and perhaps their partner, that physical closeness equals emotional closeness. But you and I know that proximity isn't the same as intimacy, and the partner on the other side of the glass who longs to be close feels the ache of emotional distance.

The avoidant partner sends mixed messages: *Stay with me, but don't get too close.* They may want connection but react defensively when it's offered, retreating into emotional absence or retaliating with hurtful behavior. Their avoidance doesn't mean a lack of feeling. Rather, they keep relationships on the surface to escape the discomfort of introspection. Beneath these reactions, a defense was formed long ago to protect against pain. For some, being vulnerable once meant getting hurt. Surface-level relating became a safer choice.

For those seeking emotional intimacy, their partner's superficial way of relating is painful and confusing. They may ask themselves: *What's wrong with me? Why doesn't my partner care about my feelings? Do I have the right to expect more?* Over time, the effort to be emotionally close can blur the line between their true self and the self they've created to cope with their partner's shallowness.

To break down the emotional glass wall between them, both partners need to confront their fears and misconceptions. They must have honest, open conversations about their deeper feelings and the reasons behind them. Len and Sienna give us an example of the glass wall paradox.

They have two school-aged children, one from each of their prior marriages. Sienna's vibrant personality and sexual allure captivate Len when they first meet, while she finds Len's kindness and humor irresistible. Len feels as though he has finally found someone with whom he can connect both emotionally and physically.

However, Len notices that Sienna is often distracted during their first year of marriage. She takes on excessive volunteer work at her children's school, which gives her an excuse to come home late and stay away on weekends. In their quiet moments together, when Len tries to have an intimate conversation, she reaches for her phone or insists she has a task that can't wait. Often, she downplays their lack of emotional intimacy by starting an impersonal debate or saying, "It's no big deal.

We're fine." Initially, he attributes Sienna's behavior to her high energy and adult attention deficit hyperactivity disorder (ADHD). He struggles with his loneliness as he considers how to cope with it.

When Len calls a meeting with Sienna to discuss how they can better manage their work, children, and relationship, she agrees to make some changes. However, she doesn't follow up with action. Instead, she gaslights him by claiming she doesn't remember or didn't agree to their plan.

Len is confused. Sienna wants him close physically but not emotionally. He longs for her to see, hear, and understand him, hoping they can be a couple in every sense. He keeps trying to connect with her but gets the same empty responses. Sometimes, he questions whether his needs are valid, wondering if he's asking too much of her. To ease his pain, he tries to reassure himself that their relationship gives him enough of what he needs in a partnership. Nevertheless, his frustration and unhappiness drain his ability to be the kind of father, husband, and friend he wants to be.

What's happening with Sienna? Unbeknownst to Len, Sienna is deeply affected by unresolved abuse trauma from her past. She is seeing a counselor for ADHD, but she also needs therapy to process her complex trauma. If her counselor understood how serious Sienna's condition is, he would see the extent of her fear, shame, and guilt. He would refer her to a trauma therapist who could help her dismantle the emotional glass wall she has built around herself. With this support, she could realize that she's subconsciously keeping Len at arm's length in an attempt to make sure she won't be the one getting hurt this time. The trauma therapist could help her understand that she is no longer in danger.

If Len and Sienna want to escape this paradoxical cycle, the one that leaves them staring at each other through an emotional glass wall, they must confront what's holding them back. Only then can they start to reach for each other in ways that feel genuine, where both partners are truly seen, heard, and understood.

7. *The Trial by Fire Paradox*: Someone's deep-seated fear of rejection can drive them to keep testing their partner's love, which results in the very rejection they're trying to avoid.

When one partner's fear of emotional connection drives a need to "test" their partner's love through irrational and harsh demands, the other partner typically responds in one of two ways. They either keep trying to get closer or pull away. Both reactions are attempts to protect themselves from the "test" and to alter how they interact with their partner.

The trial by fire paradox shows up when the fearful or insecure partner demands constant reassurance, becomes jealous or suspicious, or criticizes their partner for not doing enough. These behaviors usually don't come from a desire to hurt their partner. Instead, they grow out of a deep worry that "I'm not lovable" or "You'll leave me."

The painful irony is that the more the fearful partner tests, the more hurt the other person feels. The partner on the receiving end is left in a bind. Sometimes they lean in, trying to reassure and prove their love. At other times, they pull away because the pressure to prove themselves is exhausting. Either way, whether they put in more effort or step back, they can't keep up with the demands of the trial. They may develop echo behavior, trying to reshape themselves to appease their partner, or they might defend themselves by getting angry, fighting back, or shutting down entirely.

And here's what keeps the trial by fire cycle going: no matter what the reassuring partner does, it's never enough. The fearful partner always finds more reasons to doubt, question, and demand. Because the real issue isn't whether love is present. The love is often very much there. Rather, it's that the fear of losing love can't be soothed from the outside.

When the desire for both partners to feel secure in the relationship turns into a trial by fire cycle, it keeps the one being tested on guard for the next offense, argument, or accusation. This heightened level of anxiety can lead them to feel self-doubt, shame, and guilt. It shifts focus and energy away from their work, other relationships, activities, and personal fulfillment. Charlie and Jordan give us an example of how this happens.

Charlie and Jordan are young men in love who have been together for six years. They have separate homes but spend a lot of time together. Charlie struggles with low self-worth and a fear of abandonment caused by emotional neglect during childhood. When he was five, his parents divorced, and he was separated from his mother. He went to live with his workaholic father in another state, whose second wife, a stern and unloving woman, raised him. As an adult, Charlie still fears being abandoned by the one person he allowed himself to get close to. He doesn't feel worthy of Jordan's love, so he constantly tests Jordan to prove it. Charlie texts Jordan throughout the day and late into the night when Jordan is on business trips as the head of a consulting firm. If Jordan isn't available at any time of day or night, Charlie gets angry and punishes him with blame and accusations, refusing to speak to him when Jordan gets home.

Unsurprisingly, Charlie's attempt to protect himself from getting hurt backfires. Jordan tries his best to reassure Charlie of his love and spends more time with him. However, Jordan can't mend the hole in Charlie's heart. He begins to resent Charlie for his irrational demands on Jordan's time and rough treatment when Jordan can't comply.

As the weight of the paradoxical cycle becomes too much to handle, Jordan fluctuates between feeling inadequate as Charlie's partner, questioning whether his complaints are warranted, and pulling away by arranging more out-of-town business trips while ignoring Charlie's texts and calls. Jordan believes he needs to protect himself from Charlie's demands, but his distance only deepens Charlie's insecurity about their relationship. Charlie can't understand why his efforts to keep them connected are tearing them apart.

Healing starts for partners in the trial by fire paradox when they're both willing to shift from a fear-based way of relating to a trust-based connection that lets each person flourish. Like the other couples in the stories illustrating each paradox, Jordan and Charlie must recognize that the patterns they've created in their relationship are significant barriers to achieving their shared goal of feeling close, secure, and happy with each other.

These seven paradoxes often emerge when our deepest desires for love collide with our greatest fears. As we've seen, sometimes we end up behaving in ways that create the very outcomes we fear most, leaving us feeling like outsiders in our relationships. In our efforts to nurture the bond, maintain peace, or hold on to closeness, we give so much of ourselves that we forget to look after our own needs. We might also weaken the boundaries that keep us safe or turn away from difficult truths, unintentionally creating more distance in our relationships.

Recognizing these paradoxes opens the opportunity to make changes, which is best addressed with the help of a professional therapist. However, if therapy isn't an option due to financial or insurance barriers, lack of access, cultural biases against therapy, or a controlling partner, we can pursue self-guided work. Let's look at some options.

Therapy
One Way out of Paradoxical Cycles

Therapy can be a powerful tool that helps bring the truth into focus and encourages clear thinking. An experienced psychotherapist creates a safe space where both partners can share their feelings, explore their fears and frustrations, and develop a deeper understanding of themselves and each other.

Before discussing the importance of therapy, I would like to address some common obstacles that prevent people from seeking it. When fear, ingrained beliefs, or cultural biases prevent one or both partners from seeking therapy, they need to understand that they are prioritizing personal beliefs over their relationship.

For example, if they believe therapy is only for weak people or those with a more liberal mindset, or that it conflicts with their religion, they might find it hard to see how their past affects their present lives and why they are struggling with personal and relationship issues. They may miss an opportunity to improve themselves and their relationships. When the partner who withholds intimacy refuses therapy, it sends a clear message about their priorities.

Admittedly, therapy can be tough because it asks us to face uncomfortable truths. But those difficult moments are a part of the journey, and avoiding them will only prolong the pain, sometimes for a lifetime. By digging into the root causes of our relationship struggles and working through them, we can move forward. As we've seen, when partners act hurtfully or accept hurtful behavior, it's often because patterns of thinking from the past continue to influence the present and have never been challenged. Early experiences involving trauma and loss, and persistent neglect, dismissal, criticism, and inconsistency can leave emotional scars that show up in our adult lives.

One common ingrained pattern of thinking in a partner who behaves in hurtful ways might be: *If they love me, they'll do what I want.* Or, *if there's a problem, it's their fault, not mine.* On the other hand, someone with a sense of inadequacy and low self-esteem might tend to overgive. They might tie their self-worth to their role as a caretaker or "people fixer."

Of course, not everyone who faces hardship in childhood carries those wounds into their adult relationships. Many grow into strong, compassionate, and capable partners, drawing on the resilience they have built through life experiences. They learn through trial and error what healthy love requires, such as trust, honesty, and empathy, and they deliberately practice these qualities. Over time, they cultivate relationships where both partners feel safe, valued, and deeply connected, demonstrating that early pain need not affect the ability to love someone.

Those who haven't yet learned these lessons might keep repeating familiar patterns of thinking and behavior, even if they cause issues and prevent them from fully loving someone and accepting love in return. Healing comes from understanding that past experiences and embedded beliefs often cause underlying relationship problems, and true healing involves replacing false perceptions with healthy ones based on what is true now.

Therapy can be a beacon of hope for many. However, I must emphasize an important warning: When abuse is present in a relationship, couples counseling (rather than individual therapy) can sometimes cause more damage than good. Why? Because a partner who fears emotional intimacy may feel justified in keeping their partner at a distance by any means and show no remorse. They might depict themselves as the reasonable, wounded one while discrediting their partner. They may also use information disclosed in therapy to intensify their distancing behavior. As a result, the partner on the receiving end can feel invalidated and, in some cases, retraumatized.

For these reasons, I suggest a different approach. Instead of traditional couples counseling, each partner should undergo individual therapy with professionals who can, if both partners agree, collaborate with each other. This allows therapists to share insights and ensure that therapeutic efforts focus on safety and addressing core issues, rather than just the appearance of "working on the relationship."

At this point, you might be thinking: *There's no way my partner will go to therapy.* Maybe you've even suggested this solution before and been met with resistance. It's certainly not uncommon for someone who hurts their partners and avoids intimacy to shun therapy. They may do this because, whether consciously or subconsciously, they fear exposing the unwanted thoughts and feelings they've been hiding. Another reason is that they lack empathy and don't see a need for therapy. They might view their relationship issues as entirely their partner's fault.

When one partner isn't willing to engage in therapy, the other partner, who feels unseen in their relationship, should still seek treatment. Whether you're working with a therapist or not, this book can serve as a trusted guide in your healing process. Each chapter aims to help you see your relationship with fresh eyes, understand the patterns that erode your sense of self, and recognize when the dynamic has shifted into emotional abuse. You'll find practical steps to rebuild your confidence, strengthen your boundaries, and reconnect with yourself. You can begin to reclaim your voice, your sense of self-worth, and your ability to be in a relationship without losing yourself.

When Therapy Is Not an Option

If therapy isn't available to you, you can still begin protecting your sense of self by changing how you respond to your partner's distancing behavior. Start by noticing the moments when their words or actions make you feel small, silenced, or unsure of your own reality.

Pay attention to how you tend to react, whether you get angry, blame yourself, minimize your feelings, or stay quiet to avoid conflict.

As you observe these patterns, consider how they may be connected to earlier relationships, where these reactions may have once helped you feel safer. Understanding this connection with the past empowers you to choose new responses that honor who you are today. Each time you express your real feelings, needs, or boundaries, you reclaim a piece of yourself.

This book and its exercises will support you in that process, offering tools and insights to help you rebuild a stronger, clearer sense of self in your relationship.

Choosing to Leave or Stay

Thinking about whether to leave or stay? Whatever you decide, remember that it's okay to take some time to make the right choice for you (unless your situation is not safe). As you become more aware of how you have compromised your identity, you will likely see your partner's controlling and distancing behavior more clearly. Accepting the reality of what has happened in your relationship and what it will take to reclaim yourself may lead you to conclude that leaving is the best course of action.

If you choose to stay in the relationship, healing will be more challenging depending on the intensity of your partner's distancing behavior and their willingness to make positive changes. The same patterns in your relationship that caused the harm can hinder your recovery. For healing to happen while remaining, there must be no emotional abuse or distancing behavior. Without these conditions, staying usually means the harm will continue, and healing will be limited.

In the next chapter, we'll look at common echo mindsets that can lead to unhealthy relationship patterns. By understanding what drives our echo thoughts and behaviors from a subconscious level, we can start to interrupt harmful cycles. As we uncover previously unseen reasons for losing ourselves, we may experience a full range of emotions, including anger, sadness, fear, love, and longing. There may also be moments of relief and renewed hope, reminding us that recovery is possible.

Self-Reflection: Identifying Paradoxical Cycles

1. Do you feel there is one or more paradoxical cycles in your relationship? If so, which paradoxical cycle(s) resonate with you? How does recognizing their presence feel to you? How does each paradox affect your ability to be fully present in your relationship?
2. Consider whether there are similarities between your current relationship and an earlier one, such as with a parent or another authority figure. Are those similarities positive or negative? How have these similarities affected your relationship?
3. Do you have clear personal boundaries in your relationship? What are those boundaries, and how do you enforce them? Does your partner respect them? If not, how do they violate your boundaries? How do you respond?
4. Do you feel that your partner sees and accepts your authentic self? Can you have emotionally open conversations with them? Do they share their feelings respectfully, or is their typical reaction to intimate talks one of anger, frustration, or withdrawal? How do you feel after discussing important matters with your partner?
5. Do you ever feel like your partner has a pattern of "testing your love" and wanting you to prove it? If so, how does it make you feel in your relationship? Have you tried discussing their behavior with them? What was their reaction?

CHAPTER FIVE

Inside the Echo Mindset

WHEN JEFF'S FAMILY points out how his wife, Emma, puts him down in front of others, he brushes it off. "She's high-strung. That's just her way," he explains, more to convince himself than to convince them. At home, Jeff relies on the same defenses. When he attempts to talk to Emma about how she always has to be right, she dismisses his feelings and gaslights him by denying her behavior. *Just let it go. It's not worth getting into an argument*, he tells himself. Sometimes he thinks, *Maybe she's right. Maybe it's my fault she acts this way toward me.* These are the stories Jeff repeats to soften the sting of Emma's actions. However, her demeaning behavior toward him erodes his confidence. Over time, he feels less like himself. And still, he convinces himself that excusing her behavior is safer than facing what it might reveal about him, her, and their relationship.

In Jeff's relationship, the harmful pattern isn't just about how Emma treats him. It's also about how he responds. By minimizing or excusing her hurtful behavior, he unintentionally allows it to continue and eventually adapts to it.

This coping strategy helps him avoid conflict and hold onto what he wants to believe, but it comes at a high cost. His sense of self becomes shaped more by how Emma treats him than by his needs and values. He tries harder to please her, while justifying or explaining away her actions. To break these patterns, Jeff must learn to recognize when he is relying on unquestioned beliefs and defenses to avoid confronting the truth.

In this chapter, we'll explore how we can get trapped in an echo mindset that keeps us feeling unseen and unheard in our relationships. Echo reactions cause us to downplay our pain or dismiss the seriousness of the situation, even when we sense that it's not right.

But we don't have to be driven by these subconscious mindsets. In the following section, I'll explain two types of powerful mental traps that keep people stuck in emotionally unsafe patterns: cognitive bias and defense mechanisms. These traps are subtle, convincing, and often seem like the truth. But once we learn to recognize them, we can start seeing our situation more clearly and stop shaping our behavior based on our partner's refusal to truly see, hear, and understand us.

As you read this chapter on the echo mindset, I encourage you to observe the dynamics in your relationship more closely, especially those you tend to overlook. Think about whether you might have a bias based on existing beliefs that needs to be challenged, or if you're using a defense mechanism to bend the truth. You can do this by noticing daily moments when you feel ignored, controlled, or emotionally distant and how you respond to them. Facing those moments can be uncomfortable, perhaps more so than you're willing to admit. But it can also help you stop minimizing your pain and recognize what's actually happening. Seeing clearly allows you to make choices based on truth, rather than fear, habit, or unquestioned beliefs.

The Trap of Cognitive Bias

Sometimes, those of us in relationships with emotionally withholding partners undermine ourselves by hanging on to what feels true rather than what *is* true. We tend to trust what's comfortable and aligns with our existing view, even when the facts contradict it. Why do we do this? Research by psychologists Daniel Kahneman and Amos Tversky shows that our thinking can be influenced by unconscious biases that distort our perception of reality.

In the early 1970s, Kahneman and Tversky introduced the concept of cognitive bias to explain how our brains take mental shortcuts when making judgments or decisions. These biases are mostly subconscious and come from the brain's attempts to simplify a world that is extremely complex. In many cases, these shortcuts can be beneficial. They enable quick decisions, conserve mental energy, and allow us to respond efficiently in familiar or urgent situations. Without them, daily life would be slowed down by constant, exhausting analysis. However, the same shortcuts that help us navigate the world can also distort reality, leading to shallow views, poor judgment, and flawed decisions. When we recognize these biases, we can reevaluate how we formed our beliefs and seek evidence to verify their accuracy.

In relationships, cognitive biases can cause us to project our hopes onto someone new, convinced they possess the emotional maturity, empathy, or commitment we seek, even if there is not yet solid evidence to support it.

At the beginning, we tend to focus on glimpses of ideal qualities in our love interest—like kindness, attentiveness, and vulnerability—and fill in the blanks with what we hope is true. When their behavior contradicts our image, such as controlling behavior, criticizing, or withdrawing, we rationalize it. *They're really not like that.* While occasional criticism or withdrawal can be normal, these actions can develop into patterns that cause harm.

Sometimes, it's true that a person is just stressed and their behavior improves. However, there may be a larger issue at hand, one that we may overlook or excuse. In time, excusing our partner's unacceptable behavior becomes a trap. That's because we're invested in an image of that person that exists more in our minds than in reality, and we lose ourselves trying to make the relationship work. We continue to believe we have a deep emotional connection with our partners despite mounting evidence that the connection we thought we had was never truly there.

Let's look at several types of cognitive biases in relationships that cause us to give up parts of ourselves that define who we are. Each bias type is described and illustrated with vignettes featuring real-life couples.

Confirmation Bias

One common form of cognitive bias is confirmation bias, the tendency to seek out or interpret evidence in ways that support or confirm our desires or expectations, while ignoring or dismissing evidence that contradicts them. When we experience confirmation bias, our brains are more likely to label as accurate information that fits with our existing beliefs. Our brains quickly filter out contradictory evidence because it threatens our current beliefs and forces us to reevaluate our views. In this way, confirmation bias acts as a mental gatekeeper, preventing us from facing difficult truths.

When we realize that qualities in a person, such as integrity and respect, are missing, we must acknowledge that our thinking may be flawed. Here are some common confirmation biases in relationships and the truths they hide:

- Misreading our partner's mistreatment as occasional rather than a pattern of behavior.
  Chronic mistreatment is deliberate and will persist if not addressed.
- Failing to deal with issues in our relationship by telling ourselves they will eventually go away.
  Issues must be resolved, or they will establish a precedent in the relationship.
- Prioritizing our partner's needs over our own to be a "good partner" when it's not appropriate. *Overgiving can cause us to lose ourselves.*
- Taking the blame for our partner's mistreatment because we believe they love us and wouldn't intentionally hurt us.
  If there's no genuine remorse after mistreatment, and it happens consistently, it's abusive.
- Taking responsibility for our partner's behavior as an act of empathy.
  Empathy doesn't mean being responsible for another person's unacceptable behavior.
- Believing that our partner's frequent criticism is intended to help us.
  Demeaning criticism is a method used to control someone and create emotional distance from them.

- Holding onto hope that our partners will change, despite the lack of evidence to support this expectation.
  Change requires taking responsibility and acting in ways that produce lasting results.

Janet and Mark's story illustrates how her confirmation bias about him causes her to give up an activity that energizes and fulfills her. Believing his comments are well-intentioned, she doesn't realize they are the beginning of a pattern of treatment designed to undermine her sense of self so he can better control her.

Janet and Mark

The Discouraged Artist

Janet, a single woman in her forties, returned to creating the artwork she had abandoned years before when her mother insisted that she major in business rather than art in college. Now she gets a lot of encouragement from her friends, who recognize her talent for abstract art. Shortly after she resumes her artwork, she meets Mark, who also appears to support her creativity by going with her to art museums and paying for some of her art supplies. However, as their relationship progresses, he downplays her art, saying things like, "I don't know why you would call that art. Anyone could do it." He claims her friends are "being nice" when they compliment her work.

Janet's hurt feelings reveal a deeper truth about Mark: He is not an emotionally safe partner because he dismisses something very meaningful to her. His lack of support not only disrespects her values but also her emotions. However, her confirmation bias about Mark leads her to believe that he genuinely cares about her and wouldn't say anything untrue. He strengthens her bias by claiming he's protecting her, like when he says, "I'm just being honest with you so you don't make a fool out of yourself." In response, she doubts her abilities and questions whether her mother was right to discourage her from pursuing her creative interests.

By listening to the wisdom in her hurt feelings and comparing her beliefs about Mark with his actions, Janet will be better prepared to stand up for her right to create art without his negative comments. She might even realize that his belittling remarks are strong signs of his insecurity and desire to control her. If she doesn't, Mark's lack of support could be the start of a pattern of behavior that allows him to manipulate her actions and feelings, preventing emotional intimacy. Besides a confirmation bias, there's also a boundaries paradox (Paradox #4 from the previous chapter) at play here: Mark is crossing a trust boundary that lets Janet pursue her passion free from his derogatory remarks.

When she sees through her confirmation bias and recognizes the crossed boundaries in their relationship, she will realize that creating art is essential to her personal growth and sense of self, and that she has every reason to embrace it. It's okay for Mark to voice his opinion about her art, but it is not acceptable for him to do so in a way that discourages her from doing what brings her joy and serenity.

When confirmation bias leads people to believe falsehoods, it can have more frequent and harmful effects. Read on to see how other types of cognitive bias can show up in intimate relationships and contribute to a loss of self.

Anchoring Bias

Kahneman and Tversky introduced a second bias, known as the anchoring bias, in a 1974 research paper published in the journal *Science*. Anchoring bias involves clinging to the first piece of information we receive and sticking with it, even when circumstances change. In relationships, this bias can appear as someone holding onto happy memories from early experiences, believing that if they try hard enough, they can recapture that joy. Even when the relationship becomes toxic or emotionally hollow, they don't want to acknowledge how much the dynamic has shifted. This warped perspective makes it harder to confront the truth and address the deeper issues driving their loss of self. Lucas and Terrence's story shows how anchoring bias plays out in relationships.

Lucas and Terrence

The Honeymoon Phase Anchor

Lucas and Terrence meet during a sun-soaked summer vacation in Cape Cod, where they feel an immediate attraction to each other. Fun-filled days with friends and evening walks along the beach seem like a dream come true. Lucas feels sure he has found the one he has been waiting for. Both live in New York and are determined to turn their whirlwind romance into a lasting relationship. Upon returning home, they spend a lot of time together.

As the months go by, however, Terrence's behavior toward Lucas begins to change. Instead of the growing emotional closeness Lucas expects, Terrence becomes irritable and fault-finding. He snaps at minor issues and makes hurtful remarks. Claiming only that he needs space, he goes away for a week at a time without providing any details about where he's been. Lucas takes Terrence's behavior personally, thinking he might be responsible for Terrence's emotional distance. Although he's puzzled and distressed by the change in his partner, Lucas holds on to the memory of those perfect two weeks in Cape Cod. He believes that if he is more patient, more understanding, or more *something*, they will be able to recapture their bliss.

Over time, Lucas molds himself to match Terrence's preferences. He quits his poetry book club after Terrence mocks it as pretentious and keeps his thoughts and feelings to himself, worried that revealing too much will push Terrence further away. Lucas's compromises to please Terrence make him feel disconnected from his true self. He longs for a more independent life where he can be himself and find happiness with Terrence.

Lucas's cognitive bias about Terrence keeps him anchored in the belief that Terrence will return to the warm and emotionally transparent man with whom he fell in love. However, they find themselves in a glass wall paradox (Paradox #6 from chapter 4), with Terrence keeping Lucas physically close but emotionally distant. Unbeknownst to Lucas, Terrence suffers from internalized homophobia, in which someone with same-sex attraction turns the negative attitudes of others against themselves. Terrence wants to be with Lucas, but he can only reveal glimpses of his vulnerability in a vacation setting that doesn't require him to maintain long-term emotional intimacy with another man.

Lucas faces a critical turning point in his relationship. He can continue to relinquish his sense of self around Terrence to sustain their bond, or he can bravely confront Terrence with honesty and compassion, encouraging both to seek professional help. But first, Lucas needs to recognize the bias that distorts his perception of Terrence, understand the true meaning behind their struggles, and challenge his belief that hiding himself will prevent Terrence from leaving. He also needs to recognize that the man he first met only revealed part of who he truly was, and now, in this later stage of their relationship, the patterns that have developed prevent the love they both want. From that place of clarity, Lucas can make an informed decision about whether to stay with Terrence or leave to find a relationship with someone who can love him freely and fully.

The Halo Effect Bias

The halo effect bias is the tendency to form a positive impression of someone based on a single characteristic, such as success, charm, or physical attractiveness. Social psychologists Richard Nisbett and Timothy DeCamp Wilson at the University of Michigan in 1977 expanded on Edward L. Thorndike's introduction of this effect by demonstrating the power of first impressions. They filmed two interviews with the same college instructor, one in which he acted warm and friendly, and the other cold and distant. When the instructor appeared warm and friendly, people not only liked him more overall, but they also thought he looked better, moved more smoothly, and even had a nicer accent. However, when he acted cold and distant, those same traits were judged more harshly. What's remarkable is that participants didn't realize their overall impression influenced their judgments.

Psychologists Carlota Batres and Victor Shiramizu furthered the research in 2023 by studying the "attractiveness halo effect" in forty-five countries. Their study showed that faces rated as more attractive were also rated more positively on traits such as confidence, intelligence, sociability, and trustworthiness, demonstrating the effect's cross-cultural presence.

The halo effect bias shows how our minds tend to focus on one positive trait of someone we like and let it shape our overall view of their character. This can help us quickly trust or form good relationships, because we associate being friendly and communicating well with being capable and dependable. But it can also be risky because it might cause us to overlook flaws, forgive harmful actions, or disregard evidence that conflicts with our first impression. When the halo effect occurs, it becomes hard to change our opinion of someone, even when strong evidence suggests otherwise.

Similar to the anchoring bias, the halo effect can lead us into a relationship with someone we don't fully know. We might assume their kindness also means they are trustworthy and capable of a close and supportive partnership. When their behavior doesn't fit with our view of their character, based on just one standout trait, our bias makes it hard for us to accept the truth, adjust our impression, or leave the situation. Instead of expecting the other person to change their behavior, we might alter our thinking and actions in ways that weaken our sense of self in the relationship.

Once again, we see that allowing bias to influence our decisions puts us at risk of developing the Echo complex. The relationship between Olivia and Ethan illustrates this phenomenon.

Olivia and Ethan

The Successful Partner

Olivia married Ethan thirty-two years ago. She was initially drawn to his caring attitude toward others, believing he would continue to treat her well and become a successful doctor. She guessed the physician part right. He eventually became the head of a division at a major hospital, but not much else has gone well in their relationship.

Ethan is not the type to rage, but his cold demeanor keeps Olivia at an emotional distance just as effectively. She said he had always been a "take charge" type, but after their children were born, his controlling behavior became more obvious. From then on, he insisted on telling her what to do, kept their finances secret, blamed her for things beyond her control, and undermined her parenting. Whenever she expressed her hurt feelings, he gaslit her by denying his actions and accusing her of self-pity. His lack of empathy toward Olivia was difficult to understand, especially given his kindness and caring toward others.

Olivia's halo effect bias (and the effect of the relationship's paradoxical cycles) leads her to believe she is to blame for Ethan's behavior. She develops a less favorable view of herself and often thinks, *What's wrong with me? Maybe what he says is true. Maybe I am doing what he says I am doing.* She used to be open with her thoughts and feelings, but she describes herself as having been "tongue-tied for years."

Their daughter, now an adult with a young family of her own, lives nearby and has some of her father's vindictive tendencies. Because her father treats her well and convinces her that her mother is the problem, she defends him. When Ethan deliberately causes trouble and upsets Olivia, she blames her mother, calling her "moody." Olivia wants to tell her daughter the truth, that living with him has caused her years of silent suffering. But fear holds her back. She believes speaking out against Ethan will damage her relationship with her daughter.

Olivia is "tormented" by how Ethan treats her. The difference between his public and private personas makes her feel like she's living in two separate worlds. Recently, she has considered leaving him and has spoken with a family attorney. However, she hasn't worked for many years and worries about living alone, as well as how a breakup might affect her family. She has developed tachycardia and sometimes feels dizzy and faint. She says she "doesn't have the stamina" to leave the relationship. Meanwhile, Ethan's drinking worsens, and he falls into "dark moods" where he's angry and depressed.

When Ethan is cited for a DUI, he seems to regret his actions, and Olivia believes it might be a good time to push for couples therapy. He agrees to go, but only pretends to participate in the therapy sessions. Before each session, he dictates how Olivia should change, what to say, and how to treat him during the sessions. Afterward, he uses the content of their sessions to berate her.

When Olivia can no longer endure her anguish, she joins a women's therapy support group where she meets others with similar struggles. Through the group's support and shared experiences, she discovers a possible reason why Ethan's public image doesn't match his private behavior toward her.

Ethan likely has narcissistic personality disorder, which occurs when someone has an exaggerated sense of their importance and constantly seeks admiration, but shows little genuine empathy for others. They tend to see relationships in terms of what they can get rather than what they can give, and often overlook or dismiss others' feelings if they don't benefit their own needs. People with this disorder generally view others as the source of their problems.

Ethan definitely fits this pattern. Behind his facade of extreme confidence, he's vulnerable to even the slightest criticism. He's skilled at crafting an image of how he wants others to see him when they don't know him personally. However, beneath his friendly exterior, there's a man who is unable to have an intimate relationship. His lack of empathy allows him to betray Olivia through his actions without feeling remorse.

Armed with her new knowledge and insight, Olivia reevaluates her situation and musters the courage to leave Ethan. After an acrimonious divorce and a period of adjustment to her new life, Olivia focuses on rebuilding her confidence and surrounding herself with supportive people. Her experience with Ethan leaves her with emotional wounds. But it also teaches her something else: the importance of self-respect, honoring her emotions, and the danger of judging someone based on an attractive façade that conceals deeper truths capable of causing irreparable harm.

The Shared Reality Bias

The shared reality bias is the tendency to believe something is more real when others see it the same way. Social psychologists C. D. Hardin and E. Tory Higgins, in their article for the *Handbook of Motivation and*

Cognition: The Interpersonal Context, define the shared reality bias as the idea that if we keep our thoughts, feelings, or experiences to ourselves, we may feel uncertain about them. But if we share them with someone and they say, "Yes, I get that," it feels true. In other words, things feel more real and valid when we experience them with others.

Having a shared reality bias can be a healthy way to build social connections through common feelings and concerns. In relationships, a shared reality helps foster a sense of unity, as what both partners believe to be true forms a central part of their identity. In their book, *Love and the Expansion of Self: Understanding Attraction and Satisfaction*, social psychologists Arthur and Elaine N. Aron argue that in close relationships, partners expand their sense of self by incorporating each other's perspectives, identities, and experiences. So, what feels personal becomes a shared reality. Essentially, when someone becomes part of your "expanded self," their world becomes your world too, and both of you develop a more connected, validated sense of reality together.

But shared reality can also be maladaptive. In *Shared Reality: What Makes Us Strong and Tears Us Apart*, Higgins explains how our shared realities can make us vulnerable to intergroup conflicts and emotional issues. Shared reality bias can occur not only between romantic partners but also between a partner and their close friends or family. In my experience, I've seen one partner use this bias to gain control over the other, both inside and outside the relationship. For instance, when someone makes negative comments about their partner, whether directly to them or to others, the person being criticized and those who hear the comments may start to believe the criticism is valid. This creates an imbalance in the relationship and makes the mistreated partner feel undervalued. In the story that follows, Lily and Ryan demonstrate the negative side of shared reality bias in close relationships.

Lily and Ryan

The "Overly Emotional" Woman

Lily's ability to openly express her feelings has helped her develop a grounded sense of self. However, after seven years in a relationship with

Ryan, she has begun to question whether her feelings are valid. When she gets upset by his actions, like canceling plans at the last minute or mocking her opinions, he shifts the blame onto her. "You're being ridiculous," he says. "You get so emotional over things that don't really matter." If she presses further, he sighs and adds, "Is it that time of the month?"

The repetition of Ryan's claim that Lily is "overly emotional" prompts her to reconsider her reactions to his remarks. *Am I wrong to feel hurt that Ryan didn't acknowledge our anniversary and brushes off my repeated objections to his overspending?* Lily's acceptance of Ryan's depiction of her leads to a shared reality bias. Her conflicted feelings about what she *should think* leave her uncertain about whether to confront Ryan.

At social gatherings, Ryan exaggerates stories about Lily's "emotional outbursts," portraying her as overreacting and unable to control her emotions. During an outing with friends, he recounts a recent night when he got irritated with their young server for bringing him the wrong dinner entrée. "It was no big deal, but Lily got really mad at me and didn't speak to me for days." Their friends chuckle, subtly supporting Ryan's version of Lily's behavior. However, Lily remembers the incident differently. Ryan humiliated the server by calling her a "bimbo" and asking for the name of the restaurant's manager. Afterward, Lily complained about Ryan's rudeness and went to apologize to the server. Lily was so disappointed in Ryan's behavior that she stayed silent on the way home.

Another time, Ryan's brother, Jarrett, pulls Lily aside and tells her she has to stop "being so hard" on Ryan. Lily is dumbfounded. She realizes that Ryan's comments about her being overly emotional are affecting others' opinions of her.

Ryan continues to reinforce this shared reality bias. After dinner at their apartment one night, he invites their friends to play pool and leaves all the cleanup to Lily. She sits in the kitchen, weighed down by unspoken resentment. She wants to tell Ryan how she feels about his actions, but she hesitates. *Maybe I should just do the cleanup and stop obsessing over it*, she thinks. Just then, a friend walks into the kitchen and offers to help. She sees the serious look on Lily's face. "I'd be pissed off too if my husband left all the cleanup to me," says her friend. "It's disrespectful. I'd tell him that's not okay."

Her friend's comments validate Lily, prompting her to start working with a therapist to address her self-doubt and Ryan's behavior. During these sessions, she realizes that Ryan's accusations are not about her emotions. Rather, calling her overly emotional is a tactic to disguise his attempts to control her thoughts and feelings. He crafts a narrative that keeps her at an emotional distance by shaming her, and allows him to feel superior and in control. Recognizing Ryan's manipulation, along with other flashpoints in their relationship, makes Lily angry and boosts her confidence.

At the next gathering with friends, Ryan tells Lily to go upstairs and get him another beer. "Get it yourself," she responds. As expected, he protests. "What's the big deal? Why are you being so crabby?" He looks around at their friends as if to say, "See what I mean, she overreacts." But Lily stands her ground. "I'm not being crabby," she says firmly. "I'm calling you out on patronizing behavior." Ryan tries to laugh it off, but this time, seeing Lily's determination, their friends stay silent. Lily feels a surge of empowerment. By taking control of the situation, she sets a new standard that reinforces her boundaries against Ryan's disrespect and controlling behavior. By recognizing their shared reality bias and changing her reaction to his behavior, she begins to regain her voice and inspire those around her to challenge their assumptions about her "overly emotional" temperament, reinforced by Ryan.

Loss Aversion Bias

Loss aversion bias, also identified by Kahneman and Tversky, describes our tendency to feel the weight of a potential loss far more strongly than the satisfaction of an equivalent gain. Kahneman was awarded the Nobel Prize in Economic Sciences in 2002 for their concept and related contributions to behavioral economics (Tversky passed away in 1996, and the Nobel Prize cannot be awarded posthumously). Together, he and Tversky demonstrated how easily human judgment can be influenced, showing how we misjudge probabilities, underestimate risks, and let emotions guide choices we believe are rational.

This loss aversion bias can also show up in relationships. Even when a partner withholds emotional intimacy in harmful ways, the person affected may see leaving not as a step toward healing and freedom, but as a loss too heavy to handle. What's at risk isn't just the relationship, but also familiar routines, shared history, the identity built around being part of a couple and family, financial stability, and even the hope that things could get better. Loss aversion makes these perceived losses seem larger than the benefits of safety, self-respect, new opportunities, and reclaiming a sense of self. In this context, loss aversion bias explains why someone might stay in a relationship that causes distress and a loss of self. The fear of losing what's familiar can be stronger than the prospect of a healthier, more fulfilling future.

Marlene and Jerry exhibit loss aversion bias in a long-term relationship. She remains in an empty marriage, although she has sacrificed her well-being and that of her children. The fear of losing what she knows is greater than the benefits of leaving an oppressive relationship.

Marlene and Jerry

The Self-Sacrifice Mindset

Marlene and Jerry met in their mid-twenties and married within a year. She mistook his impulsiveness for passion and his moodiness for sensitivity. She was unaware that he had a drinking problem.

Jerry was the youngest of six siblings in a dysfunctional family with a workaholic father and a mother who mostly confined herself to her bedroom. He started drinking at the age of fourteen. What began as sneaking beers with older boys during middle school evolved into getting drunk at high school parties and binge drinking in college. His lack of parenting and excessive drinking led to arrested emotional development. Now, as an adult, he refuses to get therapy and continues to carry the impulsivity and self-centeredness of an emotionally neglected adolescent boy.

Marlene and Jerry start a family, and his corporate job supports them well. But all the home and child-rearing responsibilities fall to Marlene. He says it's necessary for him to work late, socialize with his colleagues and clients, and travel for the company. But much of his absence is used as an excuse for heavy drinking.

By the time they have three children, Jerry has become unpredictable—reasonable one day, reproachful the next. He throws tantrums when upset, shames the children, and blames Marlene for the kids' misbehavior. Dinners turn into a battleground. The kids get into trouble at school.

Marlene worries about the impact of an absent, ill-tempered husband on her kids, but she doesn't know what to do about Jerry. She kindles a glimmer of hope that his troubles stem from work stress and that his behavior will eventually improve. She focuses on her activities with the kids while neglecting her own care. There are times when her chronic stress and anxiety become overwhelming, and she fantasizes about leaving Jerry and taking the kids with her. Yet she stays because she feels that dismantling their shared life would tear their family apart. How could she put her children through a divorce? How would they divide their assets and explain things to others? Her fear of starting over keeps her in a marriage she believes requires her to sacrifice her well-being for her children.

As she enters the autumn of her years, Marlene is increasingly aware of her age. At sixty-five, Jerry is retired but still the irresponsible person she married. He spends his time in his workshop, gets "stupid stoned," and stirs up conflict with her and their adult children. Although the kids are grown now, the effects of their upbringing persist. Their son reflects his father's judgmental and argumentative nature, always believing he's right. Their older daughter nitpicks Marlene's home environment when she visits, mocking her for not living up to the daughter's standards, like having a larger kitchen sink or replacing older furniture. Their daughter is also quick to blame her for things that aren't her fault, like the problems of Marlene and Jerry's son. Their younger daughter continues to get involved with men who don't treat her well. Poor communication skills and unresolved anger, hurt, and resentment among parents and siblings have severely strained their family relationships.

Marlene feels a crushing sense of guilt, realizing that although her intent was to raise her children well, her self-sacrifice has had the opposite effect on them. Her guilt and self-blame keep her stuck in unhealthy habits, like letting her older kids talk to her disrespectfully and giving her youngest daughter, who can't keep a job, money whenever she asks for it, as if she can compensate for the turmoil they experienced in their childhood. She spends her days at home, feeling listless and unmotivated. Her body aches, she has gained weight, and she cries without knowing why. She also sleeps too much.

Then one day, she takes a bold step and begins therapy. Gradually, with her therapist's support, she begins to share her memories of years of pain and self-denial. She discloses her deep shame and guilt regarding how her decisions have impacted her children. She talks about her regret for all the boundaries she allowed Jerry to cross, not only her own boundaries but also those of her children.

Over time, therapy helps her make better choices. She confronts Jerry about his behavior and demands that he leave the house until he stops causing problems and treats her with respect. After months in a separate apartment, Jerry takes some responsibility for his actions and pleads with her to let him return home. Marlene refuses but agrees to go on a few dates with him, and when he treats her well, she allows him to return to their house. Although he admits to some of his problematic behavior, he continues to speak and act without considering the effect on others, such as divulging Marlene's confidences to their adult children. His cannabis habit often leaves him dazed and confused.

Marlene doesn't feel ready to face the world alone, but she finds ways to take small steps toward independence. She reaches out to an old friend, starts attending a book club, and volunteers once a week at a local food bank. This isn't the life she envisioned, and those activities sometimes remind her of what she has lost. However, they also give her the chance to improve her well-being and develop the self-compassion needed to forgive herself for past mistakes and accept herself as she is now.

In each of these sketches illustrating various types of cognitive bias, there's an opportunity for awareness and positive change. It begins by comparing our beliefs about our relationships to reality and examining how we compromise ourselves to fit false notions. The self-reflection questions at the end of this chapter can help you identify any biases in your relationship. What matters is giving yourself a chance to pause and notice. However your relationship unfolds, remember that truth lays the groundwork for healing, and from there, new opportunities begin to open up.

The Trap of Defense Mechanisms

Cognitive biases and defense mechanisms share a common trait: they both distort the truth, but in different ways. Biases influence how we perceive and interpret information, while defense mechanisms shape how we respond to what we already know or suspect. Together, they can create a kind of double distortion, first in how we perceive things, and then in how we respond to them. By becoming aware of and pushing back against these patterns, we can make more informed decisions to avoid the Echo complex.

Having to defend ourselves against emotional pain in an intimate relationship might seem unnecessary. Partners who feel safe and emotionally connected can still hurt each other, but they are less likely to distort the truth. Instead, they resolve issues and strengthen their connection by having open and honest communication.

However, when a relationship lacks open and honest communication, our brains are wired to seek temporary relief from emotional pain when we face problems that are too difficult to accept or handle. We might develop defense mechanisms to cope with the distress of feeling disconnected from our partners. But using defense mechanisms that hide the truth is like painting over deep cracks in a wall. It appears fine for a while, but the cracks keep spreading.

While defense mechanisms offer temporary relief, avoiding what's real leads to self-doubt and uncertainty. We can identify these mechanisms, which mostly occur in our subconscious, by noticing when and why we use them. Clinical psychologist Mariagrazia Di Giuseppe from the University of Rome and her colleagues view defense mechanisms as key factors in how people adapt in relationships. They contend that developing mature defenses and recognizing less adaptive ones helps individuals handle relational stress without distorting reality, leading to more genuine repair and closeness.

Freud introduced the concept of psychological defenses in the late nineteenth century, and his daughter Anna Freud expanded on them and added her own concepts in the early twentieth century. Since then, their work has played a key role in developing treatment programs that address a variety of psychological conditions, including anxiety, depression, grief, and relationship issues. Psychiatrist Frederic N. Busch and his colleagues dedicate a chapter on defense mechanisms in their manual, *Psychodynamic Treatment of Depression*, published by the American Psychiatric Association. They demonstrate how to directly address defense mechanisms to reduce symptoms and the risk of relapse.

When we understand our defense mechanisms, we see how they may have helped us cope in the past, but also the high cost of skirting the truth. By identifying not only what we do but also why we do it, we can respond more consciously, rather than repeating old patterns that undermine our sense of self.

How Defense Mechanisms Lead to the Echo Complex

Many of my clients initially question whether their relationships are as bad as they think or if they're overreacting. They come to realize that their use of defense mechanisms to cope with their partner's distancing behavior explains why they're confused about themselves and their relationships. Sometimes this means pretending the problem isn't there, convincing themselves it isn't that bad, or explaining it away with a convenient excuse. At other times, they separate two conflicting truths in their minds so they don't influence each other, or turn a forbidden feeling into its opposite by showing acceptance instead of anger. One of the most hurtful defenses is when someone turns their partner's criticism inward and assumes the problem is their own fault. At first, it seems safer to blame themselves than to confront the unsettling truth that the person they rely on might not have their best interests at heart.

I have observed seven common defense mechanisms in my clients that lead to a loss of self. Each explanation includes a brief vignette of the same couple to illustrate how these defense mechanisms unfold in relationships. I use the same couple for the vignettes because it's typical for all these defense mechanisms to occur when one partner creates emotional distance from the other.

Denial involves blocking external events from awareness because it's too much to handle. Even when there's clear evidence that something is true or actually happened, people using this defense mechanism refuse to accept it because it's too scary to face. Denial is a kind of negotiation we have with ourselves, such as thinking, *If I ignore this, I won't have to deal with that.* But it only postpones the inevitable. If we don't listen to our feelings, they'll eventually surface in unhealthy ways. Failing to confront reality plays a significant role in developing the Echo complex.

Example: When Ezra snaps at her with yet another demand, Marlee feels hurt but quickly steels herself: *I'm strong. I can handle this.* When friends raise an eyebrow at the way he talks to her, she brushes it off. *They don't understand him like I do.* Letting herself see his behavior as abuse feels unbearable. That truth would mean her world isn't safe. So she leans harder on denial, telling herself stories that keep the fear at bay, even as she drifts further from what she really feels.

Minimization helps us lessen the severity of a problematic issue in our minds. For example, we might make excuses for our partner's childish tantrums by blaming work stress or having too much to drink. Or we might question whether we are responsible for our partner's behavior. Assigning less serious reasons for their offensive actions feels less painful than facing the truth about having a partner who lacks the character traits we want them to have. We might also downplay how those actions affect us, like feeling bad about ourselves and losing vitality and motivation. Even if we acknowledge these effects, we may not fully grasp the impact of minimizing our partner's actions.

Example: When Ezra interrupts Marlee at a party during a story she is telling about a recent experience she enjoyed as if it were boring or unimportant, she lets him. *My story isn't that great anyway*, she thinks. By minimizing the significance of the moment, she avoids the discomfort of conflict. She pushes aside her embarrassment and convinces herself that she doesn't need to get upset over something so trivial.

Rationalization is a way our minds protect us by turning difficult truths into explanations that sound rational, making them easier to accept. In other words, we explain our partner's distancing behavior as reasonable, excusable, or even caring instead of facing what's actually happening.

Consider a female partner who often yells and makes accusations. We might tell ourselves, *She only gets upset because she cares. If she didn't love me, she wouldn't get so emotional.* If the outbursts are rare and we're trying to understand a partner who is temporarily overwhelmed, that can be an act of empathy. But if the yelling becomes a regular pattern, triggered by something minor, such as forgetting to pick up the dry cleaning, it crosses the line into abusive behavior. Rationalization, in this case, prevents us from recognizing the harm being done. Being with someone who is judgmental and has a quick temper can cause significant daily stress for everyone involved.

It's not just single incidents that get rationalized. We can also justify bigger patterns in a relationship. If our partner pulls away emotionally, we might excuse it by blaming ourselves, thinking, *Maybe I deserve it. I push their buttons sometimes.* Or we might focus on how to bring them closer instead of recognizing that their withdrawal is due to a deeper issue that needs to be uncovered and addressed. By doing this, we avoid setting boundaries or holding them accountable, which lets the unhealthy dynamic continue.

Example: When Ezra takes over her finances without asking, Marlee thinks, *He's just better with numbers. This will make my life easier.* By reframing his controlling actions as smart and practical, she can accept his inappropriate behavior as the best way to handle their finances, but at the cost of suppressing her own unease and reinforcing his control.

Compartmentalization is a defense that creates mental rooms with locked doors, each holding feelings, memories, or truths we're not ready to face. This is our mind's way of saying, *Not now*, to overwhelming emotions. When we compartmentalize, we shift from feeling overwhelmed to feeling more capable, which helps us function at work, care for others, or get through the day despite carrying a heavy burden.

But no matter how hard we try to keep mental doors shut, they never stay locked. Life eventually pushes them open with a hard conversation, a sudden realization, or a moment that forces two truths to collide. We feel both at once, like our partners' tenderness alongside their cruelty, which indicates a serious issue in the relationship. Facing what's inside is hard, but it's the only way to stop splitting ourselves in two. By letting the truths in those mental rooms coexist, we return to an honest place where we can finally see clearly and make better choices.

Example: Marlee separates her life with Ezra into two parts. In one, she holds onto the warmth of his affection, their shared plans, and the moments he makes her feel wanted. In the other, she tucks away his cutting remarks, rigid rules, and the way she shrinks around him. She works hard to keep those mental rooms separate because if she opens the doors to both of them at once, the picture of their relationship becomes too stark to face.

Introjection happens when we absorb ideas or habits from those around us, particularly from loved ones and those we depend on. When our partners blame, criticize, or accuse us, the painful truth is: *This person I trust is hurting me.* But realizing that truth is overwhelming because it threatens the relationship, our sense of safety, or even who we are. So introjection takes over by turning the blame inward. Instead of facing the scary possibility that our partner is controlling or harmful, our mind insists, *This must be my fault. I'm the problem.* By accepting our partner's criticism as truth, we lessen the pain by thinking, *If I am the problem, I can fix it, regain love, and feel safe.* In this way, introjection helps us avoid the greater risk of recognizing that the relationship is damaging or unstable.

These influences may also show up as a punishing inner critic, making it difficult to tell the difference between who we truly are and who we're trying to be for our partners. By trusting our instincts when something feels wrong, we can question whether these voices truly reflect our thoughts or are echoes of someone else's expectations. We can pause and ask ourselves, *Is this me speaking, or am I repeating someone else's script?* If it's the latter, we can set it aside and replace it with words that align with our own values and truth. The more we practice honoring our instincts and identifying what is ours, the stronger and clearer our authentic voice becomes, making it harder for external influences to drown it out.

Example: When Ezra tells Marlee she "overanalyzes" everything, she feels hurt that he doesn't understand her, but soon his words become her own. She begins to think, *Maybe he's right. Maybe I think too much.* Her thoughts echo his criticism instead of honoring her own feelings.

Reaction formation happens when we cope with distressing feelings by expressing the opposite emotion. When the true emotion feels too threatening or unacceptable, the mind reverses it, turning anger into exaggerated kindness or fear into bravado. This reversal helps us avoid the discomfort of the truth, both in our own eyes and in the eyes of others.

Picture feeling overwhelmed by your partner's arrogance toward you. Rather than confronting the fear or resentment that's really there, you respond with kindness, humor, or small talk. On the surface, it looks like you're being supportive, but deep down, it's a way to shield yourself from discomfort, hide your shame, avoid conflict, or push aside frustration. This isn't exactly lying. It's more like self-protection. But over time, the gap between your true feelings and how you act creates emotional distance, pulling you away from your values and making it tougher to be genuine or trust yourself completely.

Example: When Ezra dismisses Marlee's opinions, she swallows her anger and shows up with a calm voice and a cup of coffee. Instead of expressing her hurt and frustration over Ezra's disrespect, she covers it with warmth as if their upsetting exchange never happened.

Displacement is redirecting strong feelings, like anger, frustration, or fear, away from their true source and onto something safer or less threatening. The real target might feel too risky to confront, so the emotion spills out elsewhere. Instead of addressing the conflict directly, which could lead to resolution, we lash out at a supportive friend, snap at our kids, or slam a door. Sometimes the reaction doesn't even match the situation. We might explode over a small inconvenience, not because it deserves that level of intensity, but because it's easier than facing the deeper cause of our stress. Displacement offers temporary relief, but it leaves the underlying issue untouched and can strain the relationships we value most.

Example: After a tense night with Ezra, Marlee fires off a sharp reply to her sister's casual text. Without realizing it, she redirects the anger she feels toward Ezra onto her sister, who seems like a safer target. But venting her emotions on the wrong target doesn't resolve them or her issues with Ezra.

As you can see, relying on defense mechanisms to avoid confronting our feelings can cause more harm than good. These impulses can create all sorts of chaos in our lives, such as getting stuck in the Echo complex or a paradoxical cycle in our relationships, or evading painful truths that, when accepted and addressed, could lead to healing and new possibilities.

Letting go of defense mechanisms begins with recognizing when we use them to deceive ourselves. We can pause, take in the facts, and ask: *What's true here? What might I be avoiding? And what could the consequences be if I keep avoiding it?* These questions encourage us to slow down, think more carefully, and face reality rather than hide from it.

Recognizing and confronting cognitive biases and defense mechanisms that lead to an echo mindset can help put us back in the driver's seat in our relationships. Psychologist Aaron T. Beck, known as the father of cognitive therapy, explained that distorted, automatic thoughts contribute to emotional distress and harmful behaviors, and that by identifying, challenging, and reframing these thoughts, individuals can achieve lasting improvements in mood and functioning. In other words, when we choose to respond consciously and intentionally to our partner's distancing behavior and attacks on our sense of self, we can prevent ourselves from developing the Echo complex.

Writing in a journal can be helpful here. (You can use one you already have or start a new one.) Here's an exercise you can try: Create two columns, one listing how you *typically handle* an issue with the way your partner treats you, and the other listing a better way to handle the issue that helps to safeguard your sense of self. Doing this will help you use your wisdom and the insights in this book to guide you. The more we practice honoring our feelings and intuition, the stronger our authentic voice becomes, making it harder for external influences to drown it out.

As you continue to read and understand the material in this book, I encourage you to confront any discomfort and work toward liberating yourself from the limitations of faulty thinking. I wish I had known this in my first marriage. Since then, I've learned that whether we choose to stay with our current partner or move on, learning how to keep ourselves grounded in a strong sense of self and explore the potential for a strong, thriving relationship is truly worth the effort. Each step we take to identify and challenge an echo mindset is a step toward restoring our self-worth, emotional balance, and capacity to love without losing ourselves.

Just as vital as understanding our mental and emotional patterns is recognizing how relationship stress impacts our bodies. In part 2 of the book, we'll explore how to heal from the loss of self, starting with the powerful role the nervous system plays in that process. In the next chapter, you'll discover how our relationships can rewire us on a biological level, creating either harmony or disconnection, and what it means to close the gap between emotional distance and genuine connection. When you learn to work with your body's responses to stress instead of against them, you can begin to restore safety and create lasting change from the inside out.

Key Points

1. Making decisions based on rash assumptions instead of getting the facts can unintentionally compromise us.
2. Confirmation bias causes us to seek or interpret evidence in ways that align with our existing beliefs, desires, or expectations about someone, even if those beliefs, desires, or expectations are inaccurate.
3. Recognizing our cognitive biases can help us avoid downplaying and enabling our partner's distancing behavior.
4. The anchoring bias occurs when we rely too much on a positive early experience with someone, even if that experience is based on a superficial understanding of the person.
5. The loss aversion bias occurs when the fear of losing a relationship, even an unfulfilling or harmful one, outweighs the potential joy of building a healthier, happier life.
6. The halo effect bias in relationships occurs when a single positive trait influences one partner's overall impression of the other.
7. Defense mechanisms provide temporary relief from painful situations, but they can also prevent resolution and healing.
8. Recognizing the use of defense mechanisms and facing the truth about relationships can help us protect our sense of self or regain it if we already feel a loss of self.
9. By trusting our instincts when something feels wrong, we can question whether our thoughts truly represent our own or are echoes of our partner's demands and expectations.
10. Changing how we think can alter how we feel about ourselves.

Self-Reflection: Recognizing False Perceptions

1. Have you ever been in a relationship with someone who you later discovered was very different from your first impression of them? If so, describe your first impressions and how they might have been influenced by cognitive biases that you weren't aware of at the time.
2. Did the examples of people with different types of cognitive bias in this chapter resonate with you? If so, describe aspects of your relationship that are similar to the relationship examples. How do they impact your relationship and your sense of self? If you've left your relationship, write about your experience with cognitive biases in your former relationship and how they affected you.
3. Can you identify specific defense mechanisms you have used to avoid confronting difficult issues in your relationship? List them and explain how you used each one. How do these defenses impact your relationship and sense of self?
4. Do cognitive biases and defense mechanisms keep you from being true to yourself in your relationship? If so, what are some ways you are not fully present in your relationship?
5. Identify three or more steps you can take to recognize cognitive biases and defense mechanisms you might be using to cope with relationship issues. Reflect on ways to address matters you've previously ignored in your relationship and how you can change patterns of behavior that affect your sense of self. For example, when your partner criticizes or ignores your feelings, you might think, *It's not that bad compared to other relationships*, which can minimize the seriousness of the situation. To counter this, consider what a healthy, respectful interaction with your partner would look like. Identify one small boundary you can enforce, such as ending a phone call if shouting begins.

Part II

Healing from Loss of Self

CHAPTER SIX

Echo Reactions and Our Bodies

JAMIE USED TO wake up feeling lighthearted, eager for the day's opportunities. Now, after three years with George, he often wakes up with a heavy mind. He lies in bed staring into the distance, his mind filled with doubts about his relationship. His neck feels stiff, and a tightness spreads across his chest, reminders of the weight of feeling unseen, unheard, and worn down by the one person who should make him feel safe.

After years of Gloria's relentless fault-finding, Dan feels on edge, always bracing himself for her next criticism. What started as small corrections turned into reproach, and the stress he's under has caused him to gain a lot of weight.

Two decades with Casey have left Jill trying to cope with his angry outbursts and her declining health. She's learned to comply with his demands to keep him calm, rather than provoke more anger. Meanwhile, chronic stress has led to an overactive thyroid that causes anxiety, a rapid heartbeat, and exhaustion.

It's no surprise that the emotional distress Jamie, Dan, and Jill experience in their partnerships also affects their bodies. That's because the quality of our relationships doesn't just shape our emotions: it rewires our biology. In his best-selling book, *The Body Keeps the Score: Brain, Mind, and Body in the Healing of Trauma*, psychiatrist Bessel van der Kolk emphasizes that when a person endures prolonged distress, fear, or loneliness, their body reacts with a biological storm of physiological changes: cortisol spikes, inflammation rises, and immune defenses weaken. In a stressful relationship, these changes don't just cause fleeting discomfort; they increase susceptibility to illness over time.

This may get a bit technical, but bear with me. The way our bodies react to stress can reveal hidden clues about our health and relationships. Even when we're not aware of it, our nervous system is always responding, such as tightening muscles, speeding up our heartbeat, or causing mood changes. These subtle signals influence how safe, connected, or threatened we feel with our partner. By paying attention to the body–mind connection, we can recognize patterns that often stay below our awareness but have a strong impact on the quality and stability of our relationships.

The Mind-Body Connection

The polyvagal theory, introduced by psychologist Stephen Porges in 1994, explains how the body and mind work together. His theory helps us understand how the vagus nerve, the body's longest nerve, influences social behavior, emotion regulation, and responses to perceived threats. The vagus nerve extends from the brain to the abdomen, innervating various organs and controlling functions such as digestion, heart rate, and breathing.

According to his theory, three primary states of our nervous system determine whether our relationships will keep us calm and content or leave us in a state of agitation. These states are social engagement and safety, fight-or-flight, and freeze. The state we're in at any given point has a powerful influence over how we feel and how we behave. Here is an overview of Porges's three states:

Social Engagement and Safety—When we feel safe and connected to our partners, the parasympathetic branch of our nervous system senses support and acceptance and responds in kind. Our heart rate, voice, breathing, and facial expressions remain steady. We can express ourselves freely and try new experiences while feeling calm and comfortable.

Fight-or-Flight—When there's conflict in our relationship, especially when we feel attacked or rejected by our partner, the sympathetic branch of our nervous system is activated, compelling us to defend ourselves. We may either want to get away from our partner or fight back with words, tone of voice, or physical reactions, such as throwing something. We experience a mix of anger, frustration, fear, anxiety, or panic. Our prefrontal cortex, responsible for higher-level thinking, like planning, organizing, and setting goals, becomes less active, reducing our ability to stay present and engage in rational conversation. During a fight-or-flight response, we tend to respond instinctively rather than with wisdom and foresight.

When something in a relationship feels upsetting, our bodies often react before we even realize what's happening. The part of the brain that acts like a built-in alarm system, the amygdala, detects stress and quickly signals to the rest of the body that we may be in danger. This sets off a chain reaction. Our bodies release adrenaline, causing our hearts to beat faster, our blood pressure to rise, our hands to get sweaty, and our stomachs to tense up. Sometimes our muscles tense or shake. These are all natural survival responses; our body's way of trying to protect us.

The challenge arises when stress like this persists over time. Our bodies aren't designed to remain in a state of high alert for extended periods. This can weaken our immune system, cause inflammation, and eventually lead to health problems like heart disease, fibromyalgia, or digestive issues. The good news is that learning to recognize these signals and find ways to calm the body can help us regain control and better protect our health.

Freeze—When we sense danger, like when a partner yells, accuses, or criticizes us harshly, our bodies sometimes enter what's called the freeze response. Unlike fight-or-flight, freeze occurs when a deeper part of us believes that defending ourselves or escaping won't work. It's our nervous system's last resort, a built-in way of protecting us from what feels unbearable.

In freeze, we may become silent, unable to find words, or feel emotionally shut down. Our minds can become foggy, our bodies may go numb, and it might feel like we're no longer fully present. Some people describe feeling trapped in their own skin, detached from their thoughts or emotions, or even as though they've stepped outside themselves. To others, we may look spaced out with eyes staring into the distance. Physiologically, our systems shift into a kind of hibernation mode, with heart rate, blood pressure, and metabolism decreasing, which can also affect immunity, digestion, and sexual function.

At first, the freeze response may appear to be submission or passivity, but in reality, it's a survival strategy. It's the body's way of saying, *This feels overwhelming. The safest choice right now is to stay still.*

When this response happens often in relationships, the distressed person shuts down their voice, feelings, and needs to prevent further conflict or harm. It's as if their mind checks out for safety, even though their body stays in the room.

In the moment, the freeze response can shield us from the sting of confrontation. But over time, it comes at a cost. When we can't express ourselves and be present, we feel unseen, unheard, and unimportant.

Psychotherapist Pete Walker identified a fourth response to threats in 2013, known as "fawning." Fawning is essentially the survival tactic of people-pleasing on overdrive. When someone feels threatened, instead of fighting back, fleeing, or freezing, they might rush to smooth things over by agreeing immediately, apologizing excessively, showering the other person with praise, or sacrificing their own needs to maintain peace.

When we're with someone who's overbearing, emotionally checked out, or even abusive, our bodies don't feel at ease. Instead, we slip into survival mode with a fight, flight, freeze, or fawn response. Our nervous system is always alert, scanning for threats to our well-being and reacting to stress. The tension in our chest, the knot in our stomach, or the sudden urge to get away are signals from our nervous system saying, *Something doesn't feel safe right now.* Tuning into our body's signals helps us respond with foresight instead of instinct and prevent repeating patterns that cause more distress.

What's confusing is when emotionally distant or abusive partners show moments of interest, affection, or calm. Episodes of tenderness and peaceful engagement can strengthen our attachment to them, and a trauma bond can form. A trauma bond happens when a relationship runs on a cycle of hurt and repair, where moments of cruelty are mixed with bursts of affection and promises of change. That mix of pain and comfort wires the brain to cling tightly to the relationship, even when it's harmful. Power imbalances, isolation, and emotional manipulation all feed the cycle, slowly wearing down self-esteem and sense of self. Over time, the highs of reconciliation can feel addictive, making it hard to walk away. While trauma bonding is often talked about in the context of severe abuse, it can also take root in intimate relationships where there's no obvious violence but the dynamics still leave one person feeling controlled, diminished, or dependent. And, of course, much of this occurs in our subconscious mind. Outwardly, we might feel confused by our reactions and behaviors. But when we view our bodies as inner guardians and listen to the messages they send, we become better equipped to protect our sense of self.

Neuroception
Our Inner Guardian

Back in 2004, Stephen Porges showed us precisely how our bodies detect safety or threat in our environment. He identified a built-in surveillance system that constantly scans for safety or danger, without us even realizing it. He called this *neuroception*. It's the mechanism that decides whether we can relax and connect, or whether we need to switch into survival mode through fight-or-flight, freeze, or fawn. If our neuroception senses safety, through warmth, connection, and attunement, we naturally soften, feel calmer, and open up to others. However, if our neuroception senses a threat, such as ongoing disconnection or aggression in a relationship, we enter these states of protection. Keep in mind that we can't control our biological responses, but we can control how we handle a threatening situation.

The following three sketches demonstrate how neuroception works and the profound impact of the mind-body connection in intimate relationships.

Mali and Marc
Biological Harmony

Mali and Marc have been together for five years, and their relationship serves as a base camp that keeps them socially engaged. Kind and respectful to each other, they have created a safe space where both can listen, respond, and validate each other. Every morning before work, they take the time to sit and have coffee together, discussing anything on their minds. Neither of them hesitates to share their experiences, concerns, and desires. Most evenings, they enjoy more conversation, hang out with friends, or sit together on the couch while watching TV or a movie. When making decisions, they respect each other's viewpoints and preferences and compromise when they disagree. Like every couple, they have arguments from time to time, but even when they disagree, they focus on the issue at hand instead of attacking each other and work to resolve their differences with mutual respect.

One of the many benefits of their relationship is the mutual support they provide in pursuing their individual goals and aspirations. The emotional balance and biological synchronicity Mali experiences allow her creativity to flow freely as a musician and songwriter. Similarly, Marc, who is developing a tech start-up, can focus on turning his ideas into action, free from the burden of relationship stress. They both attribute their professional success to the emotional safety and support they give to each other.

Think of Mali and Marc's relationship as a biological symphony. Each person is like an instrument, with their own unique sound, but when they're in tune with each other—listening, adjusting, and responding—they create a beautiful harmony. Just as a musical symphony relies on rhythm, balance, and resonance to produce harmony, a deeply connected relationship uses these elements to create a vibrant composition of two people who bring energy and beauty to each other's lives.

Elise and Alan
Biological Discordance

Elise and Alan's two-year marriage contrasts sharply with the harmonious partnership between Mali and Marc. Elise and Alan grew up as friends, and their romance blossomed in high school, but their lives went in separate directions. After Elise's fifteen-year marriage ended in divorce, she reconnected with Alan, who was still single, and they married. Elise longs for meaningful conversation, affection, and a safe space to be vulnerable.

Alan isn't comfortable with deep discussions, affection, or sharing his feelings. He realizes that Elise needs more from him, but keeps her emotionally distant by focusing on work that involves travel, and when he's home, he withdraws to the basement in their home for hours.

Elise and Alan's relationship can be described as a case of biological discordance. Elise feels unfulfilled and unsupported, while Alan feels pressured and overwhelmed. When Elise tries to break through Alan's defenses by encouraging him to express his feelings and spend more time with her, he feels threatened and enters a fight-or-flight state. He shuts down midconversation, avoids eye contact, or attends to his phone to create an emotional barrier between them. Elise views Alan's withdrawal as a threat to her emotional safety and also shifts into a state of fight-or-flight. She pleads with him for emotional closeness and transparency, and presses him with questions, but he responds with empty answers and excuses, such as being tired or needing space.

Sometimes, Elise misreads Alan's distancing behavior as a reaction to something she did, or she worries about his mental health. When he withdraws for hours, she pushes harder to understand the reasons behind his rejection of her attempts to connect. She spends much of her time wondering how to bring them closer.

Their lack of emotional connection affects all aspects of their relationship, including physical intimacy. When Alan needs closeness, he tries to feel nearer to her by making sexual overtures. While Elise enjoys their sexual encounters, she can't fully relax during them. She anticipates that the bond she feels with him during sex will dissolve when he goes to the basement to sleep, another distancing behavior that relieves his anxiety about being too close to Elise, and leaves early for work in the morning.

The disconnection in their relationship not only impacts their emotional well-being but also makes it hard for them to fully engage with life. Elise is a talented cook who hopes to compete on a popular television cooking show. However, her relationship worries drain her energy and focus, pushing her toward burnout. Alan's self-imposed isolation brings on bouts of depression.

Even when they're enjoying each other's companionship, there's an undercurrent of discord in their relationship. And this is how their relationship will remain until both are willing to explore the deeper reasons for their emotional estrangement and work toward biological harmony.

Lisa and Toby
From Biological Discordance to Social Engagement

Lisa and Toby have been together for five years, and they have a one-year-old daughter. Toby, an only child, grew up in a peaceful household with a single mom who cultivated his emotions and didn't shame him for crying when he felt sad, hurt, or scared. Lisa, on the other hand, is the youngest of six siblings, and her alcoholic father and mother often argued and yelled at their children, who also fought among themselves. Growing up in a household filled with conflict and without anyone to confide in taught her to defend herself with anger and aggression, such as arguing, refusing to admit fault, and lying when it served her purpose. She sees herself as "tough" and feels threatened by Toby's softer side. He wants to be vulnerable with her, but when he shows sadness, fear, or gets teary, she tells him to "man up." She tries to control him through anger and demeaning behavior, like gaslighting him to "win" an argument.

Toby desperately wants to tell Lisa how her behavior hurts him and affects their relationship, but his fear of her judgment makes it hard for him to find the right words to express himself. He doesn't want to come across as a "wimp." Every time he tries to talk with her, he second-guesses himself afterward, tormenting himself with thoughts about what he should have said. On her part, Lisa doesn't see her actions as hurtful. Rather, she blames the conflict on Toby's inability to be the man she wants him to be. Feeling rejected and judged by Lisa, Toby's confidence and motivation continue to weaken. He wants to start a landscaping business, but he feels it would be an uphill battle without her support.

As the cycle of Lisa's fight response and Toby's freeze response continues to be a barrier to connection in their relationship, he develops a platonic friendship with a woman at work with whom he can be in a state of social engagement. Their friendship starkly contrasts with his relationship dynamic at home, making him realize how much is lacking in his marriage. When Toby opens up to his friend about his unhappiness, she gives him her therapist's name.

In therapy, Toby realizes that his wife's contempt for him indicates her displaced anger and a shame-driven fear of vulnerability. He also understands how his past experience with being bullied at school shapes his reactions to her aggression. After gaining a new perspective on their relationship, he finds some practical ways to address the issues.

After several months of therapy, Toby feels more confident about confronting Lisa. He tells her he's been in therapy and wants to discuss their relationship. He says he loves her and wants to stay in their marriage, but it's hard for him to be in a relationship where he can't be himself and express his feelings without her judgment and resistance. As usual, Lisa feels threatened and chooses to fight. She gets angry at him for going to therapy and tells him to "grow up." She accuses him of "always complaining about me," and insists "everyone else thinks I'm nice."

But Toby is bolstered by his awareness of the underlying dynamics in their relationship and doesn't back down this time. He takes responsibility for his part in their troubles by not expressing what he needs in their relationship and insists that she take responsibility too by seeing a therapist. Lisa loves Toby and doesn't want to split up their family. After further discussion, during which Toby stands his ground, she reluctantly agrees to go to therapy.

Over time, Lisa learns in therapy that the way she treats Toby stems from an ingrained belief that she must protect herself from vulnerability. Lisa realizes that she is still using the same dysfunctional ways of coping from childhood, even though she no longer needs to. She begins to understand how her past experiences and her childhood responses continue to influence her current life.

As Toby and Lisa gain self-awareness in their therapy sessions, their biological response to each other begins to change. Lisa's neuroception, which had been sensing a threat to her defenses against vulnerability and triggering a fight response, begins to sense safety, allowing her to more often enter a state of social engagement with Toby. It takes time for Toby to open up to Lisa. But as he sees her make positive changes, he begins to feel trust and a sense of emotional safety with her.

Lisa and Toby's relationship is a work in progress, and there's no guarantee they will succeed as a couple. But their story demonstrates how exploring the past to understand its effect on the present can give couples a chance to improve a relationship that encourages both their individual and shared growth.

These three couples exemplify the range of dynamics that can develop in intimate relationships. Mali and Marc show what it looks like when two partners create biological harmony, a safe base of mutual respect, support, and validation. Elise and Alan, in contrast, demonstrate how biological discordance leaves one partner yearning while the other pulls away, trapping both in a cycle of unmet needs. Lisa and Toby reveal how a couple can shift from biological discordance to social engagement when they gain self-awareness and begin to change long-standing patterns. Overall, these stories highlight how the nervous system responds to signals of safety or danger, creating a sense of harmony and closeness or emotional distance. Learning to observe and manage these reactions can break the cycle of conflict and, if both partners are willing, help them explore ways to build a harmonious partnership that allows each to maintain a healthy sense of self.

Avoiding Echo Reactions

When our neuroception detects a lack of safety in our relationships, triggering a fight, flight, freeze, or fawning response, we may act in ways inconsistent with who we are, saying or doing things that are out of character. These are echo reactions that can break down our sense of self. But they are also important indicators that it's time to do something different, because what we're doing isn't working.

To stay calm and avoid echo reactions, we need to activate the higher part of our brain, specifically the prefrontal cortex, which is responsible for managing executive functions. We already know that executive functioning includes organization and planning, but it also involves regulating our emotions. Being fully aware of what's happening, not only from our perspective but also from our partner's, helps us separate their actions from our self-worth and react in moments of conflict without compromising our sense of self.

Responding in ways that align with our personal values means recognizing the false perceptions that work against us. Consider these questions to see through false perceptions:

- *Do I believe I've done something to cause my partner to mistreat me?*
- *Do I think I have to go against my values and intuition to make my partner love me?*
- *Do I feel like I need to tolerate my partner's behavior to keep the peace in my relationship?*

Answering yes to one or more of those questions indicates you're experiencing an echo response that can lead to a loss of self. The goal here is to be able to answer "no" because doing so can help you see through false perceptions. (You may have your own insightful questions.)

When we work on reorienting our thinking, it helps to remember that our partner's troubling behavior may not be our fault. Instead, it stems from fear, insecurity, immaturity, a need to control, or a sense of entitlement. Rather than taking responsibility for someone else's actions, we should pause to consider why our partners behave the way they do. Think about the answers to questions that focus on underlying issues:

- *Is my partner projecting their insecurities onto me?*
- *Why does my partner seem to be threatened by my need for honesty and emotional closeness?*
- *Why is there a pattern in my relationship of me pursuing emotional connection and my partner avoiding it with insensitive responses?*

When you notice yourself caught in unhealthy patterns, recognizing false perceptions and underlying issues is essential. Being prepared with more effective ways to respond is also helpful. The following scenarios highlight common emotionally distancing behaviors that are often disguised as "normal" conduct. Each example presents two possible reactions: an echo response that diminishes a sense of self and a grounded response that protects it. This distinction is important. When you react in ways that weaken your sense of self, you might experience immediate relief or avoid conflict, but over time, you lose confidence and connection to your true self. On the other hand, responding in ways that uphold your sense of self affirms your worth and integrity, even if it feels uncomfortable at first.

Understanding these two types of reactions helps you distinguish between self-eroding habits and self-protective choices. By paying attention to how each reaction feels and how it affects your relationship, you become more aware of responses that support, rather than undermine, your true self. As you read, notice the feelings each reaction stirs in you and think about how you would respond if your partner said something similar to you.

Breaking the Cycle of Echo Reactions to Common Distancing Behaviors

Scenario 1

Dismissing vulnerability
Avoidant partner: "Give me a break! Are you crying again? You're so needy—it's exhausting."

Echo reaction: "I'm sorry. I can't help it. I'm just an emotional person."

Grounded reaction: "I'm sharing something that matters to me. I need you to respect my feelings. If you don't, I'll stop this conversation now and talk to you when you can listen to me and respect what I say."

Scenario 2

Sarcasm during emotional moments
Avoidant partner: "Wow, someone's clingy tonight. Should I get you a teddy bear?"

Echo reaction: Laughs awkwardly, feels shame. "I guess I got carried away. Just ignore me."

Grounded reaction: "I'm being sincere with you, and sarcasm dismisses my feelings. If you're uncomfortable with my emotions, mocking me isn't a productive way to handle your discomfort."

Scenario 3

Picking a fight after an emotionally intimate experience

Avoidant partner: "Why do you always leave your stuff everywhere? You're such a slob."

Echo reaction: "Sorry. I didn't realize I was being messy. I'll clean it up now."

Grounded reaction: "It feels like you're picking a fight to avoid what could be precious moments of connection with each other. I'd like to talk about that instead of getting pulled into an argument."

Scenario 4

Mocking serious conversations

Avoidant partner: "Here we go again with your 'deep talks.' Can't we just watch a movie and not analyze everything?"

Echo reaction: "I guess I do tend to overthink things. Okay, let's watch something."

Grounded reaction: "Connecting emotionally matters to me. If you're not open to that right now, we can pause, but I won't allow you to belittle what's important to me."

Scenario 5

Deflecting partner's disclosure of painful childhood experience with cruel humor

Avoidant partner: "Wow, no wonder you're so screwed up. That explains a lot!"

Echo reaction: "Yeah, I guess that's true. I'm probably too much to deal with sometimes."

Grounded reaction: "That was callous and uncalled for. I need your empathy and understanding, not your judgment."

Scenario 6

Persistent criticism

Avoidant partner: "You never do anything right. I don't know why I even bother with you anymore."

Echo reaction: "I'm sorry. . . I'll try harder next time. I didn't mean to mess things up."

Grounded reaction: "I won't accept being spoken to like that. If you have an issue with something I'm doing, you're welcome to bring it up respectfully. But if you talk to me disrespectfully, this conversation is over."

Scenario 7

Gaslighting

Avoidant partner: "That never happened. You're just being dramatic again, like always."

Echo reaction: (Feeling self-doubt) "Maybe I did get confused."

Grounded reaction: "I know what I experienced, and I won't let you try to make me doubt myself."

Scenario 8

Jealous control

Avoidant Partner: "Why were you being so friendly with that guy? Is he your boyfriend or something? I can't trust you at all."

Echo reaction: "I didn't mean to upset you. I'm sorry I hurt you."

Grounded reaction: "There's no reason why either of us can't have a friendly conversation with someone. I won't tolerate you imposing unreasonable restrictions on me. If you don't trust me, let's talk about the reasons why and work toward trusting each other."

Scenario 9

Withholding affection as punishment

Avoidant partner: Ignores partner for two days after an argument, refusing to talk.

Echo reaction: "I'm sorry I did something to make you so angry. Just tell me what I did so I can make it better."

Grounded reaction: "It's not okay to shut me out when you're upset. We need to understand each other and how we can live peacefully together."

Scenario 10

Humiliation in public

Avoidant partner: Claims to be right or an authority on a topic. "You wouldn't understand. This is too complicated for you."

Echo reaction: Feels hurt and shame, but stays silent.

Grounded reaction: "There's nothing wrong with my intelligence. If you feel a need to put me down, I need to know what's driving that behavior toward me."

A Word About Reaction

When a partner uses demeaning words or attitudes to create emotional distance, it's important to recognize what's really happening, even if they don't fully admit it to themselves. Condescension isn't harmless. It's a tactic of power and control. Each cutting remark chips away at the other person's sense of self-worth, leaving them feeling emotionally unsafe in the relationship.

Sometimes, when this is happening, we might decide that the best response is no response at all. Our nonreactivity in these situations doesn't mean we're ignoring the issue or letting our partners off the hook. Instead, it means we're focusing on our goal of not getting drawn into hurtful interactions. In these moments, we might say something like, "I'll talk to you when you can listen to me and treat me with respect." Then, we can simply walk away. This is a self-respectful approach that shifts the responsibility for the other person's behavior back onto them.

Staying Calm to Avoid an Echo Reaction

By noticing what our body is telling us and pausing long enough to engage the wiser part of our brain, we give ourselves a chance to respond to a partner's hurtful behavior without making things worse.

When tensions rise and we feel our bodies slipping into a fight, flight, freeze, or fawning response, the best response is often to create a buffer zone between our partner's behavior and our reaction. Even a brief pause can give a chance to calm ourselves before responding in a way that might lead to echo behavior. This involves taking steps to ground our minds and bodies.

While pausing, consider these questions:

- *What's happening in my body?*
- *Am I in my scared, defensive place or my calm, rational place?*
- *What would make me feel calmer and more centered during this interaction with my partner?*

To help calm our bodies, techniques such as box breathing and repeating a mantra can be beneficial:

Box breathing: As you may have noticed, breathing becomes shallow when people are distressed. However, we can combat this by increasing oxygen intake, which signals our nervous system that the situation is under control. According to the *Harvard Heart Letter*, regulating our breath can lower the level of the stress hormone cortisol and may even help lower blood pressure. Box breathing is a yogic technique for controlling and regulating breathing. It's so effective that U.S. Navy SEALs use it for this purpose. The word "box" refers to the four sides of a box. Picture these sides while taking four breaths: four counts of inhaling (imagine your breath moving up the first side of the box), four counts of holding your breath (visualize your breath moving across the top of the box), four counts of exhaling (moving down the second side of the box), and four counts of holding after exhaling (moving across the bottom of the box and closing up the square). We can use this technique to support our overall health, especially during times when we sense a threat to our emotional well-being.

Repeating a mantra: Similar to box breathing, repeating a simple word or phrase can help us maintain our composure during stressful times. Phrases like *I am in control of my emotions, I choose peace over conflict*, or *I am capable of standing up for myself* can remind us that we have the power to manage our reactions. Quietly or silently repeating one of these mantras during a stressful situation helps us stay calm and respond to a partner's offensive behavior with a grounded reaction.

Initially, both box breathing and repeating a mantra might feel awkward. However, practicing these techniques over time makes them easier to use in our daily lives. Once you learn to steady yourself and stay calm in stressful situations, you create the inner space needed to respond effectively. From this grounded place, you are no longer carried away by reactive echoes. Instead, you are better prepared to speak with clarity, honesty, and confidence.

Talking Straight with Your Partner

Creating an inner space between your partner's distancing behavior and your response allows you to calm down and consider a response that feels right for you, rather than reacting with an echo response. Here's how to start: Take a deep breath and silently repeat a mantra of your choice, such as *I am wise, capable, and strong.* Make direct eye contact with your partner and keep your voice steady. If it feels right, frame your response around your love and commitment to the relationship. You can begin with a brief statement like, "I love you and want us both to be happy in our relationship. But we can't be happy together when you belittle me or dismiss my feelings. It hurts me and creates distance between us."

This statement does two things: It calls attention to the specific behavior that is the issue, rather than blaming your partner's shortcomings. It also expresses how the behavior personally affects you. At this point, your partner might get defensive and attempt to redirect the focus to you. They might say, "I don't do that" or "You're the one who's causing the problem." Keep the conversation focused by returning to the main issue. You might say, for example, "I don't think you set out to hurt me, but I need to understand something: When we start to get close, what makes you feel like you have to push me away?" By approaching the issue with curiosity instead of blame or judgment, you give them a chance to reflect rather than react impulsively.

Think ahead about what feelings might come up for you when you discuss your partner's hurtful actions. These feelings could be fear, anger, or resentment. Consider how you've handled those emotions in past conversations and set a goal to avoid repeating unhelpful responses. Plan what you'll say and when, and aim to stay relaxed during the conversation. (I get it. You may have tried some of this before, and nothing worked. But stay with me here. It's rare for change to result from sporadic attempts. The key is to keep repeating the same approach and not give up.)

Helping your partner explore the deeper reasons for their distancing behavior is best left to a therapist. But if you believe there's a chance they'll soften their defenses if given the chance, it might be worth trying. Keep in mind, though, that criticism and threats will only trigger their defenses. You're trying to address their fear of emotional intimacy, so keep the conversation brief and be ready to walk away if it's not going well. If you sense that your efforts to soften their defenses will only cause more hurtful behavior, it's best not to try doing this.

Keep in mind that while the avoidant partner may experience different emotions, they might only show their feelings through anger. Anger is a complex emotion with many layers, such as hurt, shame, and fear. It can also be a way to gain power and control, which might come from those same feelings. No matter what causes the anger, if it's the only emotion an avoidant partner shows, trying to resolve conflict could make them angrier and justify their actions, rather than taking responsibility for what they did.

A partner who keeps denying responsibility with defenses like anger is choosing to hide their vulnerable feelings or to prioritize power and control over reconciliation. In this case, you might say, "I understand that you get upset, but we have to be able to talk about things without arguing." Regardless of how your partner responds, avoid arguing, defending, or explaining. Keeping your comments brief strengthens your position and makes it harder for them to resist what you're saying.

Once you finish speaking, conclude your conversation and give them time to reflect on what you said.

When discussing your feelings with your partner to encourage an open, honest conversation, be prepared for a range of outcomes. If they show willingness to work on their issues, that's a sign of potential progress. However, if they respond with a fight-or-flight or freeze reaction and resist your efforts to connect, it might mean they don't realize the seriousness of the situation. If that happens, you could say something like, "We need to take a break from this conversation and come back to it when we're both able to listen and respond to each other calmly." (Remember to stay consistent with your message and say the same thing if this comes up again.) If they become physically or emotionally abusive, leave immediately and get yourself (and your kids, if you have them) to a safe place.

After the conversation, take time to process what happened and how you responded by asking yourself, "*What feelings came up for me during the discussion with my partner? Did I feel grounded in confidence, or did I feel self-doubt? What happened in my body? What worked and what didn't?*" Reviewing what occurred during a conversation with your partner is similar to what professional athletes do when watching their game tapes to identify areas for improvement in their performance. The more you use the tools described in this chapter and learn from what happens, the better you'll be able to handle upsetting interactions with your partner.

Choosing to Take a Stand

When a partner refuses to stop mistreating you and resists emotional intimacy, you might have to give an ultimatum, like insisting on therapy or considering separation. Sometimes, leaving immediately isn't feasible due to financial, family, or personal reasons. In these cases, careful thought and planning, such as finding alternative housing, seeking legal advice, or building a support system, are often necessary before a practical solution emerges.

If you can't separate right away, don't abandon yourself in the relationship. Instead, accept what you're facing and adjust your expectations accordingly. Give yourself permission to explore your options with patience and courage, whether by talking to trusted friends, professionals, or support groups, so you can find a way to stay safe and honor your sense of self.

In both my personal life and many years as a therapist, I've learned a hard but essential truth: People who resort to abusive behavior to keep their partners emotionally distant rarely change. This is generally not because they can't change, but because they don't see a reason to. Their behavior is rooted in deeply held beliefs about power, vulnerability, and their role in a relationship. These actions originate from a worldview that validates the emotional harm they inflict.

This truth can be painful to accept, especially if you've spent years holding onto hope that your partner will someday wake up and recognize what they're doing, see the pain they've caused you, and commit to personal growth. But in cases of emotional abuse, hope can interfere with progress.

In some relationships, when one partner finally refuses to tolerate mistreatment and starts setting firm boundaries, the avoidant partner may seem to change. They might tone down their most obvious controlling behaviors and even act more respectfully. However, this shift is often not due to genuine remorse or self-awareness. Old beliefs are hard to uproot. Instead, it signals a change in strategy. Their old tactics no longer work, so they adapt to maintain their power in new ways. What may seem like growth is often just a change in behavior, not a significant or lasting one. Without a strong commitment to inner work through therapy, accountability, and a sincere desire to grow, old patterns tend to resurface, especially when someone is stepping way out of their comfort zone or a controlling person starts to feel they're losing control.

What does this mean for you? What I've described above might seem like bad news, and in some ways, it is. But regarding the issue of losing your sense of self, it's not. Once you understand this dynamic, you can stop exhausting yourself trying to tear down the emotional wall your partner keeps reinforcing. You can stop twisting yourself into knots to prove your love, and you can give up hope that these efforts will finally bring them around to your way of thinking. Ultimately, you'll see that it doesn't matter what you do. If your partner refuses to make the necessary effort for genuine change, they will likely remain emotionally distant.

Letting go of the hope that they will change isn't giving up. It's waking up. It involves redirecting your focus from what they want to what you need and deserve in a committed relationship. It's about choosing reality over illusion and self-respect over false hope. That choice, though challenging, is a significant act of self-love.

When we grasp the profound connection between body and mind, we tune into the conversation between them. This ongoing dialogue affects not only how we feel in our relationships but also how we show up in them.

Reclaiming a strong sense of self also involves tuning into what our emotions are telling us. They indicate what matters most, where our boundaries lie, and what inside us needs respect. Just as polyvagal theory explains how the nervous system is constantly scanning for safety or danger, our emotions send signals that guide us toward what we need to honor within ourselves.

And this is where we're headed next. In the following chapter, we'll explore what happens when we stop trying to push away or control our emotions and instead learn to listen to them. Emotions then become guides that can help us heal, strengthen our relationships, and connect more deeply with who we are and who we want to be.

Key Points

1. When we feel safe and connected in an intimate relationship, we can be spontaneous and try new experiences with confidence.
2. When our bodies sense a threat to our safety and security, our nervous system triggers biological reactions that

prompt us to defend ourselves with a fight, flight, freeze, or fawn response.

3. The fight-or-flight state is associated with emotions such as hurt, anger, frustration, fear, anxiety, and panic.
4. The freeze response feels like emotional numbness, withdrawal, being tongue-tied, and a sense of being trapped.
5. When we feel rejected or threatened by our partner's actions, our neuroception sends signals to our bodies that can trigger instinctive reactions, potentially worsening the situation.
6. To remain calm during stressful interactions with our partners, we must engage a higher part of our brain that allows us to separate their actions from our self-worth and avoid feelings of shame and guilt.
7. Recognizing the underlying psychological factors at play in our relationships will help us respond thoughtfully rather than impulsively to hurtful interactions.
8. To stay grounded in upsetting interactions with our partners, recognize the difference between an echo response, which can lead to a loss of self, and a grounded response that comes from a strong sense of self.
9. Chronic isolation and rejection in our relationships can lead to a range of health issues, including adrenal fatigue, sleep disturbances, anxiety disorders, depression, chronic fatigue, and a weakened immune system.
10. A partner's reaction to discussions about their demeaning behavior, whether they take responsibility or shift the blame onto us, reveals their capacity for emotional intimacy.

Self-Reflection: Identifying Mind and Body Reactions

1. Have you noticed changes in your body and how you feel during your relationship? If so, can you name some of the changes and how they've impacted your emotional and physical health?

2. How often do you feel threatened by your partner's actions toward you? How often do you feel calm and safe around them? Describe an experience in each state and how it made you feel.
3. In distressing interactions with your partner, do you respond with an echo reaction or a grounded reaction? If you respond with an echo reaction, identify the reasons for it. Consider whether those reasons are based on truth.
4. After troubling interactions with your partner, how do you feel about yourself? Can you identify the sensations in your body that hold stress and anxiety?
5. Describe some ways you attempt to recover from conflict with your partner. What methods are effective? Which ones aren't?

CHAPTER SEVEN

Emotions Are Inner Guides

Sarah sank into her desk chair as her phone lit up with a message from her husband. "Come to the bedroom." She knew what that meant and didn't want to go. But she also knew how he'd act if she didn't: cold silence, sharp words, and behaviors meant to make her feel like she was the problem. As she had many times before, Sarah stuffed down her feelings and did what her husband wanted. She knew she had a right to choose, but didn't want to face his backlash.

She poured her energy into keeping the household calm, always working to keep things at a simmer rather than letting them boil over. But the burden of her anxiety, shame, and the neglect of her wants and needs became unbearable. And it wasn't just about her anymore. How could she explain the turmoil between her and her husband to their four-year-old son? Why did she allow it to go on? Finding herself at a loss to answer those questions, she reached out to me.

Sarah was a beautiful woman in her thirties, but I could see in her careworn face the early lines and dull eyes of suffering. Instead of viewing her husband's behavior as abusive, she attributed it to his strong-willed nature and bad temper. When I asked her to identify areas of her body where she stored hurt and resentment, she looked puzzled. I suspected she had become desensitized to the physical sensations caused by chronic stress. She mentioned that she sometimes felt a constriction in her chest, as if she couldn't breathe deeply. Her inability to take deep breaths reflected the pressure of her marriage and how she responded to it: staying small to avoid her husband's aggression.

I asked her whether she had felt similarly in a previous long-term relationship. She thought for a moment, then described her mother as someone who seemed indifferent to Sarah's needs growing up. When

Sarah was young, her mother kept her at home to help with household chores and, when her father fell ill, to care for him. She didn't allow Sarah to go to sleepovers with her grade school friends, and later, she had to return from college on weekends. She learned to comply with her mother's demands in order to gain her love and attention. I could see a strong parallel in her marriage.

In therapy, she realized that her reaction to her husband's treatment was a continuation of childhood conditioning that taught her to suppress her feelings and respond in ways that would earn her mother's approval. Learning to bottle up her emotions had led her into a marriage that repeated a similar pattern.

Sarah hadn't yet realized that emotions are vital guides to maintaining a strong sense of self. They're internal signals that warn us of danger or an impending loss of self. When we ignore them, we fail to address something meaningful in our lives that needs attention. In their research at Northeastern University, in affiliation with Harvard Medical School, psychologists Karen S. Quigley and Lisa Feldman Barrett provided evidence in 1999 that ignoring or dismissing emotions leads us to overlook essential information about unmet needs, unresolved conflicts, and relational imbalances. This neglect can trap us in destructive patterns, diminish well-being, and weaken self-direction. Their research linked emotional listening to *intentional psychological change*, meaning that self-development begins when we pay attention to our emotions, understand them, and intentionally choose new responses. In this view, emotional awareness serves as the foundation for resilience, self-regulation, and meaningful change.

As we've seen, the urge to suppress our emotions is often fueled by a fear of how our partner might react or a desire to avoid conflict. Although this coping method may seem useful and practical in the short run, it can cause harm in the long run. Unexpressed feelings contain energy that accumulates in our minds and bodies. When this energy remains trapped, it can lead to confusion, withdrawal, anxiety, depression, shame, loss of energy, and anger directed at ourselves and others. It makes sense that we start to feel a loss of self. After all, how can we be the person we're meant to be when we carry such a heavy burden?

In a groundbreaking study, epidemiologist and public health researcher Elaine Eaker and her colleagues followed 3,682 participants (including 1,501 married women) for ten years. The 2007 study assessed both cardiovascular outcomes and overall mortality and found something remarkable: women who suppressed their feelings during arguments with their husbands were four times more likely to die from any cause than those who expressed themselves. In other words, suppressing emotions during conflict wasn't just uncomfortable. It was lethal.

The study, part of the well-known Framingham Heart Study, found that suppressing emotions during marital tension significantly affected women's health, increasing the risk of heart disease and early death. Notably, the health effects of marital stress were more severe for women than for men in this research.

The message is clear: suppressing emotions during conflict might keep the peace temporarily, but over time, it damages emotional well-being and physical health. Learning to express feelings and resolve disagreements in close relationships isn't just good for connection. It can even be lifesaving.

Just as surely as holding in emotions can keep us stuck, honoring them can propel us forward. I've witnessed this countless times in my work with clients, and Sarah's story is a clear example.

For years, Sarah believed the only way to be accepted was to suppress her feelings and meet others' expectations. This mindset became so deeply ingrained that it shaped many of her choices. But once she recognized the pattern, she realized her emotions had been trying to tell her something all along: she was denying herself by giving too much to others, and it would continue if she let it.

As she worked through her pain and began reclaiming her sense of self, Sarah still felt the pull to give in to her husband's unreasonable demands, even when his behavior was hurtful. The difference was that now she could recognize those urges for what they were: part of an old mindset that no longer served her. With time, she grew strong enough to set a clear boundary, telling him directly that she would no longer tolerate his selfish and offensive conduct.

That moment marked a turning point. By giving voice to her emotions instead of burying them, Sarah found a freedom she hadn't known before. It gave her the courage to take steps she had once been too afraid to imagine. (You'll read more about Sarah's therapy and what unfolded in her marriage in chapter 9.)

The Wisdom in Emotions

When we shut off the valve to our emotions, we not only deny our feelings, we also deny ourselves. That's because our emotions influence how we think, make decisions, and take action, especially when faced with something that requires careful consideration. Research from Nadine Jung and colleagues in 2014 shows that our emotions are not separate from reasoning but deeply connected to it. In their experiments, people in anxious states, whether caused by spider phobias or the stress of upcoming exams, had trouble thinking as clearly and logically as those in calmer moods. Even positive emotions changed how participants approached problems, sometimes making their thinking more flexible. The message is clear: emotions have a significant influence on the reasoning process. When we silence or suppress them, we don't just ignore feelings. We cut off access to the inner guide that helps us make good decisions, weigh options, and take meaningful action in our lives.

Psychologist Barbara Fredrickson, best known for leading the Positive Emotions and Psychophysiology Laboratory at the University of North Carolina at Chapel Hill, provides strong evidence for this truth. She discovered that positive emotions do more than just feel good in the moment. They broaden our awareness, enhance our ability to think creatively, and help us build lasting personal resources, from stronger relationships to increased resilience. In this way, emotions act as signals, guiding us toward what matters and getting us ready to move in that direction. When we recognize and accept our feelings, as Fredrickson's work demonstrates, we are better equipped to set meaningful goals, approach problems with perspective, and nurture the connections that sustain us. They allow us to handle situations with greater intention.

Gaining emotional wisdom requires identifying our feelings and understanding where they come from. For example, when we feel fear and respond with an echo reaction to something our partner said or did, we can ask ourselves: *What other feelings are driving that fear? Is it an attempt to avoid hurt, sadness, guilt, or rejection? Is my reaction appropriate to the situation in the moment, or is it triggered by past experience?* Our answers may show us that echo reactions often stem from a fear of rejection, a need to please, or a sense of inadequacy. Or perhaps they come from never having learned to handle confrontation and conflict, or from lacking a strong sense of self. Perhaps the cause is an old, misguided belief that being tolerant of another's transgressions will somehow make us feel safer or prevent more trouble.

Recognizing these deeper emotions and their roots provides us with a new perspective on who we are and what we want *now*. We can put more thought into our reactions instead of reacting in ways that compromise ourselves.

As we get better at honoring our emotions, we realize that old wounds don't just fade away, and the beliefs we once absorbed, especially when our feelings were dismissed or invalidated, can stay with us. These remnants of the past can make it difficult to fully trust our current feelings, even when we know better.

Recognizing an old mindset can go a long way in helping us make different choices. We don't have to keep falling into patterns that once silenced us and held us back. Let's explore some practical ways to stay grounded in the present.

Separating the Past from the Present

When we doubt our feelings, especially if our partner has dismissed them, we might start to view our emotions as flawed or think of them as a decision we've made rather than a natural part of who we are. We might spend hours rehashing a painful conversation, trying to figure out who's to blame, or find ourselves pulled back into memories of regrets and past hurts that bring up shame and self-doubt, triggered by our partner's anger and criticism.

When we struggle with emotions like this, it's often rooted in an unexamined belief that it's okay for someone else to determine our worth. For some of us, surrendering this control may have been a survival tactic, one we needed during childhood. But hanging onto it now is like carrying an outdated map that only leads us in circles.

Dispensing with that old map requires having a frank talk with ourselves. We can begin by asking ourselves: *What if my past doesn't have to dictate how I am in the present? What if the way I was treated back then was a reflection not of my worth but of someone else's limitations? What if I don't have to keep proving myself to people who try to control me or take my power away?*

Even as we do this work, we might fall back into old patterns. Our partner's offensive actions could trigger our usual ways of coping, even though better options are available now. During times of stress and conflict, we can recognize faulty thinking that we've never questioned before by asking ourselves: *What past experiences have caused a similar feeling? Is my partner's behavior similar to that of someone important from my past? Am I slipping back into childhood defenses that no longer serve me?*

This introspection can be challenging and sometimes painful. However, once we recognize how old beliefs trigger emotions that keep us stuck in unproductive thinking, we extend grace to ourselves for past mistakes and struggles. We can tap into the wisdom of emotional freedom to claim or reclaim the power we have as adults. We can access the full range of choices available to us today, no longer limited by decisions made long ago. In this way, we can avoid falling into the Echo complex.

Freeing Our Emotions

Tapping into the power of introspection requires us to free suppressed emotions. How do we do that? A good place to start is by recognizing it's perfectly okay to have them.

It's all too easy to judge ourselves for feeling a certain way, especially if we think our feelings don't matter. Our partners may try to instill this idea in our minds, especially if they're controlling, but it's also true that we let them. A common challenge my clients face is getting their partners to *listen* when they try to express their feelings. This often happens in relationships where we lose our sense of self. Allowing our partners to silence our emotions is a primary cause of echo behavior. By doing this, we accept their need to shut down a core part of who we are.

Avoidant partners often interrupt, step over, mock, get angry, and resort to "whataboutism," as in, "What about my feelings?" It's true that talking about their feelings is important (especially the more vulnerable ones they hide). But to break paradoxical cycles in our relationships and reclaim our sense of self, we need to focus on expressing our own feelings, especially if we're not used to doing so. A strong sense of self requires honoring every emotion: joy or sorrow, anger or contentment, shame or confidence, or whatever shows up. All our emotions have a place in our lives. Even our more shameful emotions, such as feelings of inadequacy, self-loathing, and remorse over past mistakes, as well as those we consider foolish, are part of being human. By embracing each of our feelings without judgment, we can free ourselves to experience the full spectrum of human emotions and cultivate empathy for both our own experiences and those of others.

Research by University of Toronto psychologist Brett Q. Ford and her colleagues in 2018 supports this. They found that individuals who practice accepting their negative emotions rather than fighting them tend to do better both immediately and over time. In a series of studies, they discovered that when participants allowed themselves to experience difficult feelings without judgment, those emotions became less overwhelming in stressful situations. Acceptance not only decreased the intensity of distress but also enhanced overall psychological well-being in daily life and even years later. This suggests that by recognizing and creating space for our emotions, we strengthen our ability to remain steady, think clearly, and respond to challenges with greater perspective.

Accepting our emotions is essential for inner stability, yet our emotional lives rarely exist in isolation. Partners continually influence one another's emotional states, often without realizing it. Recognizing how deeply intertwined our nervous systems are allows us to better understand how our emotional responses during conflict affect our partner—and how their emotions, in turn, affect us.

How Couples Co-Regulate Each Other's Emotions

Although our emotions serve as a helpful internal guide, they can be unreliable when the feelings we experience are not entirely our own. Maybe you've gone through this yourself. I certainly have.

One of the most startling ways I lost myself in my first marriage was through the change in my demeanor. Before I met my first husband, I tended more toward my father's New England temperament, which kept him calm and focused, even in situations he couldn't control. My very Southern mother, for her part, encouraged me to always be kind and cordial to others. Highly emotional relationships were foreign to me, and I never pictured myself arguing vociferously with my partner and ending up crying in the closet.

But that's what happened. What I didn't know at the time is that there's a biological reason why partners have a significant impact on each other's emotions.

James A. Coan, a clinical psychologist and neuroscientist at the University of Virginia, has devoted much of his career to studying how our closest relationships affect our ability to cope with stress. In a compelling fMRI study, he asked married women to face the threat of a mild electric shock either alone, while holding a stranger's hand, or while holding their husband's hand. The results were striking: when the women held their partner's hand, especially in strong, supportive marriages, their brains showed significantly less activation in areas associated with fear and stress, such as the amygdala. Coan concluded that partners engage in a process called "co-regulation," in which they influence each other's emotional states. Supportive partners can calm and protect us, easing the burden of stress, while antagonistic or critical partners can have the opposite effect, heightening fear, increasing stress, and making us feel unsafe. His work demonstrates that intimacy is biologically powerful, capable of healing and protecting us, or, when strained, causing distress and deepening our wounds.

Emotional co-regulation is largely unconscious and can occur without our awareness. However, we can acknowledge that emotional co-regulation is always a factor to some degree when we're interacting with our partners. Recognizing this, we can choose to harness the power of co-regulation to influence the tone and outcome of the interaction. When we stand up for our rights and values in a composed manner, rather than becoming reactive, we can utilize the co-regulation effect to help calm a heated conversation and adopt a more rational approach to the encounter.

Granted, this can be a challenge. Feelings are complex. Tempers flare. Fear takes over. Habitual thinking and behavior come into play. Instead of engaging with an open mind or a willingness to resolve the issue, partners might refuse to back down or twist the blame to avoid exposing their deeper fears. When this happens, our attempts to de-escalate the conversation may not be effective.

There is also the possibility that our partners may perceive our calming attempts as invalidating or condescending. If their anger stems from feelings of inadequacy, they may interpret any attempt to soothe them as pity or an effort to fix them, which can trigger their shame. They may resist our support to avoid being seen as needy or incapable. This defensive stance makes it difficult for us to reduce the intensity of the interaction because our partner is not seeking a resolution. They're trying to protect themselves from what they see as a threat, even though we're working toward a point where we can talk calmly and rationally.

Another challenge here is to manage our own emotions. We can't control how our partner reacts, but we can be mindful of our own responses, which can influence theirs. Again, we must remember that often our partner's anger is not about us, but about their internal struggles. Instead of absorbing their hostility and shifting into a state of fight, flight, freeze, or fawning, we can remind ourselves that our partner is reacting out of a need to control rather than from coherent thought.

This shift in perspective can help us remain composed and avoid being drawn into conflict or reacting in ways that undermine our self-respect.

Modeling emotional maturity is an essential tool here. If our partner is lashing out, we can calmly say something like, "I'm here to have a conversation with you, but I can't do that when you attack me." If their anger continues to escalate, it may be necessary to disengage by saying, "I care about you, but I need to step away until we can talk more calmly." Setting this boundary can help decrease the intensity of the interaction, although it may not work the first time we try it. But doing it repeatedly sends a message that we're not so easily controlled.

Emotional maturity also underpins how we give and receive love. Let's take a moment to consider how it affects the way we love in intimate relationships.

Love Is an Emotion

Emotional maturity enables intimate partners to love genuinely and deeply. Let's explore what I mean by that, beginning with a question.

What is love, really? This is a question people have been asking for ages. Philosophers, authors, scientists, and psychologists have all tried to define love. Aristotle described the highest form of love as a virtuous friendship where both individuals genuinely wish the best for each other. Unlike temporary desire, this type of love is based on mutual respect, shared values, and the pursuit of a good life together. Writer C. S. Lewis, in his book *The Four Loves*, believed that the highest form of love is giving oneself freely without expecting anything in return. Psychologists, on the other hand, define love as a vital emotional bond, built on attachment and intimacy, that greatly affects our well-being. On a scientific level, love begins with biology. People are wired to seek connection for safety, survival, and a sense of belonging.

But love is, of course, much more complex than instinct. Fredrickson puts it simply: Love is an emotion. Not just a feeling that comes and goes, but something that's shaped by the ways people connect with each other. Real love doesn't exist on only one person's terms. It exists in the space between two people who understand each other. It's in that shared space where both partners are authentic. They listen, care, and grow together. That kind of connection can't exist when one partner acts and the other merely echoes back, ignoring their own true feelings. Love is created in the moments we share, the emotions we express, and the ways we respond to each other.

In such moments of shared emotions, people express love through a variety of feelings, including empathy, joy, affection, sadness, regret, caring, and even anger (but not abusive anger). This mutual sharing of emotions is how we cultivate true intimacy. For love to take hold and grow, both partners must be mature enough to be emotionally present and open to love without being hindered by fears and insecurity.

What happens when a pattern develops in a relationship where one or both partners hold back their true feelings? Over time, this dynamic wears down not only the relationship but also the precious qualities within each person that enable them to love each other. If both partners can't engage with mutual honesty and emotional transparency, they stay distant. The relationship might function on a surface level, but it won't be fulfilling or secure.

When we acknowledge not only the wisdom in our own emotions but also the truth about our partner's feelings, like a pattern of anger and indifference, and what these feelings reveal about their ability to love us, we can stop reacting with echo behavior. When we respond with emotional maturity, we're better equipped to acknowledge and express our feelings clearly and authentically.

Express Emotions with Confidence

The insights below help us stay true to ourselves as we express our feelings. They remind us that we can overcome fear, self-doubt, and old ways of coping that once caused us to ignore what our feelings were trying to tell us. They help us distinguish between truth and others' projections or manipulations, and in balancing empathy with self-protection. With this understanding, we can speak assertively, knowing that our emotions deserve respect. By honoring them, we open the door to a deeper connection with ourselves and, if they are willing, our partners.

1. Understand Your Fear

When we suppress painful emotions, we may do so out of fear of conflict or a desire to please our partners. We might think, *If I don't tell my partner how I really feel, they won't get angrier or punish me. I can keep things peaceful.* But when we respond to our fears by censoring ourselves, we compromise our values and set a precedent of being unheard and disrespected.

Remember, your partner's controlling behavior may be fear-based, and they aren't showing their deeper feelings either. When this dynamic is at play, partners are acting out of the same fear of rejection, just in different ways. You can, however, model something different, which is necessary if your relationship and circumstances are going to change. So speak up.

A word of caution here. Safety is always the top priority. If you're unsure how your partner might react, speaking up doesn't have to mean confronting them in the heat of the moment. It can start with small steps, such as calmly sharing your feelings in a safe setting, perhaps in a public place, drawing a clear boundary instead of apologizing, or writing down your feelings if speaking feels unsafe. Speaking up might also involve reaching out to a trusted friend or counselor when you need to be heard and validated before deciding how to move forward. The goal is to prioritize your safety while expressing your emotions, rather than carrying them around.

2. Believe in Yourself

Expressing our needs and feelings is a brave act of self-preservation, and believing we deserve the love and kindness we seek from others gives us the strength to do so. When we trust in our self-worth, that trust acts as a shield against our partner's harsh treatment. Instead of internalizing their hurtful words and actions, we can see their actions for what they truly are: reflections of their need for control, rather than accurate judgments of our worth.

Recognizing our self-worth means understanding that our inner struggles, mistakes, flaws, and the negative perceptions of others do not determine our value as human beings. We are inherently worthy of love, respect, and kindness, regardless of our imperfections. No one has the right to take that away from us, including ourselves.

One of the most meaningful rewards in my work is witnessing that pivotal moment when a client fully realizes how much they have underestimated their self-worth, whether through negative self-talk, people-pleasing, or tolerating disrespect and abuse from the person who is supposed to love them. It's an eye-opening realization, often accompanied by emotions ranging from grief (for the years lost to self-doubt) to excitement (for what's possible now). And once they start to honor their worth, they can refuse to continue living under self-imposed limitations.

What's especially inspiring is watching how they step into personal power that can change everything, not just for themselves, but also for their children, if they have them. They stop tolerating disrespect in their relationships and start advocating for their needs. They stop over-explaining, excessively apologizing, or waiting for permission to take up space. Budding confidence replaces self-doubt, and a new attitude toward self-worth replaces underestimating oneself. Life feels less like enduring and more like living with intention. This same transformation is available to you. Once you choose to honor your voice, you begin creating a different story for yourself and for those who look up to you.

3. Resist Dissociating and Fawning as Ways to Cope

Both dissociation and fawning are common echo behaviors. Dissociation is a freeze response that can leave us feeling detached from our thoughts, feelings, and bodies. When we dissociate instead of responding to a disturbing interaction with our partners, we might lose control over our actions and feel hollow or emotionally numb. We may feel as if it's impossible for us to speak, and that we're watching what's happening from outside our bodies.

Fawning, on the other hand, is marked by a strong urge to please others and an excessive need for reassurance and approval from them before making decisions. Demeaning ourselves in this way dishonors our true feelings and will never lead to a strong sense of self. (Read more about freezing and fawning in chapter 6.)

In the moment, dissociation and fawning behavior may seem necessary in situations that feel beyond our control. They might provide temporary relief by pushing aside our deeper feelings. However, over time, these responses to adversity can become ingrained patterns that happen without us fully realizing how they harm us.

When we feel the urge to dissociate or fawn, it's a sign that, emotionally, we're not fully present, so it's best to physically remove ourselves from the situation. In the moment of upsetting interaction, we can say, "I'm going to take time out to think about what just happened and consider my feelings." Then, we can walk away and find a private place to collect our thoughts and feelings. Choosing this response not only breaks the harmful cycle with a distant or abusive partner but also helps us avoid echo reactions in a situation that requires us to be fully present. By taking a step back, we create an opportunity to respond thoughtfully and clearly, rather than reacting out of fear or putting ourselves at risk.

4. Understand Projection

As we learned in chapter 3, projection is a defense mechanism that offers the mind temporary relief from anxiety. When our partner uses this defense to project their unacceptable thoughts, feelings, and motives onto us, trying to make us feel the shame they experience or have tried to suppress, we might ask ourselves, *Is this my fault? Am I the problem?* This uncertainty can weaken our confidence and make it hard to know how to respond. However, when we realize that our partner's blame may be a way to protect their hidden emotions, we can step back and evaluate whether the criticism is justified or simply a way for our partner to unload their struggles onto us.

Here are some ways to respond when a partner tries to project their feelings or personal issues onto us.

- "I sense that you're upset about something, and it feels like you're directing that toward me. Can we talk about what's really going on for you?"
- "I want to support you, but I can't take responsibility for things that aren't mine to carry."
- "I've noticed that you try to blame me when you're feeling anxious or unsure. Maybe we can find a time when you're feeling calmer to talk about what you're feeling when this happens."

As you read through these examples, consider your own situation and think about some appropriate responses you can give when your partner starts to project their feelings onto you. When you're in conversations with your partner where they're projecting onto you, keep checking in with yourself by asking, *Am I staying true to my values? Am I being manipulated or made to feel guilty for something that isn't mine?* As we've seen in chapter 7, emotional co-regulation may be happening here, so responding calmly instead of reacting impulsively can help reduce tension and promote emotional safety. Always ensure you can reach a safe place if the conversation turns abusive. (Read the safety warning at the front of the book for a safety reminder, and go back to chapter 3 if you want to review truth #3 that relates to projection.)

5. Recognize the Limits of Empathy

Empathy is an essential quality in any relationship, but it becomes problematic when it leads to excusing harmful behavior. While understanding a partner's fears about emotional intimacy and the reasons behind their defenses is important, tolerating offensive actions is not acceptable.

Healthy empathy means understanding a partner's inner struggles without letting ourselves become their emotional punching bag. When we confuse empathy with tolerating mistreatment, we risk losing sight of our own worth and boundaries. Recognizing this difference helps us stay compassionate while also safeguarding ourselves, which is what makes true intimacy and mutual respect possible.

6. Protect Against Emotional Manipulation

One of the biggest challenges in disconnected relationships is recognizing when our partner deflects attention away from their own issues by attacking our vulnerabilities. They might target our insecurities to make us feel guilty or responsible for their unhappiness. This often happens when a partner emphasizes our flaws but refuses to acknowledge their own. In such situations, we can step back and ask ourselves:

- Am I being held responsible for things beyond my control?
- Does my partner dismiss my feelings while demanding I validate theirs?
- Do I often feel like I have to prove my worth or explain myself?
- Does my partner criticize me more when they seem stressed, anxious, or insecure?

Saying "yes" to any of these questions indicates we are not to blame. When our partners create emotional distance with intimidating behaviors, they may be attempting to disown their unwanted feelings. Regardless of why they behave this way, they are responsible, not us, and their manipulative actions never determine our worth.

7. Come from a Position of Strength

When our partner pulls away or mistreats us, we might feel uncertain, confused, or even powerless. That's understandable. Anyone would feel shaken in those moments. Yet, even when we don't feel completely sure of ourselves, we still have choices. Responding from a place of strength doesn't mean we need to feel fully confident. Instead, it means living by our own values and protecting what matters to us. By honoring ourselves in this manner, we reaffirm that our feelings are genuine and deserve to be expressed.

One of the most effective ways to do this is through body language. Making direct eye contact sends a clear message that we are present, aware, and not easily intimidated. It is a silent yet powerful way to command respect. The way we speak matters just as much. Maintaining a steady voice conveys our message with strength.

Coming from a position of strength means remaining rational and composed, even when emotions run high. While lashing out may feel satisfying in the moment, it rarely leads to resolution. This is where being assertive comes in. Assertiveness is standing up for ourselves clearly and directly. We demonstrate respect for ourselves and our partner by communicating honestly without aggression or defensiveness.

When partners are dismissive or offensive, the best approach may be to disengage. Not every battle needs to be fought, especially when the other person isn't open to a respectful exchange. Walking away isn't a sign of weakness. It's a sign of wisdom. And again, if the interaction escalates into abuse, stop the conversation and get to a safe place.

In the next chapter, you'll meet Sharon, a woman with an emotionally avoidant and abusive husband. She learns to understand her fears, believe in herself, resist echo behaviors, recognize when her husband projects his insecurities onto her, set appropriate limits on empathy, and approach situations from a position of strength. It wasn't always that way. Her early life taught her to survive through self-sacrifice and silencing her voice, patterns she carried into adulthood. In her relationship with Richard, these old dynamics take a devastating toll, making her feel like a prisoner in her own home.

Sharon's story is one of pain, but it's also one of awakening. As she begins to understand the deeper reasons for her situation and her role in it, something powerful shifts. What unfolds is a journey back to the strength she always had but never knew how to claim until she faced the truth.

Key Points

1. Children learn about proper emotional expression within their families, and this understanding, or lack thereof, affects their adult relationships.
2. Our emotions serve as vital guides, offering us valuable insights into who we are and what we truly need.
3. Ignoring an emotional signal indicating danger or loss can be very costly because we overlook something important that requires our attention or fail to take steps to prevent potential harm.
4. All emotions seek resolution. Unexpressed feelings store energy that builds up inside us, weighing us down and blocking our mental, emotional, and physical vitality.
5. Unexpressed feelings show up in our minds as confusion, withdrawal, anxiety, depression, shame, a loss of vitality, and anger toward ourselves and others.
6. Emotional pain often stems from old, limiting thought patterns that were learned during early development.
7. In romantic relationships, partners co-regulate each other's emotions, meaning one or both partners can either promote calmness and a strong sense of safety or incite feelings of danger, leading to a fight, flight, freeze, or fawning response.
8. Understanding both our own emotions and those of our partners can help us avoid echo reactions and help prevent losing ourselves in relationships.
9. Making accusations or blaming us for problems that aren't our fault can be our partner's way of projecting their unwanted thoughts, feelings, and motives onto us.
10. When we assert ourselves, we manage our emotions rather than letting them drive impulsive or instinctive actions that could make things worse.

CHAPTER EIGHT

Sharon's Story

IN THE FIRST part of this book, we explored the phenomenon of the Echo complex, the subtle yet powerful forces that can cause someone to gradually lose their sense of self within an intimate relationship. We examined each factor individually, observing how they can shape the way partners relate to each other. Now, we'll see how these elements interlock in real life to form a harmful pattern of interaction that is hard to recognize when you're living through it. Following one woman's journey to see how these dynamics play out might help you recognize similarities in your own experience and understand what it takes to start making changes.

When Sharon first reached out for therapy, she had a severe Echo complex. She had given up her independence, stopped pursuing her passion for dancing and horseback riding, and hadn't stayed in touch with her friends for years. She allowed her husband to control where she went, who she spoke to, and even what she wore. She loved her husband and wanted to stay with him, but she was deeply unhappy and longed to be her former self.

When you read her story, pay close attention to what happens in her relationship with Richard. Notice how her cognitive biases, like confirmation bias, influence her behavior. Observe how she explains her husband's actions and justifies her own by using defense mechanisms like denial, minimizing, and rationalization. Take note of the paradoxical cycles present in their relationship, all of which push her toward the Echo complex. (I will note these factors in parentheses the first time they happen in her relationship with Richard to help you begin to spot them.) After finishing her story, answer the questions and complete the exercise at the end of this chapter. In chapter 9, you'll get a look inside Sharon's therapy and the outcome of her relationship.

By the end of Sharon's therapy a year later, she wanted to share her story to help others who have gone through the pain of losing themselves in their relationships. Her story is based on details from my therapy notes and my experience as her therapist. Like other therapy clients in this book, some details have been changed to protect confidentiality.

Sharon Meets Richard

Sharon, the choreographer and leader of a popular dance troupe, was invited to perform at the Person of the Year Award gala held at the city's modern performing arts center. Backstage, on the night of the event, her dancers stretched and rehearsed their moves for the closing number while Sharon watched Richard deliver his acceptance speech on stage. Prominent citizens and community leaders gathered to honor him for his efforts in bringing economic prosperity to the city. *This is what a real man is like*, she thought. *Generous. Responsible. Caring.* (Confirmation bias.) Sharon was married, but she and her husband were living separately as a result of her husband's addiction and abuse.

After the ceremony, Richard approached Sharon and introduced himself. He told her how much he enjoyed the dance performance and invited her to lunch to discuss hiring her troupe for an upcoming event. "He made me feel like I was the only one in the room," she told me when she first started therapy.

Sharon's initial impression of Richard was very different from her view of her husband, whom she'd been married to for seventeen years. Recently, she had taken out a restraining order against him to protect herself and their two teenagers. His longtime struggles with alcohol and gambling had worsened in recent years. He lost his job, stole their children's identities to open new lines of credit, and gambled away the money they needed for bills. He also lied about filing their yearly income taxes, leaving her with a $30,000 debt to the government. When she confronted him about the tax debt, he shoved her and yelled in her face.

Worrying about her problems made it difficult for Sharon to eat properly or sleep well. Nonetheless, she worked tirelessly to support her family financially and built a strong reputation as a choreographer. Even as she and her troupe performed at the city's most glamorous events, no one knew about her troubled life.

One week after the gala, she had lunch with Richard at a restaurant with a breathtaking ocean view. He talked about his friendships with celebrities and the most influential people in the state. He shared stories of his trips to India, Brazil, and Paris. He displayed his charming smile and laughed effortlessly. She felt very comfortable with him.

When she told him that she was considering taking a position in another city to escape her husband, Richard said that he knew the chief of police well and would "handle" her husband's threats. "I saw him as my knight in shining armor," she said.

That night, Sharon formed a clear image of Richard as a wise, decent, trustworthy, and kind-hearted man (halo effect bias). The next day, he followed through on his promise when two police officers went to her husband's apartment to talk to him. After that, her husband stopped making threats. "For the first time in my life, I felt I was protected," she said. "Not only me, but also my children."

Searching for Love

Sharon longed to be with a man who could provide the love she had been searching for since childhood. Growing up on a farm in California, her parents didn't place much value on nurturing her emotions or helping her develop a strong sense of self. Instead, they promoted her independence, telling her she was the only one of their four children capable of taking care of herself.

Her parents traveled extensively with her two older brothers, who competed in regional and national gymnastics competitions. When her parents were home, her father preferred his cocktails to spending time with his daughters. Sharon's mother, too, always had something else to tend to. The family home was often teeming with visitors and activities. From the outside, Sharon's family appeared to be thriving and happy, but beneath that polished image, there were issues.

One Christmas morning when she was ten, Sharon sat quietly beside her three siblings as they tore into their gifts. When her mother asked why she hadn't opened her presents, she said she didn't have any. Only then did her mother realize that Sharon's gifts had been left unwrapped in an upstairs closet.

Another time, after the family had been looking for a new car, Sharon's father asked everyone where they wanted to go to dinner. "Can I pick?" Sharon asked. "It's my birthday." She had turned twelve that day. No one remembered.

Her parents' frequent absences required her and her sister to have babysitters, one of whom molested Sharon's older sister. Another time, a drunk family friend spent the night and molested Sharon after her parents went to bed. Neither girl told anyone. Both internalized their shame and anger, which led to eating issues.

Sharon's sister's weight gain became a target for their father's criticism at the dinner table. To avoid her father's admonishment, Sharon left food on her plate, believing he would approve if she stayed thin. Starving herself became a way to turn her repressed feelings into self-directed aggression.

Sharon longed for her parents' love and attention but stayed silent about her need and bore the pain of their emotional neglect. She believed they would only love her if she didn't need them. "I had to do everything myself so I wouldn't bother my parents," she said. "I didn't want to create problems." She concealed her hurt, anger, and shame by climbing oak trees and riding horses in the fields around her family's farm.

Convinced that her accomplishments proved her worth, she worked hard to excel in school and, through her efforts, earned a scholarship to a prestigious university in Los Angeles. Unfortunately, while in college, her belief that she had to please others to be loved led her into a relationship with an unstable man. An up-and-coming rock musician she dated broke her heart by sleeping with her best friend. He was also addicted to heroin and robbed stores to fund his habit. "I tried to help him," Sharon recalled later, "but I only enabled him. I thought he cared about me, so I stayed." They split when his record label forced him into rehab.

Sharon struggled with anorexia and depression and ended up in the emergency room when she was nineteen years old. The ER doctor gave her lithium and sent her home. No one in her family was aware of her illnesses. She arrived at home later that afternoon to an empty house. In despair, certain she didn't have the ability to live a good life, she downed vodka and dumped out her bottle of lithium on her bed, intending to swallow all of the pills and end her misery. Then she had second thoughts and quickly spat out the first few she had put in her mouth. She never told anyone about the incident. Shortly afterward, she dropped out of college to join a local dance company owned by a friend's parents.

As a dancer, Sharon quickly gained recognition because of her talent and the guidance of excellent instructors. She caught the attention of a top dance company in New York, which invited her to join. Although she kept receiving praise from her instructors and fellow dancers, after several years, the stress of performing triggered a relapse of anorexia that threatened her ability to perform. She was no longer able to handle the demands of her career, so she left. In the months that followed, she taught dance to support herself while under the care of a doctor who helped her recover from her illness.

As she became more physically and emotionally stable, Sharon met a man with whom she felt a strong connection. She didn't realize the severity of his alcohol use and gambling habit until after they married and started a family. When he wasn't using, he treated her with kindness and respect. But over the years, his addictions consumed him. Instead of taking responsibility, he blamed addiction for his job losses and unexplained absences from home.

Sharon continued to focus on supporting her two children and providing a normal life for them by accepting a residential choreographer position with a steady income. But when the children were teenagers, her husband got physically violent. He pushed her out of bed and pinned her to the floor. The police arrived afterward and arrested him for domestic violence. Sharon and her husband separated several times, and each time he expressed deep regret for his behavior and told her he couldn't make it without her. Eventually, she realized that her husband wasn't going to change, and applied for jobs in other cities. She had just been offered a position as the director of a well-known dance company when she met Richard.

Falling for Richard

Charming from the beginning, Richard persuaded her to turn down the job offer. They began seeing each other. He wanted to know why she'd stayed in her marriage. "Because it was the right thing to do at the time," she told him. "It wasn't always bad, but over time it got worse. I didn't want to give up for the kids."

He told her he didn't understand why women were attracted to such low-life men and that he took his responsibilities seriously. He confided how hard he had worked to save his marriage with his "crazy" ex-wife, who suffered from depression and would not leave the house. He said that being the "stable one" in a twenty-five-year marriage had taken its toll on him.

One night, at the premiere of a film Richard brought to the city, Sharon arrived in her seat just as the lights went down. On stage as the master of ceremonies, he introduced the film's star to thunderous applause. The spotlight swept across the theater and landed on Sharon and the man sitting beside her, a world-famous actor. Richard had intentionally seated Sharon next to the film's star. Thrilled by Richard's surprise, she knew arranging such a delightful experience meant he really cared about her. *God really knows how to come through for me*, she thought, certain that she had finally found a man who could make her happy (anchoring bias).

After she filed for divorce from her husband, Sharon occasionally traveled with Richard on his business trips, when her children could stay with her parents, who lived nearby. They enjoyed luxury hotels and dining at expensive restaurants. She admired what she saw as his strength of character. A leader in his field, he spoke with authority and confidence. He appeared to be a man who could truly love her. "I never want to be without you," he told her. She didn't want to be without him either, although she didn't realize his statement meant something different to him than it did to her.

One day, while they were in their hotel room on a business trip, Richard went through Sharon's emails and found one from her male insurance agent. Seeing it, he got upset and told her, "That guy just wants to get in your pants." Getting worked up, he told her he didn't want to be with her anymore (trial by fire paradox).

Deeply shaken by the abrupt change in his behavior, Sharon decided it was best to leave. She didn't want to be in another relationship with a man who hurt her. As she headed toward the door with her bag, he grew more agitated and said that if she left, their relationship would be over. She responded by telling him that if he didn't get a handle on his jealousy, *that* would be the cause of their relationship ending. When Sharon stood up to him, he apologized and told her he loved her so much he couldn't stand the thought of her with another man. "I thought, okay, I may have to deal with some jealousy," she recalled. "I didn't like it, but I figured that was the extent of it. I never thought he would become extremely controlling" (minimizing).

Despite signs of Richard's jealousy, Sharon thought things were going well between them. She viewed him as a great man and wanted to be the woman he was proud to have by his side. Being with him gave her a sense of purpose and made her feel important as the girlfriend of a highly regarded city leader. As she considered ways to improve their relationship, it occurred to her that focusing too much on her dance career might have contributed to problems in her past relationships. By doing so, she may have held back from fully committing to her partners. Maybe something similar had triggered Richard's reaction. Determined never to repeat that mistake, she vowed to make any personal sacrifices necessary to maintain their relationship. She would put him first (Echo paradox, boundaries paradox).

Explaining Away Red Flags

Although Sharon began to prioritize her relationship with Richard, his senseless accusations and unwarranted anger continued. One evening at dinner, just after they placed their order, Sharon said she would be back in a minute. She wanted to say hello to an old friend she spotted across the room. Immediately, Richard accused her of being selfish and forbade her from talking to her friend. He jerked his chair away from the table and stomped out of the restaurant. Sharon followed. On their way home, he drove twenty-five miles over the speed limit. In shock and disbelief, unable to understand the sudden change in his attitude, Sharon apologized and promised to be more attentive to him.

Later, after a sleepless night of pondering how she could be a better partner to Richard, Sharon reached a conclusion. Beneath his vibrant and confident exterior, he harbored insecurities, but that was normal. She had seen it in other men she had been with. Once Richard realized how much she cared about him, surely, he wouldn't have such severe reactions (rationalization).

A few weeks later, after a formal press dinner at the governor's mansion, Richard accused her of flirting with a journalist sitting next to her. Sharon, who had been showering Richard with words of love and affirmation, didn't understand why he kept making accusations. He told her that his ex-wife and previous girlfriends never flirted with other men like she did. Distressed by his remarks, she questioned herself. Her attempts at being cordial didn't feel like flirting, but there must be something to his complaints. If he hadn't had these issues with other women in his past, it must be her fault. Maybe she had sent out suggestive signals without realizing it and needed to be careful about how she interacted with other men to avoid his anger (introjection).

But regardless of how Sharon compromised herself to please Richard, his controlling behavior grew worse, and she grew more compliant with his demands. When she was alone in her car commuting to and from work, he often kept her on the phone. He asked where she had been, who she had seen, where she planned to go, and who would be there. He insisted she accompany him to every social event he attended and bought her fashionable clothing and jewelry to wear (denial).

On nights when he was free, he pressured her to cancel her plans so they could be together. He brushed off her explanation that she had other commitments. If she didn't spend time with him when he wanted, he ghosted her afterward. Sharon felt intimidated and resentful, but she convinced herself that a pillar of the community like Richard hadn't achieved that level of influence without going after what he wanted. "I tried to understand his need to be with me constantly," she said. "I tried to see his intensity more as passion."

When Richard learned that Sharon and her daughter were going to move in with her parents after her son left for college, he convinced her to live with him just six months after they started dating. She felt reluctant because she didn't know him well enough yet, and she was concerned about how living with Richard would affect her daughter, but he told her he wanted to marry her, so she agreed. Surely, living with him would prove her love and help him relax into their relationship without so many demands on her time.

For a while, living together felt like they were becoming a family, and Richard seemed to grow more secure in their relationship. However, a couple of months after she and her daughter moved in with him, Sharon's brother sent her a music video on Valentine's Day featuring male dancers with bow ties around their necks and black pants, but no shirts. When Richard saw the video, he demanded that she tell her brother it was inappropriate and insisted that he apologize. Sharon enjoyed the quality of the dancing in the video and didn't find anything wrong with it. But to please Richard, she did as he asked. When her brother expressed surprise that she would object, she admitted that she hadn't thought the video was a big deal either. Afterward, Richard was furious. "I forbid you to speak to him ever again!" he said. His irrational behavior had returned with full force. But Sharon felt she had no choice, so she stopped talking with her brother and hoped Richard would forget the incident. But her decision had repercussions. When she later married Richard, her brother refused to attend their wedding celebration. "The music video incident was one of many red flags," said Sharon. "But I hung on to the fairytale that Richard was the love of my life, and that everything would be okay."

The night before Richard took Sharon to meet his mother, he told her to show him lots of affection when they were at his mother's house. True to his request, she wore a pretty dress, held his hand, and kissed him on the cheek several times during their visit. His mother received her warmly, and later Richard told Sharon that his mother approved of her. Sharon didn't know anything about his childhood but took his mother's kindness as a sign that he came from a close-knit family. After their visit, she couldn't understand his hateful comments about his mother after Richard took her to the grocery store and bought food for her.

After dropping his mother off at her house, Richard said, "What you see is an act. She pretends to love people to get things for free." He said his mother only wanted to see him so he would buy her food. Sharon thought his comments were odd. After all, he had been trying to impress his mother with his new relationship. But she didn't want to pass judgment on them. She figured Richard might also be insecure about his mother's love. She saw Richard as a caretaker, someone who stepped in to help when needed, and that role was bound to take a toll on him at times.

When Richard asked her to marry him the following week, her vision of the wonderful life they could share overshadowed her worries about Richard's behavior. She believed it was the right time to move forward with her life now that her daughter, a high school senior, was spending more time with her father, who had been doing well in recovery, and her son was away at college. Captivated by the excitement of his proposal, she overlooked her ongoing concerns about Richard. Surely, she thought, his jealousy problem would subside after they made a lifelong commitment to each other. They planned a spring wedding.

A Quick Marriage

Two months before their planned wedding date, Richard persuaded Sharon to let him go with her to the courthouse to sign her divorce papers. He said he would protect her if there was any trouble. She was worried that he and her ex-husband would get into a fight. But as usual, when in public, Richard remained composed and confident. He knew the judge, made small talk, and even threw in a couple of witty remarks to break the ice.

After Sharon and her ex-husband signed the papers, Sharon was ready to go home. But before they left, Richard suddenly suggested they get married at the courthouse that day and have a boat party on their previously planned wedding date. Overwhelmed by the emotional weight of the official breakup of her family, Sharon felt unmoored and vulnerable. She wanted a chance to talk with her son and daughter to tell them they wouldn't be able to attend her wedding. But she feared losing Richard and wanted his commitment, so she agreed. They married the same day she finalized her divorce, just eight months after they met.

Sharon counted on their marriage to improve their relationship, but things didn't turn out as she had hoped. "After we married, we had blissful moments, but I had this nagging feeling that something was deeply wrong, and I didn't know how to fix it," she said. Several weeks later, while they were driving to her parents' house, Sharon's son called. Richard insisted that she use the speakerphone so he could hear their conversation. When her son mentioned that he and his sister planned to spend Christmas with their father's family, Richard pounded his fist on the steering wheel and forbade the children from seeing their father.

After Sharon hung up, Richard said, "They're just like all the rest. They believe in the loser and forget the man who's doing everything for them!" He claimed he hadn't signed up for the baggage she brought into their marriage. Deeply hurt, she pleaded with him to reconsider. "I love you so much. I'm sorry this is difficult for you," she sobbed. "They just don't know any better. They hope their dad will change. Please don't be angry." His statements went against his promise to take care of her and her children, but she wondered what she could do about it. She felt indebted to him. Because of Richard's wealth and generosity, it was the first time in many years that she didn't have to struggle financially.

In the months afterward, she embraced her new life as the wife of a wealthy and influential man. There were elegant soirées and major city events to attend, trips to exotic locations, and a beautiful home to decorate. Over time, she began to see Richard as two different men: one who seemed to love her, and another who called her ugly names and threatened divorce and financial ruin. "I was in survival mode," she later explained. "To stay on his good side, I pushed away my fear and isolation and acted lighthearted and content. I tried to focus on the good times in our relationship" (lonely love paradox, reaction formation, compartmentalization).

Richard asked Sharon to stop working because he couldn't handle his jealous feelings. He boasted to others about his wife's brilliant career as a dancer and choreographer, but what he told her was very different. He said he hated dancers, calling them loose and immoral. "I thought that if I quit, he would stop suspecting me of wanting to be with other men," she said. "So I let another piece of myself go."

After she left her job, Richard insisted she stay home rather than visit friends and family. He told her to focus on their life together. He sent her multiple texts every day, always expecting a quick response, and frequently kept her on the phone for an hour bragging about his latest accomplishments and all the wonderful things people said about him.

Whenever she mentioned in a text that she was going to run an errand, he always responded, "Wait. I'll take you when I get home." If she didn't wait for him, she had to endure an hour-long lecture on how she had been scheming to cheat on him. She spent her days working through his list of demands and chores. She cooked, cleaned, washed windows, painted baseboards, and made all his appointments.

"Richard owned all my time and all my energy," Sharon said. "He put people in my life and took others out. He made all my decisions." Being unable to work and his constant demands on her time kept her in a high state of anxiety and caused her to feel deep discontent, even though she enjoyed a comfortable home and financial stability. This time, her relationship was free of drug addiction and physical violence, and she focused on her gratitude (silent scream paradox).

Entrenched in the Echo Complex

Before long, Richard insisted on accompanying Sharon everywhere she went. He joined her on her morning walks so she couldn't "have an affair with a neighbor." Her horseback riding gave him more chances to criticize her for talking to others. He changed her cell phone number without her permission and told her not to share it. Once, he left her at the airport in a foreign country as punishment for talking to a passenger on their flight.

Sharon tried to reason with him, desperately hoping he would stop his punishing, senseless behavior. But her desperation had no apparent effect on him. Although she felt a great deal of resentment and anger, Sharon remained silent about her feelings to avoid his hostile reactions. "Any time I expressed an emotion, he used it against me," she said. "Eventually, I lost myself to the point where I couldn't have feelings. I couldn't have needs, opinions, or make my own decisions. 'Just tell me what you want me to do' was the only response he seemed to accept."

Richard's behavior continued to be erratic, even strange. Sharon watched in disbelief whenever he threw tantrums. Once, he cried like a baby after a figurine from his large collection of Beatles memorabilia fell to the floor and got a tiny chip in it. On the day they bought a house together, he shook uncontrollably and didn't say much. When he lapsed into these moods, she comforted him as if he were a child, telling him everything would be okay. She felt torn between his hurtful behavior and his extreme need for her.

Sharon didn't tell anyone about Richard's strange behavior or the way he treated her. He was the leader of a major organization, and she believed that if any of his colleagues knew how he acted privately with her, they would think he was crazy. The truth might cost him his job and reputation. "I felt responsible for all his emotions. It was like he was obsessed with me and needed me like a drug." Sharon alternated between loving and hating him. At times, she thought about leaving him, and these thoughts filled her with guilt and sadness.

To protect herself emotionally, she began to pull away. But as she grew more distant, his grip on her grew more intense. Still, things weren't always bad. Once, Richard surprised her with two purebred puppies, and he supported her passion for horseback riding by encouraging her to compete in dressage events. "I wanted so desperately for us to be the two people who were deeply in love at the beginning of our relationship. It was hard for me to give up on him," Sharon explained. "But all his moves were strategic, never based on a true sense of giving and unconditional love."

Stress Takes a Toll

Unsurprisingly, Sharon's health worsened. Just days before Christmas, she found out she had breast cancer. She knew she wouldn't be able to meet Richard's needs during her surgery and recovery. Concerned about how he would react, she kept the news to herself until after the Christmas holiday. It turned out she was right about his reaction.

"You're giving me your bad karma!" he said. Sharon thought, *Why isn't he holding me, telling me he will be with me all the way to protect and support me? Where is the man I met years ago? How could I have been so deceived?*

One week after Sharon's mastectomy and reconstructive surgery, Richard already expected her to resume managing her household and administrative duties. When she felt weak, he responded coldly, as if she had no right to neglect him while she recovered. A short time later, while trying to regain her strength, she lost her balance on a treadmill and fell backward. Frightened, hurt, and clutching her swollen chest, she asked him to take her to the hospital. He reluctantly dropped her off and then headed to work.

After her emergency surgery for a hematoma, he picked her up outside the hospital. Sharon blamed herself for not being more careful. She desperately needed his comfort, but he refused to speak to her except to say, "What do you do for me? All you do is take." Feeling weak and defenseless, she coped with Richard's heartless treatment by convincing herself that he was venting his frustration with her and didn't truly mean what he said.

"I just blocked out my emotions because I needed him to survive," she later explained. Eventually, she discovered that Richard had been seeing another woman during her surgery and recovery.

A few months after her surgery, Sharon began regaining her strength and discussed with Richard her desire to see a therapist together so they could better understand each other. He suggested that she have an individual session with his therapist first, and then, if his therapist recommended couples counseling, he would attend. Feeling hopeful, Sharon thought maybe the therapist could help Richard understand the harmful effects of his behavior on her and their marriage. Perhaps she could help them get back on track. But during Sharon's session, the therapist told her that Richard had a "type A personality" and she needed to understand him better. She advised Sharon to stop dwelling on the past. Feeling unseen, unheard, and deeply hurt after the therapy session, she realized that Richard had portrayed himself as a victim in their marriage, and the therapist had bought into it.

Beginning of the End

When Sharon's son joined the military and her daughter went away to college, she felt great relief that they were at a safe distance from the turmoil in her life. She was concerned that her daughter had witnessed some of the trouble with Richard, and it was hard to explain why she stayed with him. Her son, when visiting, had a tense relationship with Richard and didn't trust him. Now that both of her children were gone, Sharon tried once again to discuss Richard's hurtful behavior with him. But he refused to consider her feelings. After that, Sharon said she stopped showing her emotions around him. "I didn't smile. I didn't cry. I didn't yell. I was a zombie."

One day, as Sharon and Richard drove to a business meeting in another city, he insisted that she hang up the phone when her daughter called. Sharon's daughter sounded upset about something, but she assured her mother she was okay and would call back later when Sharon was alone. The next day, Sharon spoke with her daughter, who shared a harrowing story of being a mile from shore with three friends when their boat sank. Only two life vests for four people left them fighting for their lives as they nearly drowned trying to get back to shore. Sharon sobbed with her daughter over the phone. She couldn't bear that her daughter had almost lost her life, and she hadn't been able to talk to her afterward. She vowed this would never happen again.

The final straw came when Sharon found out she had a sexually transmitted disease after being faithful to Richard for eight years. At that moment, she realized how emotionally distant Richard had been during their marriage and understood that she could no longer go on as she had. A wave of despair came over her as she absorbed this truth. She knew that if she wanted to find a better life, she had to leave him. But she would have to return to supporting herself, and she had never lived alone before. She didn't want to think about leaving her dream house and the lifestyle she was used to. "Even though I knew I had to protect myself from further harm, I was terrified of leaving. I just didn't know if I had the strength left to build a new life." So, she decided to put off making a decision (loss aversion bias).

Getting Therapy

After some time passed, Sharon decided to find her own therapist and made an appointment with one she could see online when Richard was not at home. As her therapist, I helped her see that her husband likely had unresolved complex trauma from childhood that led to narcissistic personality disorder and episodes of age regression. His intense fear of being vulnerable and his lack of empathy made him incapable of emotional intimacy, which he considered a threat to his self-image. Being vulnerable would require exposing his insecurities and deep-seated feelings of inadequacy. I recommended educating herself on the challenges of being in a relationship with a narcissistic partner. I wanted to ensure she understood the severity of what she was dealing with and how she could protect herself.

As she worked on healing, Sharon learned how her own past influenced her present. She realized that, as a child, she needed a parent to help her process her experiences, perceptions, and emotions to develop a healthy sense of self. No one was there to help her make sense of her parents' neglect, recognize that she had always been worthy of love, or tell her that the sexual abuse she endured was not her fault. No one was there to validate and reflect her feelings or to teach her how to love and be loved. As an adult, she still held the same unrealistic, self-sabotaging beliefs she had from childhood: that people would only love her if she became a reflection of their needs and ignored her own.

Her pattern of stuffing down her emotions and her unresolved shame led her to lose herself in a relationship with a man who couldn't love her. Every time she ignored her feelings to meet Richard's (unrealistic) expectations of her, she became a source for his narcissistic needs, eventually abandoning herself and becoming an echo of him.

If Sharon had chosen a partner capable of giving and receiving love, she would have felt trust, intimacy, and autonomy in the relationship. She would have had a secure base—a base camp—for self-reflection and personal growth. But Richard's mental and emotional state made all of that impossible. And Sharon wasn't the only one to experience this in her relationship with Richard. His daughter from a previous marriage had recently told Sharon that he had forced her mother to stay home too, that his bullying had led to her mother's emotional breakdown, and that she still suffers from depression.

Gathering Support

As Sharon accepted the truth about her relationship and her role in it, she reached out to her parents and sister to share what had happened in her marriage. She decided to file for divorce from Richard and found an attorney who would protect her rights and safety. Meanwhile, she refused to travel with Richard, and while he was away, she collected evidence of his abuse and other essential documents to use in her divorce case. When she found out he had used phone apps to track her movements, she got her own cell phone.

Richard sensed something was wrong. He kept an eye on her movements using hidden security cameras around the house and knew whenever she left the premises.

Sharon kept a packed bag in case she needed to escape if he became violent. Her family urged her to leave him immediately, but she had decided that she would not be the one to leave. "All my fury at him exploded like a bomb," said Sharon. "I wasn't going to be pushed out of my own home by a mentally unstable person who wanted to ruin me. I would not leave. He would."

In the divorce petition, Sharon's attorney requested sole possession of their home, temporary alimony, attorney's fees, and a motion preventing Richard from moving any possessions or transferring funds in or out of accounts. The petition also mentioned that any violence, even though there had not yet been physical violence, against Sharon would be considered a criminal offense.

When served with the divorce petition at their home, Richard, visibly upset, backed down. He asked if he could stay overnight, as he had nowhere else to go. She told him he could stay in the back bedroom, but he had to find a new place to live the next day. After he left in the morning, Sharon put her two dogs in the car and drove to the beach for the day. "It was exhilarating and scary," she said. "I wasn't just breaking the rules, I was shattering them. He wasn't going to control me anymore."

Sharon drew a line to stop Richard's controlling behavior, but her feelings for him did not go away. After they separated, she couldn't resist the urge to check his social media accounts, and she wept when she saw his photos with other women. The person she had to push away was the same person she still loved. She knew he felt lost without her and stayed concerned about his welfare.

Sharon sought comfort from her loved ones after he left. "If it weren't for the love and support of my friends and family, I would have had a nervous breakdown," Sharon said. "It was so difficult to accept the pain of being mistreated after all I had done for him." They all welcomed her back with open arms.

Relapsing into the Echo Mindset

As Sharon moved toward freedom and away from Richard, he tried to pull her back in. She blocked nearly all communication but allowed him to continue emailing her about legal and household issues. He exploited this by urging her to reconsider their divorce, claiming their "forever love" was worth saving. "It was painful to see him so desperate, like starving in front of my favorite food," Sharon admitted. "It was an ache in the pit of my stomach." To avoid being drawn back to him, Sharon took walks, rode horses, and visited family. She knew that if she gave in, she would go back to the same nightmare, and her kids would be pulled back into the chaos. The possibility of a cancer recurrence was also something she wanted to avoid, and stress could weaken her immunity.

One day, Sharon had a sudden thought that Richard would be alone during the upcoming Thanksgiving holiday. So she made some food items she knew he enjoyed and waited for him in the lobby of his office building. Richard hurried out of the elevator and wrapped her in his embrace. "Oh, how I've missed you," he said. "I haven't been with anyone else." As they talked, his phone rang. Sharon could see on Richard's screen that the caller was one of the women he had been seen with on social media.

Sharon walked away. "I let my guard down and got sucker-punched," she said. "Opening up to him again was incredibly painful. I felt it on all fronts." Driving home, she wept bitterly. The next morning, she couldn't get out of bed.

Reclaiming Her Voice

As Sharon continued her healing work, she experienced episodes of intense sadness and paralyzing fear of being on her own. She was plagued by thoughts of how she allowed Richard's cruelty and felt disoriented by the loss of her identity as his wife. The sorrow of her fractured fairytale demoralized her. She felt utterly alone in her large house, and she struggled with self-doubt.

Gradually, however, as she allowed herself to release the emotions she had long suppressed, freedom from his oppression began to feel like taking deep breaths of fresh air. Writing down her thoughts, feelings, and experiences in a journal helped her learn to trust and express her emotions and to practice loving herself as she would a cherished friend. She forgave herself for repeatedly giving in to Richard and for neglecting herself just as her parents had neglected her. She found that she could take control of her inner life by tuning in to the wisdom of her emotions and acting on them, and by recognizing that the harsh inner voice demanding perfection stemmed from absorbing others' judgments. Her dream of partnering with a man who would champion her in ways her parents never had was over. But in time, self-reflection helped her create a new dream, one where she could be her own hero.

After a year of therapy, Sharon gained a new sense of purpose and fulfillment. She made significant changes in her life, including surrounding herself with family, friends, and dance colleagues who treated her with great respect. "I know now that I must believe in myself," she said. "I am worthy of love and confident in who I am, and I will never again allow someone to take that away from me."

Sharon is no longer anyone's echo.

This chapter highlighted some of the steps Sharon took in her life to break the cycle of the Echo complex and build a strong sense of self. One of the most crucial steps she took was engaging in therapy. Many people feel unsure about how therapy can help them change seemingly unchangeable situations, so seeing it in action can be very helpful.

In the next chapter, you will enter the therapy room to witness powerful moments when lasting change begins to take hold. You'll see how Sharon comes to accept herself, the reality of her relationship, and whether or not she leaves Richard. All three clients in the therapy chapter—including Sarah and Derek—uncover false perceptions shaped by their pasts that caused each of them to lose themselves in their relationships. They start to see their world clearly, reclaim parts of themselves they had hidden, and remove obstacles to a healthier, happier life. Their stories give us a glimpse of healing from the inside out and what's possible when we face the truth.

Self-Reflection: Recognizing False Narratives That Lead to Loss of Self

1. Describe several cognitive biases that Sharon demonstrated in her relationship with Richard. What are some ways she could have avoided her false perceptions in each situation?
2. Describe several defense mechanisms Sharon used to cope with the distress caused by Richard's behavior. What might have happened if she hadn't relied on defense mechanisms in her relationship?
3. What warning signs did Sharon disregard in her relationship with Richard?
4. Describe one or more situations where Sharon's misguided responses to Richard's treatment were a result of suppressing her emotions.
5. Identify at least three of the twelve truths from chapter 3 that played out in Sharon's relationship. Next, describe one or more paradoxical cycles from chapter 4 that occurred in her relationship.

CHAPTER NINE

In Therapy for Loss of Self

WHEN TRUST AND emotional safety are lacking in a relationship, our instinct may be to react in ways that preserve the image of our relationship, but this only causes more harm. For example, we might stay silent to keep the peace, even if it means betraying ourselves. We might turn our pain inward through self-criticism or outward by blaming others. Or we may deny, downplay, or make excuses for behavior that hurts us because facing the truth feels too overwhelming. These are echo behaviors that feel like a protective response in the moment, but they don't lead to healing.

Recovery starts when we stop echoing others' expectations and begin listening to our true feelings and desires. This chapter explores what happens when someone chooses to go beyond just surviving in a relationship and begins taking steps to reclaim their true self. The following conversations from three therapy sessions illustrate how this process happens.

Each of these three clients entered therapy with the Echo complex, their sense of self diminished by psychological forces they couldn't yet see. Over the course of treatment, each person experienced shifts in perspective that helped them realize how their unresolved emotional issues—old patterns of compliance, fear, shame, and guilt—had subconsciously caused them to become an echo of their partner's unresolved issues. Most importantly, they recognized that they no longer had to carry this burden. They let me share their stories because they wanted others going through similar situations to realize how enlightening therapy can be in helping them tap into their inner strengths and resources.

As you read the dialogue taken from their therapy sessions, I invite you to pay attention to your thoughts and feelings. Notice what feels familiar in what they say. Maybe it's a feeling or a pattern you recognize in yourself. Maybe it's a description of something their partner did and their reaction to it. These moments of recognition can be uncomfortable, but they're signs that something within you is awakening. Change begins with seeing things clearly, even when it hurts. Because once we understand how we have disconnected from ourselves, we can start to find our way back.

Therapy for Loss of Self

Like Sharon, the other two clients in this chapter were susceptible to entering relationships with emotionally unavailable and controlling partners due to unresolved childhood issues and experiences. However, losing a sense of self in a relationship doesn't necessarily indicate a troubled childhood. Even those with a healthy sense of self can become involved with someone who avoids emotional intimacy through harmful behavior.

When I begin working with a new client, I ask them to tell me the story of their relationship. Often, their confusion and despair over what's happening, along with how they cope, make it hard to see how much of their true self they have lost in the relationship. Sometimes they leave out details they're ashamed of and add them later once they trust I won't judge them. As they tell their story, we start to piece together the truth and the significance of what happened. Along with their mix of emotions, they feel a great sense of relief that someone finally understands what they've been through. Many have been alone with their despair for a long time.

When they first share their story, they sometimes don't reveal their emotional pain because they've learned to hold back, as if they have no right to their feelings. I encourage them to open up by asking reflective questions and offering brief, supportive comments. During the session, I direct them back to points in their dialogue that present key opportunities for therapeutic exploration. The intent here is to guide them toward the insights and resources they need to begin healing and make positive changes in their lives.

The dialogue in each session is based on my therapy notes and memory, with some details altered to maintain confidentiality. For clarity and to emphasize key moments in therapy, I include a thread of dialogue from a single actual session, while occasionally adding relevant exchanges from other sessions to provide context.

Sharon's Therapy

As Sharon (chapter 8) recounted her story, she didn't blame herself for falling in love with Richard. She had seen qualities in him that she valued in people: an outgoing personality, professional success, and a good reputation. As we read earlier, she wanted to believe she'd finally found the great love she had longed for, so she kept justifying his behavior to fit her perception of him even as his actions grew more callous. When she started therapy, she hadn't yet realized how strongly her sense of self-worth was connected to her ability to meet Richard's expectations. She contacted me when she realized that relying on Richard to feel worthy of being loved only led to emptiness and despair.

Amy: What's it like living in your marriage?

Sharon: I am two people: a heavy rock that just sits there when I'm with him and a creative person who wants to express my ideas and energy when he's not around. It's the way I survive.

Amy: How does it feel to be a heavy rock?

Sharon: I feel like nothing, just empty, numb. But underneath, I'm hurting and resentful.

Amy: So you hide those feelings from him instead of telling him how you feel?

Sharon: Yes, I'm afraid that if I do, he'll hurt me even more by not caring about how I feel. He tries to control my thoughts and feelings to fit in with what he wants them to be. But it's not really me he's talking to. He doesn't see who I really am. He doesn't even notice that I never laugh anymore.

Amy: What's it like for you when he doesn't see you?

Sharon: I feel like a fake. I'm not connecting with him. Our conversations are never about me; they're always about what he wants. I'm not important to him unless I'm doing what he expects me to do.

Amy: Is this how you felt as a child when your parents were emotionally and often physically absent?

Sharon: Yes, in many ways, it feels the same. My brothers were the stars in my family, and my sister played the piano and sang. I had nothing. I felt like I was small, not important, a spectator. But I felt deeply hurt that I wasn't worth my parents' time and didn't have talents like my siblings, so they could be proud of me too.

Amy: How did you cope with your feelings?

Sharon: I felt like I had to prove myself. I thought, I'll just take care of myself! But I didn't know how.

Amy: Where did that lead you?

Sharon: I remember when I was fifteen years old, my mother had been gone for several weeks, and I missed her so much. During that time, I lost my virginity, got drunk, and smoked cigarettes.

Amy: You turned your hurt and anger against yourself. Is that what you're doing now by tolerating Richard's abusive treatment?

Sharon: (*Crying*) I try to go along with Richard so that I don't create more problems. I keep thinking, *If I can make him happy, he will love me.*

Amy: Just like you did with your parents. (*Pause*) Do you see the pattern here? You're using the same coping skills you did as a child. The child in you doesn't want to create problems, so she goes along with what she thinks is expected of her.

Sharon: (*Still crying*) I've caused myself a lot of problems by thinking I can get love and approval if I hide myself.

Amy: It's an old belief with a strong critical voice. But that's all it is. It's the voice of a child who wasn't yet mature enough to make sense of emotional neglect.

I decided to give Sharon an exercise to help her bring herself into the present as a mature and capable woman. The purpose of the exercise was to help her understand that her critical voice came from how she interpreted her experiences as a child, and that she could now reevaluate those experiences with the insight and perspective of an adult.

I asked her to recall an experience that triggered her critical voice and write her initial thoughts about the event. She gave me the example of a time when Richard accused her of flirting with other men.

Amy: What were your first thoughts when Richard accused you of flirting?

Sharon: I felt guilty that maybe I was too friendly and gave men the wrong impression, that it was my fault. I needed to keep reassuring him that he was the only man I loved and wanted to be with.

As suspected, she immediately blamed herself and felt defective. Next, I asked her to think of a more reasonable thought, that of a woman who looks at her childhood beliefs as just that, the logic of a child who blamed herself for her parents' emotional neglect.

Sharon: When I try to think more rationally about his behavior, it's hard. A critical part of me tells me, *You're not allowed to think that.*

Amy: So you took the blame and tried to comfort him. Yet even when you apologized to him and reassured him of your love, he didn't hear you. He kept you up half the night, criticizing you and insisting he can't trust you, and demanding that you stay home unless he's with you. How did you reconcile your belief that you just needed to love him more with his unwillingness to hear you and accept your love?

Sharon: It has never occurred to me that the critical voice in my head comes from that little girl whose parents weren't around, and who had to figure things out on her own.

Amy: You believed the critical voice inside your head, not questioning where it came from.

Sharon: I did and still struggle with it. But it makes sense that I reacted to Richard the same way I did to my parents, trying to be a good girl. Now I can see that doing that never got me what I truly needed, and it's the same now with Richard.

Amy: I know that's hard to accept, Sharon. But it's a crucial insight for healing from painful childhood experiences and understanding the misguided beliefs you formed about yourself as a result.

Sharon needed more time to process what she had uncovered about the profound influence of her past on her present before she could begin to move forward. In the sessions ahead, the focus shifted to tracing the origins of her childhood voice and finding practical ways to lessen the hold that the negative thought patterns it created had on her.

Amy: Let's take a closer look at how your critical voice reacts when Richard makes unreasonable demands and accusations. You're quick to apologize even though he's clearly at fault.

Sharon: I'm afraid that if I don't give him what he needs, he'll want to be with another woman.

Amy: You told me you suspected him of cheating on you. Do you believe you can control his choices by hiding yourself in the relationship?

Sharon: I guess I do. But doing that seems crazy, now that I'm talking about it with you.

Amy: Help me understand what happens when your critical voice tells you to disregard yourself to avoid problems—like Richard's cold-hearted behavior—but doing so doesn't make the problems go away.

Sharon: When Richard tries to control me in some way, I go to that little girl part of me, the one that does what he wants. He seems to like that part. Then, when he's feeling down or scared, I go to the part of me that comforts and reassures him because I don't want him to go through the pain I felt when I was all alone growing up.

Amy: So it's like there are parts of you that you show Richard because he needs them, and other parts of you hide because, as you say, those parts create problems that bring on his callous behavior. But you realize now that denying parts of yourself will never get you what you want most in a relationship. What you want is for all of you, and not just parts of you, to be seen, accepted, and loved.

Sharon: Yes, that's how it feels.

As I got to know Sharon better, it occurred to me that her confident, creative side as a successful dancer could be a potent force in her healing process. She remained passionate about dancing and even sent me a video of an outstanding performance that showcased her skills as both a choreographer and a dancer. She told me she occasionally received calls from former dance colleagues who encouraged her to get involved in their projects, but she felt she had to turn them down. Richard would never support her return to a career in dancing.

Amy: Tell me about your creative part.

Sharon: My creative part dances, rides horses, paints, and writes songs. I love that part of me. It fills me with joy, hope, and purpose.

Amy: Where does your critical voice go when you're being creative?

Sharon: It goes quiet, I guess. A different, strong voice shows up that wants to blow my critical voice out of the water!

Amy: Tell me more about how that happens.

Sharon: Well, I was always good at dancing and felt confident in my ability professionally. I had relationships with people who made me feel special.

Amy: How do you feel when you're dancing and riding your horses?

Sharon: Like I'm in my own world where I can be free to create and be who I am. I feel strong and confident. Richard doesn't want me to be strong. He wants me to be weak so I'll be dependent on him.

Amy: Where does your strong voice go when you're with Richard?

Sharon: It's still there, somewhere, but I push it down and ignore it.

Amy: Do you feel loved when you're with your horses and dancing in front of an audience?

Sharon: Yes, I feel valued, like I'm capable of anything. Everyone appreciates my work and my creativity. They're so caring and supportive.

Amy: Your friends love you for who you truly are. They see your heart, your strength, your spirit, and they respect you because of it. But with Richard, it's different. And this will be hard to hear, Sharon. Richard has serious mental disabilities that drive his irrational wants and needs. It's not likely he'll ever be able to see you beyond what he expects of you. Your lack of understanding of his mental disorders, along with suppressing your feelings and trying to prove your love, has caused you to lose yourself in the relationship. You must understand that nothing you do will change him. He's not capable of providing you with the love you want and need. You will need to get fully informed about what happens in a relationship with a narcissistic person, the effects on you, and, if you chose to stay in the relationship, how to protect yourself as best you can.

With her new understanding, Sharon realized that hiding parts of herself in her relationship with Richard not only harmed her but also enabled his harmful behavior. Comparing the despair she felt with him to the warmth and ease of her relationships with others, she began to see that love is not meant to be earned through sacrifice or self-erasure, but something to be given freely through acceptance, kindness, and a genuine desire for the other's well-being. This realization helped her see herself, Richard, and their relationship in a new light.

Sharon let go of her unrealistic vision of his character and their relationship, and stopped her echo reactions to his demands and accusations. As she did, she began to reconnect with parts of herself she had given up and started choosing herself over him. She no longer apologized for upsetting him when he made false accusations and held him accountable for his abusive behavior. When he insisted that she travel with him, she declined. She went to a coffee shop, dressed in the yoga pants he had forbidden her to wear in public, and didn't answer his texts.

As Sharon reclaimed her power in the relationship, she began to feel a more complete sense of herself. He responded to her new attitude by allowing her to make some decisions on her own. Even though she held anger and resentment toward the way he had treated her, the change in his behavior and her newfound sense of agency gave her hope that their relationship could improve. She still had a deep bond with him and felt responsible for his care, so she put their divorce proceedings on hold.

Soon, Richard fell back into his old ways. He held the divorce over her head like the sword of Damocles, using it when he wanted to control her. He threatened to "crush" her when she refused to go to an event with him. But instead of an echo reaction, Sharon agreed to divorce him. It surprised her when, instead of attacking her with more accusations, he backed down.

Amy: I can see that you're feeling more confident. What have you learned that is helping you feel stronger?

Sharon: I've learned that the more I express who I am—what I feel, what I want, what I value—the less power he has over me. His threats no longer have any influence on me because I don't feel the need to please him anymore.

Amy: How does that feel for you?

Sharon: It feels great. I'm reacting with my authentic, powerful self. I no longer feel invisible.

Amy: Does your critical voice still come up?

Sharon: I do have moments when I feel insecure and hear my critical voice say, *Are you sure you're doing the right thing?* But I know now that it comes from a distant time in my life, and from a place that doesn't have control over me anymore.

Amy: Do you hear Richard's voice in your head, berating you, telling you what to do?

Sharon: Yes. I still hear his voice even when he's not with me. But I recognize it as his voice.

Amy: You realize how empowered you are by seeing through the stories you used to tell yourself, by seeing the truth.

Sharon: Yes. I was giving up who I was. But as hard as all this has been, it's also taught me a lot and is making me grow. The person I am getting back is better than the person I left.

As Sharon grew stronger and more self-aware, she grieved for her dream of Richard as her knight in shining armor; for the way she lost herself in the relationship; and for her children, who had suffered from distress, instability, and chaos. She grieved that he never saw her for who she is, didn't seem capable of loving her or of acknowledging her love, and never believed in her as she believed in him.

As of this writing, Sharon has not left Richard. When she understood how psychologically wounded he was and that he would back down when she confronted him, she wanted to give him a chance to get into therapy for complex trauma. Meanwhile, even though she is still at risk of the Echo complex, she has made significant progress in holding her boundaries against his demands and mistreatment. Some of the changes she made in her life were harder than others. Her adult children were adamantly opposed to her staying in her marriage, and there was no guarantee that even if Richard entered therapy, he would change enough to do his part in building a viable relationship with Sharon.

However, by staying grounded in the truth instead of mistaken beliefs and expectations, Sharon found the strength to begin breaking free from the exhausting cycles that had kept her trapped. She started relating from her authentic self—and being fully informed about Richard's character—rather than a need to preserve the relationship. The shift that brought Sharon back to herself gave her a renewed sense of hope that no longer depended on changing him, but on her own healing.

Derek's Therapy

When Derek came in for his first therapy session, he said he felt like he was living life as someone else, not who he was or wanted to be. Over the past few years in his relationship with Ella, his blood pressure, weight, and anxiety had all gone up. He had acid reflux and headaches that he described as feeling like "a tight band around my head." He said his mind felt like a jumble of mixed emotions, and he couldn't concentrate on anything. He used to handle stress well, but reported that now "I crumble under pressure."

Derek told me that after meeting in college, he and Ella dated on and off in a long-distance relationship for five years before marrying two years ago. He began therapy because he wanted to know if her behavior toward him was emotionally abusive. When I asked him to describe her actions, he said she was suspicious of his friends and family and had forbidden him from contacting them. She criticized him for being naïve. When he tried to talk to her about her senseless restrictions and the way she treated him, she twisted the blame onto him. Recently, when she got angry with him, she grabbed him, screamed in his face, and ripped his clothing. She also harped on him about gaining weight, even though she knew her criticism shamed him.

Although they both had professional careers, he handled all the household chores, including cooking and running errands. He said that when he did everything Ella wanted him to do, she told him he was a wonderful, supportive husband. But he felt a total disconnection from her, emotionally, physically, and sexually.

Amy: Tell me more about how you feel when you're with Ella.

Derek: I feel like she's constantly judging me. It makes me anxious, like something bad will happen if I step out of line. Last Friday, I told her that her comments about my weight were rude, and she woke me up the next day at 7 a.m. by saying, "Good Morning, Jerk Face!"

Amy: How do you respond when she treats you that way?

Derek: The way she treats me makes me want to stay silent. She won't accept that I might have a different opinion or feeling than she does. She always has to be right.

Amy: How do you feel about living in a relationship in which you have no voice?

Derek: I have a lot of self-doubt. I know the way she treats me is wrong, but somehow I feel responsible.

Amy: Have you tried talking to her about your right to see your family?

Derek: When I told her I wanted my mom to visit us, Ella went off the rails. She got a hostile look on her face and told me I could go visit my mom and take my girlfriend with me. Then she shoved me out of the front door of our apartment. She was always accusing me of having a girlfriend, but there's no way I would even think about doing that. I don't even know how she came up with that idea.

Amy: Forbidding you to see your family and friends is just another way to disregard you and your needs. What's it like for you, not being able to see or communicate with your mother and father, with your brothers and old friends?

Derek: I really miss them and feel guilty about the way I'm treating them. But I comply with her demands 100 percent. I keep my mouth shut even though I'm angry and resentful.

Amy: How do you handle your anger and resentment?

Derek: (Voice breaking) I drive to a private place and cry and scream in my car. Sometimes I work out or go for a walk in the park.

Amy: I can see that your relationship causes you a great deal of emotional pain. Have you tried to talk to her about the way she treats you?

Derek: I've tried several times to reason with her about her behavior. One time, I told her that she was abusive. But instead of taking responsibility, she got really angry and denied that it was true. She insisted that I apologize for what I said. I just can't get through to her.

Amy: That must be pretty frustrating for you. Tell me about how you and Ella were at the beginning of your relationship.

Derek: When we started dating, I admired her a lot because she was this beautiful woman who was in medical school studying to be a cardiac surgeon. I thought she was a good person. It seemed like she was right about everything, and she seemed to have much stronger feelings and opinions than I did, so I set mine aside and just went along with hers.

Amy: Sounds like you idealized her, and had some false impressions and beliefs about her character. What effect did that have on you?

Derek: I let her make all the decisions. For a while, I thought that I was becoming a better person with her influence, even though I had no say in the relationship.

Amy: How does it feel to hold yourself back in the relationship?

Derek: It was okay for a while, but now I feel nervous, stressed, angry, puzzled, and disappointed. I feel an emptiness, like I'm invisible.

Amy: What feelings bother you most?

Derek: I feel like I let myself down. I not only abandoned myself. I also abandoned people who love me. I wanted to be such a great husband.

Amy: Why do you continue to abandon yourself?

Derek: It seems easier than having to withstand Ella's anger. But I ask myself every day, "What am I doing?!"

Amy: How would it feel now to open up and show her your authentic self? To express your resentment, anger, and sadness, your need for her love and approval?

Derek: I couldn't do that. She'd go ballistic. She would mock me, criticize me.

Amy: Do you remember when you first began hiding yourself? Did this start in an earlier relationship or when you were growing up?

Derek: (Looks down and stays silent for a moment.) I got bullied a lot from middle school to high school by a guy I went to school with. It was mostly about my weight. It was really hard. I thought it was my fault. I tried to put the bullying out of my mind, but I had a lot of resentment and anger. I cried a lot.

Amy: How did you react to the bullying?

Derek: I just tried to get away and didn't fight back. I was too afraid and embarrassed to tell my teachers or my parents. Having to change clothes in the locker room during gym class was traumatic for me. I refused to go on class trips. No one knew what I was going through. I felt alone and hopeless about stopping the bullying.

Amy: You suffered a great deal of pain, Derek, and felt you had no one to talk to about it. It seems you're doing the same thing now in your relationship with Ella. You're coping with your fear, shame, and embarrassment by not fighting back.

Derek: I hadn't thought about it that way. I can see how those two experiences have some similarities, even though they're quite different circumstances.

Amy: How did the bullying affect you?

Derek: I had really low self-esteem. When I got older, I didn't feel comfortable with dating. But when I met Ella in college, I was drawn to her because she was this amazing woman who showed an interest in me. I thought if she wanted me, that meant I was worthy in some way.

Amy: So you thought Ella saw something worthy in you and could heal your pain of feeling unworthy. But knowing someone's worth requires knowing their authentic self. From what you've shared about her, it seems like she doesn't see you as an individual with your own distinct personality.

Derek: She doesn't know me at all.

Amy: So you're with a woman you chose because she made you feel worthy, but she doesn't know you at all, and you don't feel worthy when you're around her.

Derek: I guess that's true. But I would really miss her if I left.

Amy: Do you miss yourself in the relationship?

Derek: Yes! I want it to be like it was before. I feel a deep longing to be me again.

Amy: You mentioned that you have a good friend who would be supportive if you confided in them about your relationship. What would you say about your relationship with Ella if you could talk to this good friend?

Derek: It would be hard to talk to anyone. I've hidden it for so long.

Amy: Are you afraid that if you told your loved ones that Ella is physically and emotionally abusive, it would make it true?

Derek: That sounds right. Lots of times, I've asked myself if what I'm thinking about Ella is really true. Is she to blame? Is it really a problem? I imagined I was neglecting her in some way.

Amy: Would talking to your good friend be a relief to you? Would it ease your self-doubt?

Derek: Yeah. I think it would.

Amy: Talk to me about your relationship just as you would to your good friend.

Derek: I would say I'm in an abusive relationship. I can't see my family, and I can't say what I want or how I feel, and I haven't told anyone.

Amy: How would it feel to be able to voice those words to a good friend?

Derek: It would be scary, but what a relief it would be.

Amy: Can you arrange to talk to your friend?

Derek: I couldn't do that because Ella makes me report to her all the conversations with other people where her name comes up. If I didn't tell her, then I'd be being dishonest.

Amy: Aren't you being dishonest with her by hiding yourself in the relationship?

Derek: I hadn't thought about it that way.

Amy: If you long to be yourself again and you feel like Ella wouldn't accept the real you, that means you've chosen her over yourself. A relationship is not a choice between one or the other. It's a partnership between two individuals. Do you feel like you can be free to open up and be your authentic self in other relationships?

Derek: Mostly, I feel free to be myself with my friends. But it's different with Ella because I feel like she wouldn't accept me if I showed her who I really am. I want to be myself, and I think about leaving her all the time. But I feel like I would be deserting her, and I couldn't live with the guilt.

Amy: So what you're saying is that you would feel guilty about deserting a woman who rages at you, imposes her way of thinking on you, rejects your opinions, feelings, and needs, and physically attacks you. And even though you've deserted yourself in the relationship, you believe it's okay to stay.

Derek: That sounds crazy, but it's true.

Although confiding in his good friend terrified Derek, he followed through after our session and felt glad that he did. He reported back that the conversation was very affirming for him. His friend was supportive and shared his own experiences in an abusive relationship.

Derek's conversation with his friend and the insights he learned about himself and his relationship in therapy helped him recognize the underlying forces and his role in them. He began to view his relationship with Ella from a different perspective, which gave him the confidence to be honest with her more often about his thoughts and feelings.

One day during a session, Derek shared two steps that he had taken to stop betraying himself in his relationship. First, he had insisted on visiting his family. And second, he'd told her that her nagging him about his weight was rude, and she needed to stop. To Derek's surprise, he discovered that as he became more confident, Ella became more receptive to him, and her angry outbursts became less frequent.

This realization changed how he saw Ella. He used to view her as having control over him because she set the rules of their relationship. Now, he saw her as more of an insecure and fearful woman who needed his reassurance and might respond to his authority in certain circumstances. With this new understanding, he realized that both of them showed strong defensive behaviors that kept them from revealing their emotional lives to each other. In Ella's case, this appeared callous and controlling, whereas in Derek, it manifested as self-abandonment.

Derek's therapy marked a significant shift in how he showed up in his relationship. But it would require both of them working together to confront and resolve their unresolved relationship issues and to open themselves to the emotional connection each wanted but feared. And Derek was still at risk of having the Echo complex. At the end of therapy, he chose to stay in his relationship to give himself a chance to approach it with his new perspective.

If You Feel Overwhelmed While Reading

Take a moment to pause your reading if you start to feel pain or experience upsetting memories. Try to sit in a comfortable position with your feet flat on the ground, your hands resting in your lap, and breathe in slowly. Then breathe out even more slowly. Repeat this deep breathing a few times. Remind yourself: *I'm safe right now.* You can also repeat a calming affirmation like, *I can face this and still be okay.* Let each breath and each word help you find your center. If you feel like crying, find a private place and allow yourself to cry. Crying is a powerful release that can be cleansing and freeing. Be proud of yourself for having the courage to face the truth. Every moment of honesty is a step forward.

Sarah's Therapy

In our first therapy session, Sarah wanted to clarify whether her marriage was as bad as she thought or if she was overreacting. She worked full-time as a product manager for a digital products company, providing the majority of financial support for her husband and their four-year-old son while also managing all the childcare and household tasks. She felt intensely unhappy and had no life outside her family, yet she endured his brutish behavior to prevent further conflict.

By the time she came to see me, however, she had had enough of giving herself to a husband who disregarded her needs and feelings and demeaned her with condescending treatment.

Amy: Tell me more about how your husband treats you.

Sarah: If I refuse to do what he wants, he gets mad and retaliates against me. He breaks things, swears, and won't talk to me.

Yesterday, while I was on the phone with a client, he kept making banging and crashing noises. The other night, he pushed the button on the carbon monoxide detector and woke up our son. Last weekend, I had sex with him even though I didn't want to because I knew if I didn't, he would mess up our son's birthday party the next day. It's just easier to do what he wants, even though I feel angry and repulsed by the way he acts.

Amy: How do you handle your feelings?

Sarah: I have a tendency to block my emotions and deal with them later, but they never get resolved. I question myself a lot.

Amy: What do you question yourself about?

Sarah: Well, sometimes I think he may be right. Like when he yells at me about the house being a mess. It *is* a mess. I know from a logical standpoint that it's because I do everything and get no help from him, but there's also some part of me that believes I should be able to do better.

Amy: So you take the blame for his bad behavior?

Sarah: I have a fear that something will happen to him if I don't give him what he needs. He says things like, "You won't be seeing me anymore," and I think, "Oh my God! He's going to hurt himself." Whenever I think I could lose him that way, it's incredibly painful. It brings back memories of losing my father when I was twenty years old. He was diagnosed with Parkinson's disease when I was twelve and had a long illness.

Amy: What goes through your mind when you feel this way?

Sarah: My first thought is, "Did I push him too far?" The idea that I did makes me feel like a failure.

Amy: Sounds like you base your thoughts and decisions not on what you need, but on how you think he's going to react.

Sarah: I do that a lot. But the abuse isn't always obvious to me. I've always had the idea that my needs are less important. I don't like to cause him pain. I think I've babied him a lot. I just feel like I owe people.

Amy: How does your fear of causing him pain affect you?

Sarah: There are things I want to do for myself, but I don't have time because I'm always at home, waiting for whatever he's going to order me to do. I have to be 100 percent available to him. I know it's wrong, but I do it anyway.

Amy: What are some things you want to do?

Sarah: I want to focus more on my career, work out, do artwork, and see my friends. I also love celebrating the holidays, but he refuses to let me have a menorah. And when I dress up, if I look too nice, he says, "Who are you trying to impress?" so I change my clothes. I even eat what he wants to eat, even though I don't want to. I just do whatever I need to do to avoid drama.

Amy: Where did you learn this way of thinking? Tell me about what it was like growing up.

Sarah: My father was African American, and my mother was an Orthodox Jew. We lived in an Orthodox neighborhood, and I felt like I didn't fit in.

Amy: In what ways did you feel you didn't fit in?

Sarah: I loved my dad, but I was embarrassed that he was Black and the other parents weren't. I was also embarrassed that our family wasn't religious. Whenever he took me to school, I didn't want to be seen with him, so I wouldn't let him come into the school with me. All the girls wore long dresses and had huge families. I didn't know all the prayers, and we didn't follow the rules that the other kids' families did, like not using electricity on the Sabbath. I was the only Black girl, and my hair was kinky instead of smooth like the others. I didn't feel free to be myself. I came home from school crying every day.

Amy: Were you able to talk to your parents about how you felt?

Sarah: My mom didn't know how to handle my emotions. When she saw I was sad, she would say, "I don't know why you feel that way." My dad took my side when she didn't understand, but I lost his support when he got sick.

Amy: What was it like to live with your father's disease growing up? How did it affect your life?

Sarah: As his health got worse, I had to help my mother take care of him. I didn't go out or do the normal things kids do at that age. I just went along with what my mom wanted me to do. I became a people pleaser. It was really hard to lose my dad, because he understood me and loved me. But when I was still a teenager, he had a lot of cognitive impairment and had trouble remembering and finding the right words to express himself.

Amy: What was your mom like?

Sarah: She said things that made me think, "Being white is better than being Black."

Amy: What did she say that made you think that?

Sarah: Mostly comments that sounded critical, like, "I don't know what to do with your hair," and ones meant to sound like compliments, like "You look like you have a tan."

Amy: How did that feel for you?

Sarah: I felt unlovable, like my mom didn't understand or accept me. My violin teacher from grades five through eleven screamed at me, and she let him. I got the message that if I went along with what my mom wanted me to do, she would love me.

Amy: Did you have any friendships growing up?

Sarah: I liked some of the girls I knew, but I never had the chance to get together with them much. I was always at home. College was a bit better than high school, but I still didn't have many opportunities. I went home every weekend to take care of my dad. My mom knew how to guilt me into doing what she wanted me to do. I felt like I had to be there to help her, not only with my dad but also emotionally. She wouldn't let me visit friends, enjoy being young, or have a life for myself. She'd say, "This is what you do for your parents." Her mom, my grandmother, was like that, too.

Amy: How did you meet your husband?

Sarah: I met him online. I was disappointed in him on our first date because he let me pay for my dinner. But I kept seeing him even though he was moody because I thought he was the only one who would want me.

Amy: And you've been married for seven years. How do you feel about your marriage?

Sarah: (*Crying*) I feel trapped, angry, sad, frustrated, and disrespected. I'm conflicted about him. There were layers of issues from the beginning. I did everything and just took care of him. I knew something was wrong. But I mostly blamed myself.

Amy: Have you talked to him about how you feel?

Sarah: I've tried, but it's really hard. I get flustered every time. He gets mad and accuses me of nitpicking at small things, and I start to think that maybe I'm wrong. Part of me thinks that he's always been like this, and I'm the one who's changed. When I think that, I tell myself it's not so bad. Things could be worse. I'm so used to doubting myself.

Amy: How have you coped living with a man who treats you as though you're there to serve him?

Sarah: I'm a very empathetic person. I care about his welfare and think he would have trouble being on his own. He says he loves me, but he doesn't act like it.

Amy: Do you feel loved by him?

Sarah: (*Crying*) I don't have a frame of reference for what that feels like. He says he loves me sometimes, but he never seems to care how I feel or how his behavior affects me.

Amy: What about your needs, your feelings? Who takes care of you?

Sarah: When I think about what I need, I hear this voice in my head that says, *Who are you to put yourself first?* I think I'm being selfish.

Amy: Whose voice is that in your head, shaming you?

Sarah: I guess it's my mom's voice. She talks to me that way even today. In her mind, I'm still the child who has to respond to her demands to "do this, do that."

Amy: You're responding the same way to your husband. Do you see how you've lost yourself by holding onto a childhood belief that you must push away your needs and feelings to give others what they want from you? You must realize that you have choices now.

Sarah: I feel valued when I take care of other people. Sometimes I feel like if I'm not helping other people, then who am I?

Amy: It sounds like your sense of self is tied to your ability to care for others, even when they mistreat you. What about caring for yourself?

Sarah: I haven't taken very good care of myself. I still want to be a caring person, but I also want my own life.

Amy: You will have your own life when you care for yourself by honoring your needs and expressing your feelings. While you were growing up with a controlling and self-focused mother, you got the message that your feelings weren't important and that you had to put others' needs first. In school, you learned to hide yourself because you felt you didn't fit in. These early experiences led you into a marriage with a selfish and immature man who exploits your belief that you must always put others first. You didn't know any better as a child, but now that you're an adult, you have the freedom to be your own person. Are you ready to claim your own life?

Sarah: Yes. I really want to change.

In therapy, Sarah learned to recognize cues in her thinking that told her to, *Give him what he wants* and replace them with questions like, *What do I need*? and *How can I take care of myself*? She realized that she could still care about her husband without enabling his abusive behavior. As her understanding changed, she began to set boundaries against his abuse and to enforce them. She asked him to contribute more money to the household, moved into a separate bedroom, and stopped responding to his demands. She also insisted that he help with their son and household chores.

As Sarah continued to reclaim her sense of self, she eventually decided she didn't want to stay in the marriage. She felt no hope that her husband would change, and there were too many painful memories in their relationship. When she informed him that she wanted a divorce, he took partial responsibility for their issues and said that he loved her.

He became more accommodating, and he stopped breaking things when he didn't get his way. However, he didn't acknowledge the severity of his harmful behavior, and he continued to be moody and selfish.

On a different front, Sarah's therapy helped improve her relationship with her mother. She told her mother to stop treating her like a child and to stop ordering her around. Initially, her mother didn't react well, but as Sarah held her ground, her mother began to treat her with more respect.

Sarah filed for divorce from her husband and purchased another home near the one they had shared, so they could co-parent their son. She still had strong feelings for him, though, and she mourned the loss of their relationship. She worried about his well-being and felt the urge to care for him. As she transitioned away from her marriage and began a new life free from oppression, I asked her how she felt.

Amy: What's it like to have your own place and not have your ex-husband around?

Sarah: I feel so much freer now to be myself and make my own choices. I'm no longer on edge all the time. Before, I'd wake up in the morning and never know what version of him I would be getting that day and what I would have to put up with. I wanted to be truthful, tell him how I felt, but I worried constantly about his reaction, his anger.

Amy: Can you be truthful with him now?

Sarah: I can be truthful with my feelings because I know how harmful it is when I'm not. But I still hold back and give him only the information I have to, because he can make things difficult in co-parenting our son. I often let things go when he ignores my emails to schedule our son's activities, simply because I want to avoid more of his adolescent behavior. But I don't blame myself for his actions anymore.

Amy: Tell me more about your feelings of freedom.

Sarah: I'm really happy coming home to my own house. I feel like my home is a safe bubble where I can control my environment.

There are things in my life that give me joy, but that I could never have before when we were together. I had no control over anything. Just watching my own choice of TV show is so great. He always insisted on watching what he wanted and got mad at me for watching the programs I liked.

Amy: Do you still have the feelings of shame and guilt that you had before you left?

Sarah: I'm still coming to terms with the damage my marriage did to me. He put a lot of stuff in my head, and I allowed him to. My emotional fence is a mile high now because of what I've been through. But the guilt that made me feel like I couldn't leave him isn't as strong, even though I worry about his well-being and his ability to pay his bills. I see him going into a pit of loneliness, but I accept that he did this to himself. I still care about him and want him to be happy, but I know I can't go back to where I was. I understand that there's nothing I can do to help him.

Amy: You see the truth now, Sarah, and the truth, along with your courage and determination, has freed you to move forward in your life. He is the only one who can decide whether he wants to do the work necessary to mature into a responsible man or continue living with arrested emotional development.

As Sarah wrapped up her therapy, she still felt moments of guilt about leaving her husband. At times, she slipped back into old habits, such as allowing her ex-husband to wait until the last minute to make plans to see their son and taking her mother's daily hour-long calls, even though her schedule as a single, working mom left little time for herself. But Sarah had broken free from the Echo complex and the paradoxical cycles that once kept her stuck in an unhappy marriage.

While focusing on building a strong sense of self, she stopped believing she had to meet everyone's needs to prove her worth. Letting go of that old mindset freed her to stand on her own. As she continued to recover, she felt a new wave of energy that eventually led her to a man who cares deeply for her and treats her with utmost respect. Her young son is doing well, she loves her new home, and she's very happy in her new relationship. She is grateful every day for the courage she had to leave a marriage that kept her trapped in the Echo complex and prevented her from moving on to a much more fulfilling life.

As Sharon, Derek, and Sarah became more aware of their relationships, they realized what had led them to partners who were controlling and emotionally distant. They also saw the harm they'd caused themselves by giving up parts of their personalities in these relationships. This insight gave them the strength to make choices based on truth rather than distorted beliefs. Each of them began to let go of self-doubt, release misplaced blame, and realize that meaningful change in a relationship requires effort from both people. Through this process, they came to understand the importance of showing up fully in relationships by honoring their own needs and overcoming the fear of rejection that had been holding them back.

Their stories offer a glimpse of what's possible for you, too. By applying the insights from this book and tapping into your existing strengths, you can rebuild a sense of self that genuinely reflects your values. From there, you'll step into the future with greater clarity, confidence, and a sense of purpose that feels truly your own.

In these final pages, the ideas in this book come full circle, providing you with practical tools to protect your well-being, cultivate self-love, and begin breaking free from the negative influences of the past, so you can move forward with determination.

Key Points

1. Childhood beliefs and behaviors shaped by early experiences can form subconscious patterns that persist in adult relationships.
2. Submitting to a controlling or emotionally abusive partner is not an effective strategy to avoid emotional pain. Rather, it results in increased suffering.

3. Trying to prove we are worthy of a partner's love leads to emptiness and despair.
4. An irrational fear of rejection can lead to a loss of self in an intimate relationship.
5. Concealing our true selves in a relationship to manipulate our partner's decisions is dishonest and won't lead to an emotional connection.
6. When our sense of self is tied to taking care of others, it can lead to neglecting our own well-being.
7. Healing from the Echo complex starts with confronting the truth about ourselves, our partners, and our relationships.
8. Understanding how and why we've become disconnected from our true selves can be a catalyst for reclaiming our authentic selves.
9. Focusing on our interests, talents, and abilities inspires us, builds our confidence, and gives us purpose.
10. Sharing the experience of emotional abuse and the loss of self with a trusted friend, family member, or mental health professional (or all three) can be a crucial step toward healing.

Self-Reflection: Exploring Hidden Feelings and Beliefs

1. Describe how you feel about yourself in your current relationship. How do these feelings compare to the feelings you had about yourself before the relationship? Compare your feelings before and after to determine any changes in your sense of self.
2. Do you ever feel like you have two different personalities—one when you're with your partner and another when you're with others? Describe both personalities. How are they different? How are they similar? Which one feels more like you?
3. Do you think your partner fully understands and acknowledges who you are? If not, which aspects of yourself does your partner fail to see and know?

4. Do you feel that your partner often judges you in some way? If so, describe a specific incident in which you felt judged by your partner. How did that judgment affect your self-perception? How did it influence your feelings toward your partner? How did you respond to this judgment? How did your partner react?
5. Do you feel that you need to prove your worth to your partner to receive their love and attention? If so, can you identify a few ways you do this? Do your efforts to prove yourself get the reaction you hope for from your partner? What would happen if you stopped trying to show that you're worthy of love?

Exercise: Taking Small Steps to Reclaim Yourself

Review the key points and your answers to the questions in this chapter. Think about how you've disconnected from your true self in your relationship, and identify two or more small steps you'd like to take to feel more like yourself.

CHAPTER TEN

From Self-Loss to Self-Love

YOU MIGHT HAVE reached this final chapter with a new understanding of yourself and your relationship, and you're motivated to make changes in your life. On the other hand, you might feel like the woman in chapter 1 who looks in the mirror and sees a faded image of herself, unsure how to move beyond how she's been living in her relationship.

No matter where you are in your healing journey, and I've experienced both extremes myself and seen it in many others, I can tell you that building a healthy relationship with yourself will move you from self-loss to self-love. Doing this isn't easy. It takes courage to face the truth, reflect on how you've been hurt, and confront the circumstances—including your own role—that contributed to it. Now that you understand the Echo complex and how it happens without you fully realizing it, you can see how easily your good intentions led you into it. Let's examine how that typically occurs.

A Hindsight View of Echo Relationships

When you first entered your relationship, your intentions were likely rooted in love, hope, and a desire to build something meaningful. No one walks into a partnership with a roadmap that shows how things will unfold. Who among us can predict how a relationship might shape us? We can't foresee how our past will affect our present and the conflicts that will arise from loving someone.

Over time, you became entangled in difficulties you didn't expect and couldn't fully understand. Perhaps you prioritized your partner's needs so much that when you spoke, you no longer knew whether it was with your voice or theirs. Maybe you compromised your values and did things that went against your nature, gave up your needs and desires, and found yourself in a lonely place in your relationship. Through it all, you did what many in your position have done—you made choices that felt right for you at the time. That doesn't make you weak or foolish. It makes you human. You were doing your best to navigate a painful situation without the clarity that only hindsight can bring.

But here's what matters now: You can either get caught up in shame, or you can see yourself as a student of life and use the valuable insight you've gained to focus on your sense of self. You've learned important lessons through your experiences, not just about your partner, but also about yourself. That knowledge will serve you well in the future. You can now view yourself differently, not as someone who lost parts of themselves in an attempt to get what you originally intended to have in your relationship, but as someone who didn't have the insights and experience you have now. The blinders are off now that you have a name for what you've been through, the Echo complex, and its effects on you and your relationship.

Today, you're newly equipped to make better choices, see yourself and your partner with more precision, and recognize when your good intentions work against you. You're more aware that when something feels wrong, you must speak up and act in ways that honor your true self. You can say, *I know more now. I understand myself better. I know what I value. I know what I will and won't accept.* That's not just growth. That's power.

You understand, too, how important it is to stay curious—not just about your partner and relationship—but also about what happens within yourself. You have the knowledge to recognize when your reaction to your partner is more of an echo of their distancing behavior and less of what you need and want. This is not about blaming yourself. Rather, it's about resisting the urge to believe what you want to believe, even when the evidence contradicts your belief, or when you explain things away before asking the right questions. Questions like: *Why do I feel responsible for my partner's emotions? Why do I push aside my own needs to avoid conflict? Why have I gone against my values to keep this relationship together? How can I navigate my relationship while maintaining my self-respect?*

When you ask and answer these questions truthfully, your choices will become clearer. You can let your fear and old ways of thinking shape your story, or you can create a new one that reflects a strong sense of self. You can answer out of shame, guilt, or self-doubt, or you can come from a place of self-compassion and self-respect. You can try to "fix" the dysfunction, or you can step out of it. In this way, you can see that your strength lies not in how much you can endure, but in how fully you can face the truth and take the right action to honor your needs and feelings and stay true to yourself.

As you choose the path that feels right for you now, you may notice that what once felt like loss begins to feel more like space, room to breathe, to choose differently, and to rebuild. Let the wisdom from lessons learned guide you toward shaping a life that feels more like your own.

The Importance of Self-Compassion

I understand what it's like to lose your sense of self, and I also know what it's like to reclaim it. Not only did I emerge as a stronger and more perceptive woman during recovery from my first marriage, but I also found a way to use what I had gone through to help others. That has been one of the most fulfilling experiences of my life. Wherever you go from here, remember this: you're not starting from scratch; you're starting from experience. And that makes all the difference. Every painful moment, every tear, every sleepless night, every time you silenced your needs, has given you wisdom. You know what it feels like to lose yourself, and that knowing makes you less likely to do it again. You've seen the cost of giving too much, and you've learned truths you can't ignore. You can recognize the signs of what makes you a lesser version of yourself. You understand the difference between love and senseless sacrifice, between care and control, between passion and chaos. This awareness can help you forgive yourself for what happened and guide you toward self-acceptance. You are embarking on a new story with a fuller understanding of who you are, marked by the highs and lows of being human.

In this chapter, we will explore how self-compassion helps us overcome the Echo complex and how the wisdom gained from our experiences enables us to reclaim ourselves. We will take a closer look at the inner critic that fills us with self-doubt and learn ways to challenge it. We will discuss how to let go of past mistakes to prevent them from drowning us in shame, guilt, and remorse. And we will recognize the value of celebrating our strengths and affirming our right to work on our weaknesses without judgment.

The Seven Stages of Reclaiming Selfhood

Reclaiming your sense of self is a journey. It takes time to heal, just as it took time to lose parts of yourself in the relationship. The seven stages below offer a roadmap, based on key insights in this book, to guide you and help you track your progress through each stage. Each of the seven stages is an invitation to pause, reflect, and take small but meaningful steps toward reconnecting with your true self. As you move through them, you'll begin to see new possibilities for creating the life you want to live.

There's no single "right" order and no stopwatch running. Healing rarely follows a straight line. Instead, trust your own wisdom and use your answers to the questions at the end of each chapter, the exercises you've practiced, and the stories you've read as your guide. As you go through the stages, notice where you feel drawn to stay a while and where you're ready to take another step forward. As you return to the seven stages over time, you may be surprised by how much progress you've made, and also how much stronger and more authentic your relationship with yourself is becoming.

Seven Stages

1. Be Aware and Accept Truth
   Recognizing and accepting how and why you are losing your sense of self. Understanding the full impact of your relationship and your role in it.
2. Take Action
   Starting to make deliberate choices, no matter how small, that respect your personal values, needs, and boundaries rather than conforming to someone else's.

3. Tell Your Story
   Breaking the hold of silence and shame by sharing your story with a trusted confidant. Revealing your experiences is validating, restores your voice, and gives you a clearer perspective.
4. Honor Your Feelings
   Allowing yourself to feel everything—grief, fear, anger, and shame—without guilt. These emotions demonstrate that you are claiming truth and strength.
5. Confront Old Beliefs
   Identifying and confronting misguided beliefs about yourself and others that come from early experiences, fear, self-doubt, and unresolved emotional issues. Replacing these with what is true now promotes healing.
6. Open to Self-Compassion
   Taking care of yourself just as you would care for your loved ones. Working on forgiving your past mistakes and letting go of shame.
7. Embrace Self-Discovery
   Reconnecting with who you truly are, beyond roles, rules, or expectations. Following your curiosity and trusting your intuition. Letting your needs, feelings, and desires guide you as you live your life freely and fully.

What's vital to know here is that even when our lives feel uncertain or out of our control, our inner world is ours to claim. Our thoughts. Our self-talk. Our capacity for kindness toward ourselves. That's where the power of self-preservation lies. And when we tap into that power with self-compassion instead of judgment, we create the conditions for being true to ourselves in a way that feels real and sustainable.

I have personally experienced this transition and guided my clients through their evolution from self-loss to self-love. I know that self-compassion is not just a feel-good concept. It works.

Understanding Self-Compassion

Self-compassion means treating yourself with the same kindness and understanding that you would offer a dear friend. Consider how you would respond if your closest friend confessed to experiencing the same pain you've felt. You wouldn't question, minimize, or reinterpret their feelings. You wouldn't shame them. Rather, you would believe them, comfort them, validate their feelings, and remind them of their worth. You deserve to show that same tenderness to yourself.

Think of emotional wounds as needing the same care as physical ones. Imagine you cut your finger while cooking. You would feel pain, and even if you could keep going and pretend you were okay, you wouldn't really do that. First, you'd clean the wound and bandage it to help it heal. You'd also find a way to prevent yourself from cutting again. Emotional wounds deserve similar attention. Too often, people hurt by someone they love try to ignore their pain or blame themselves, which only makes the wound worse. But just as caring for a cut helps it heal and prevents further injury, practicing self-compassion can ease our pain and promote healing.

If it feels unnatural to treat yourself with kindness, try this exercise: Imagine the most compassionate person you know (real or fictional) speaking to you. What would they say? Perhaps they'd tell you, "You've been through a lot, and you have every reason to feel the way you do. But you're not defeated. You will get through this and come out of it with wisdom and foresight." Let those words become your own. By practicing this exercise, you begin to replace the harsh inner critic's voice with a gentler, supportive one that helps you stay on your own side.

Self-Compassion as an Agent of Change

As you practice self-compassion, you will feel like you're stepping forward out of the chill of someone else's disapproval and into the warmth of your acceptance. Psychologists have observed that individuals who develop self-compassion can acknowledge their imperfections without letting those imperfections dictate their worth. In other words, you can admit *I messed up here*, while still knowing *I am worthy*. Any mistakes you've made or ways you've become an echo of your partner are not permanent stains on your character. They are natural missteps on the path of growth. Instead of punishing yourself for what you could have done differently, you can forgive yourself for not knowing what you didn't know at the time.

Embracing this mindset is liberating. It's like opening a window in a dark, airless room and feeling fresh air and light pour in. You can start to acknowledge that you deserve a better life than the one shaped by your past choices. Where once you felt like an echo of someone else, you can find the courage to speak in your own voice. Where you previously absorbed blame, you can now respectfully say, "This burden isn't mine to carry."

Grabbing the Brass Ring of Self-Compassion

Think of a time when you felt empowered—maybe a moment when you stood up to someone who treated you badly, or when you felt proud of handling a difficult situation skillfully. Or, like when Sharon danced, you felt joyful and empowered doing something you love. That strength has always been inside you. You are your greatest source of power. Remember who you are. You've got this. You only need to reach for it.

Once, you may have thought that prioritizing self-care was indulgent. Now, as you embrace self-compassion, you understand that self-care isn't selfish or indulgent. It's necessary. It's like watering a plant. As you pour kindness and care into yourself, you regain your vibrancy. The real you—the one who laughs freely, speaks your mind, and feels joy—begins to show up.

You have been wounded, yes. Make no mistake: Being with an emotionally avoidant partner who doesn't see you and pushes you away through harsh or hidden behaviors, and having the Echo complex as a result, is traumatic. But the same experiences that seemed like they might break you can transform you into a stronger self. Many of my clients tell me that, despite the trauma of what they've been through in their relationship, they are a better person than they were before they began it.

There is much evidence to support such outcomes. Trauma research had previously been centered on the negative consequences of trauma. However, in 1995, psychologists Richard Tedeschi and Lawrence Calhoun, with the University of North Carolina at Charlotte, introduced the term post-traumatic growth (PTG) to explain that the struggle with trauma can bring about positive psychological changes. Since then, there has been growing interest in resilience and the potential for positive psychological outcomes of trauma.

One study by psychiatrist Liliana Dell'Osso and her colleagues at the University of Pisa's Department of Clinical and Experimental Medicine in Italy advocated for a balanced view of trauma that acknowledges both its debilitating and liberating potentials. According to their 2022 research, individuals with traumatic experiences reported enhanced self-awareness, increased self-confidence, meaningful relationships, a deeper appreciation for life, and greater openness to new possibilities.

These studies give you a sense of what's in store for you. Rebuilding your sense of self after falling into the Echo complex means returning to yourself with greater wisdom from the painful experiences you've been through. It's about realizing that treating yourself with kindness, especially when old feelings of shame or self-doubt tug at you, gives you a way forward. Even though those feelings will inevitably reappear, you'll know it doesn't mean you're failing. It means being human can be complicated.

What's different now is that you're not meeting those moments empty-handed. You've been learning to listen for that softer voice inside, the one that says, *I see you, I'm with you, we'll get through this.* You've come to understand that mistakes don't make you unworthy. They make you real. But now, you carry the commitment to honor yourself with acts of self-compassion that remind you of your worth. That's what you're building here, not perfection, but the ability to return to yourself, again and again, with warmth instead of criticism.

This journey you're on is no longer an accounting of what happened to you. It's about who you are choosing to become. You are growing into the fullness of who you are, not a past version of yourself, but a new self, crafted with experience, wisdom, and self-love. The next chapter of your life is yours to write, and you are going to write it with the self-love and confidence you have fought hard to reclaim. Each day that you choose self-compassion over self-criticism, you reinforce your worth—and this will continue until you feel whole again. When you look in the mirror, instead of seeing a faded image, you will see the self you were always meant to be.

Coming up, you'll find practical tools to help you nurture more kindness and compassion toward yourself that you can start using right away.

Banish the Inner Critic

Let's start by talking about that little voice in our heads. You know the one I mean. The one that second-guesses us, criticizes us, and makes us feel like we're not enough. That voice is our inner critic, and we all have one. If left unchecked, that voice can lead us directly into the Echo complex, causing problems in our lives and leaving us feeling disconnected from ourselves and others.

As we've seen in this book, that voice didn't just appear out of nowhere. It starts forming in childhood, shaped by experiences and the messages we take in from those around us: a parent who is too busy, a teacher who focuses on mistakes instead of progress, a school bully, or more traumatic events. A child who feels unseen or unworthy often grows into an adult who views themselves through that same lens.

As we develop, our inner critic influences our decisions and actions. And if we believe everything it tells us, we end up in situations that reinforce old, limiting beliefs, like feeling we must prove our worth to our partners.

Here's something we need to understand: Our inner critic isn't a voice of truth. And while it's loud and persistent, that's not the same thing as being right. On the contrary, it chatters away in our minds, tossing out judgments, criticisms, and worst-case scenarios without bothering to verify whether any of it is true.

How do we know when our inner critic is speaking rather than an inner voice of truth? Here's our clue: it usually feels like we're getting punched. We make a mistake, forget something important, say the wrong thing, and suddenly we hear, *I'm such an idiot*, or *Why can't I ever get it right?* That voice is seldom neutral. It's harsh, blaming, and unforgiving. That's our signal: The critic has entered the chat.

Remember, the critic is not wisdom. It's fear and shame disguised as guidance. However, once we recognize the critic for what it really is, an outdated voice on loop, we can begin to turn down its volume. We can challenge those old messages. We can say, *No, that's not how I talk to myself anymore.*

Once we create that space, we can start to amplify a different voice. One that sounds more like, *This is hard, but you're doing your best.* Or, *You're allowed to get it wrong sometimes. It doesn't mean you're deficient.* This voice is kind. It's supportive. It believes in our worthiness, not because we've earned it or proved it, but simply because it's true.

The more we practice self-compassion, the more it frees us from the exhausting cycle of shame and self-doubt. The next time we feel inadequate, anxious about making a mistake, or worried about looking foolish, we can pause and remind ourselves, *Oh, there it is—that's just my humanity showing up. And I welcome it because being human means being imperfect.*

With all this in mind, let's look at four ways to banish the inner critic.

First, we can rewrite the old script in our minds by becoming *attentive listeners* to our thoughts. Tuning into the internal monologue that runs unchecked requires being fully present and engaged in the moment, a state known as mindfulness. By becoming more aware of our thought patterns, we can begin to notice the frequency and content of our self-critical thoughts.

When I ask my therapy clients to write down their daily negative thoughts about themselves in a journal, they're often surprised at how often their inner critic comes up. They didn't realize the power their inner critic had over them. Writing in a journal about thoughts, feelings, and experiences is a simple but revelatory way to notice and reflect on them. We can draw parallels, make conclusions, and identify opportunities to practice self-compassion. By recognizing all the thoughts that arise from our inner critic and how frequently they appear, we can identify what causes our shame and self-doubt.

Spoken phrases also provide a way to address critical thoughts through the practice of *positive self-talk*, such as affirmations of self-worth, counterarguments to our negative thoughts, or evidence of their inaccuracy. Affirmations act as antidotes to the poison of the inner critic. Repeating statements like "I am worthy," "I am capable," or "My needs and feelings matter," through speaking or writing can help rewire our brain's pathways, replacing the critic's voice with a positive one. It's essential for these affirmations to feel genuine and personal, as their strength lies in resonating with our core beliefs about ourselves. So be sure to choose ones that feel deeply true to you and are relevant to the circumstances of your life.

When you practice affirmations, you give yourself the opportunity to change your self-talk. Instead of letting self-doubt take control, you start planting seeds of self-acceptance. Over time, these small, consistent words of encouragement help you distinguish who you truly are from your partner's criticism or your self-judgment. With practice, affirmations become more than just words. They're like a steady hand on your shoulder, guiding you back to yourself. They help build confidence, boost emotional resilience, and remind you to face life's challenges by loving yourself first.

Affirmations for Self-Compassion

Affirmations are short, powerful statements that help combat an inner critic and reshape negative thought patterns. When repeated regularly, they rewire the brain to adopt healthier, more self-affirming beliefs. Affirmations can reduce stress, boost resilience, and improve self-esteem. By including them in our daily routine, we can cultivate self-compassion, even during challenging times. Affirmations work best when they're personalized to our individual lives, which is why I recommend writing your own. When you're creating your own affirmations, consider the following:

1. Use present-tense, positive language:
   Instead of saying, "I won't let them hurt me anymore," say "I choose to protect my peace and well-being."
2. Make it personal and meaningful:
   Affirmations should reflect what a person needs most. If you struggle with self-doubt, try repeating an affirmation like "I trust myself and my instincts."
3. Focus on self-compassion:
   When your inner critic tries to bring you down after a mistake or bad decision, practice forgiveness with an affirmation like, "I am kind to myself, just as I would be to a friend."
4. Repeat and reinforce:
   You can say affirmations out loud in front of a mirror, write them in a journal, or set them as reminders on your cell phone. I recommend doing all three. The more we reinforce these messages, the more they will shape our mindset.

Here are some examples of positive affirmations to inspire you:

"I deserve to be fully seen, heard, and understood in my relationship."
"I deserve love, respect, and kindness."
"I'm the one who defines my worth, not my partner or anyone else."
"I choose to put my well-being first."
"My emotions and needs are valid."
"I accept myself without judgment."
"I am letting go of any guilt, blame, or shame that does not belong to me."
"I have the strength to set boundaries and safeguard my inner peace."
"I have abundant love for myself and for others who can love me back."

Positive self-talk alone, however, is not a cure-all. Practicing self-compassion also requires us to step back and view our thoughts and feelings with curiosity rather than judgment. When our inner critic speaks, instead of engaging with it, we can observe it as a separate entity, acknowledging its presence but not its authority. This detachment allows us to create an inner sanctuary where we can comfort and reassure ourselves, rather than feeling shame.

Once we become aware of these thoughts, the next step is to challenge and reframe them. This means first *challenging* the validity of our inner critic's story. For example, if the critic says, *You're not good enough*, we might ask, *According to whom?* Or, *what evidence supports this judgment?* Then find evidence that supports the opposite of what the critic claims. Often, the inner critic's claims are based on outdated or exaggerated beliefs we hold that don't stand up to scrutiny. By questioning these thoughts, we can reduce their influence over us.

Reframing involves viewing a situation from a different perspective. Instead of accepting a self-critical thought at face value, we can approach it with self-compassion. For example, if the thought is, *I always mess things up*, we could reframe it as, *I've made mistakes, like everyone does, but I also have many successes.* This shift helps create a more balanced self-view that acknowledges both strengths and weaknesses.

Another empowering technique is to *create a character* for the inner critic. Giving it a name, a persona, or even a cartoonish image can help weaken its influence over us. When our critic starts in with negative chatter, we can counter it by saying, *Thanks for your input, (character name), but I choose not to believe that today.*

As we learn to quiet the critic and replace it with our compassionate voice, we become less likely to accept inequality in our relationships and more inclined to stand up for ourselves. The path to healing may not always be clear, but every time we quiet our inner critic, we create another chance to shine, resilient and whole.

Forgive Our Past Mistakes

Carrying the weight of shame from past mistakes can be a heavy burden, one that drains us of our energy and joy. Shame can keep us tethered to the past, hinder growth and healing, and push us further away from resolution. On the other hand, forgiving ourselves for past mistakes—whatever they may be—allows us to acknowledge the complex circumstances we faced, our emotional state at the time, and the mindset that led us to make poor choices. Self-forgiveness can help us move beyond anger and grudges to find new meaning in difficult experiences. Forgiveness doesn't mean that we free ourselves from responsibility. It means that we allow ourselves to use the wisdom we gained from those experiences.

Forgiving ourselves can bring much-needed relief, but it can also spark change. When we release ourselves from the shackles of past mistakes, we reclaim the energy that guilt and shame had consumed. This transformation changes how we see ourselves and how we engage with the world around us. It might be reconnecting with our values and goals, building new relationships or restoring old ones, or taking steps to leave a toxic situation. Forgiving ourselves can lift the burden of past mistakes and help ensure that we don't lose sight of our worth as we grow and go in new directions.

Embrace Strengths and Passions

How many times have we told ourselves that we were finally going to sign up for that art class, learn to play golf, plan that dream trip to Italy, join a book club, or start a new business we've been planning? We all possess strengths and passions that bring us to life, but the life we're living in can make us forget them. If we want to reconnect with a vital part of who we are, we must first remember how much we value the passions and strengths that we've been away from, and then embrace them.

The beauty of *strengths* is that they show up in both small and large ways. We might, for example, possess a natural ability to be a loyal and loving friend or have a wonderful sense of humor. We might be great problem solvers or possess a special talent. People who are empathetic find joy in comforting a friend or caring for an animal. Those with a sense of humor can bring levity to difficult situations and brighten the days of those around them. Skilled problem solvers find purpose in organizing community projects or leading a team at work. Individuals with special talents find happiness in doing what they love and can inspire others to do the same.

Our *passions* are natural companions to our strengths. They're one of the things that improve the quality of our lives, whether it's painting, playing music, rock climbing, gardening, writing poetry, or traveling. These aren't just hobbies. They're lifelines.

Passions offer a healthy escape from stress, a way to breathe easier when life feels suffocating. When we tap into what lights us up inside, we bring something into our lives that comes straight from the depths of our being. And when we find peace in nature, we connect with something bigger than ourselves.

Engaging in an activity that stirs our passion takes us into a state of flow—a magical space where everything else fades away, leaving only the moment we're in. Flow is much more than a pleasant distraction. Deeply connecting with what we love fosters emotional resilience, allowing our daily stresses to have less impact on us. It serves as a reminder that we are whole, vibrant individuals whose existence extends beyond our relationships.

By embracing our strengths and passions, we can push back against others who try to make us feel insignificant. When we understand what we bring to the world and what truly inspires us, it's much harder for someone else's negativity to take root. This inner confidence enables us to set boundaries, seek out individuals who genuinely support us, and, if necessary, gather the courage to leave a relationship that isn't good for us.

So, get involved. Sign up for that art class, book the trip, start the new business, and step into the sunshine! When you pour your energy into what excites you, you create a life that's rich with meaning, momentum, and possibility.

Cultivate a Better Relationship with Ourselves

When we banish our inner critic, forgive ourselves for past mistakes, and embrace our strengths and passions—in other words, when we don't let our shortcomings define us—something magical happens. We find a great new friend, and their name is "me." Our relationship with this great new friend makes a big difference in whether we continue to lose ourselves in the chaos of an overbearing relationship or find our center in a robust sense of self.

Research consistently supports the idea that individuals who understand their personalities, strengths, and weaknesses are better equipped to manage stress and are less likely to experience depression and anxiety. Brené Brown, a renowned researcher on vulnerability and shame, emphasizes the importance of self-awareness and self-compassion. Her work underscores the concept that a strong relationship with oneself cannot be given or taken away by others. It is cultivated from within. Accepting ourselves and our imperfections can be a sustaining force when our relationships with others become harmful. It is the source of the inner voice that affirms our worth, even when our partner's misguided actions attempt to convince us otherwise.

Building a strong, compassionate relationship with ourselves starts with making a conscious choice. This work involves self-reflection to gain a deeper understanding of our personal needs and to make a firm commitment to honor them. The process demands time and effort, but the benefits are well worth it. Here are eight life-giving benefits that come from cultivating a strong relationship with ourselves:

1. We hold onto personal identity: Rather than allowing others' expectations to influence us, we maintain a strong sense of who we are.
2. We recognize unfair criticism: The ability to distinguish between constructive feedback and the projections of others enables us to reject blame that isn't ours.
3. We protect our reality: Our own perceptions hold more sway, making it easier for us to resist manipulation.
4. We make empowered choices: Our confidence in decision-making grows, improving our well-being, whether those decisions involve setting boundaries, seeking support, or ending a relationship.

5. We set an example for children: The self-respect, emotional resilience, and healthy boundaries we model provide a precious example of healthy self-love for the younger generation.
6. We become emotionally independent: As we nurture our relationship with ourselves, we discover ways to fulfill our emotional needs.
7. We establish personal boundaries: Healthy self-love helps us clearly define what is and isn't acceptable in a relationship.
8. We build resilience and recovery: When we can be our own source of emotional support, we can face challenges, heal emotional wounds, and move forward confidently.

Considering these life-giving benefits, it becomes clear that caring for ourselves through self-compassion is no longer optional. It's essential. Choosing to put our well-being first is a bold decision, one that requires strength and determination. It means saying, "I deserve better," and refusing to back down from that truth.

That's just what the people in the following stories do. They show us what's possible when we make that commitment to ourselves. Their self-compassion does so much more than provide comfort. It's the spark that ignites action, leading them from being an echo of their partners to finding their own voice.

Finding Our Voice Through Self-Compassion

David
Taking a Stand

David felt he had to be careful about what he said and did when around Julia. Her moods were unpredictable, and when she got angry, her words could be scathing. If he came home late, she accused him of avoiding her. If he didn't respond immediately to her texts, she questioned who he thought was more important than her. Not much he did seemed to satisfy her. Over time, her voice became his inner critic, causing him to second-guess himself. He no longer knew how to be in his relationship without trying everything he could to keep her calm.

One evening, after another barrage of her complaints, David sat alone in the kitchen, watching funny YouTube videos on his phone to distract himself. But thoughts about his relationship disrupted him with a piercing thought, '*I've given up so much of myself trying to please her, I don't like who I've become.*' As he let this realization sink in, grief, anger, and a sense of betrayal followed, not just directed toward Julia, but also toward himself, for allowing her demeaning treatment to go on. "I'm better than this. I deserve to be seen and heard in this relationship," he said to himself. He realized that the only way to change his relationship was to stop tolerating her unwillingness to connect with him through respect and transparency.

The next morning, Julia scolded him for how he had loaded the dishwasher. Usually, David would have apologized and tried to do it "right." But something shifted in him. He looked up at her and said, "Julia, do you realize how often you speak to me like I'm a disappointment? Like nothing I do is good enough for you?" She blinked, startled. "There's always something wrong with me, isn't there?" he continued. "But I'm starting to think the problem might not be me. Are you even happy in this relationship? Because I can feel your unhappiness every day, but you won't tell me the real reasons why, and I'm done pretending it's all my fault." It was the first time he had ever said anything like that. And he didn't back down. When Julia started in on him, he walked out of the house.

In the days that followed, David stopped rushing to reply to her messages. He no longer apologized for the imagined offenses she attributed to him. When Julia tried to provoke an argument, he refused to get drawn into it. At first, she pushed back even harder, accusing him of being distant. But David remained calm. "I still care about you," he told her one night, "but I'm not going to keep abandoning myself just to keep this relationship going. That's not love. It's survival." For the first time in a long while, Julia didn't lash out. She looked at him, quiet and uncertain. Something in his honesty reached her in a way his silence never had.

It took time, many difficult conversations, and countless moments when David held his ground. Julia's entitled attitude and tendency to justify her anger didn't change, but because of David's newfound self-respect and setting boundaries on how she treated him, she gradually started listening more and criticizing less. As he continued to find his voice, David began to reclaim himself. He knew that no matter what happened next, he would never go back to believing he could change himself to fit her version of who he should be.

Kim
Deciding to Leave

The glow of the television cast moving shadows across the couch in the dimly lit living room as Kim and Alana watched their favorite crime drama. Kim gently took Alana's hand and moved closer to her. As Kim rested her head on Alana's shoulder, she sighed, "I wish we could be like this more often," she murmured. Alana stiffened, pulling away. "Here we go again," she snapped. "Nothing's ever enough for you, is it? We're spending time together, and you're still complaining. Why can't you just be happy with what we have?"

Kim knew she was taking a chance on getting rejected, as had happened so many times before when she needed to feel emotionally close to Alana. "I wasn't complaining," she said quietly. "I just meant . . . I love being close to you like this." But Alana wasn't listening. She stood up abruptly, turned off the TV, and glared at Kim. "You always want more—more time, more attention. It's exhausting. I can't keep up with it." Before Kim could respond, Alana stormed out of the room.

Kim felt beads of sweat form on her upper lip as her heart raced. The warmth she had felt for a moment vanished, replaced by a hollow ache. Once again, Alana had twisted her words, leaving Kim feeling small and dismissed. As she sat there, a sinking feeling took hold as she realized the issue was deeper than merely a disagreement. Alana's outburst was the latest in a pattern of pushing her away, making her feel like her needs were too much and her desires unreasonable. For the first time in the five years they had been together, she realized that their relationship would probably always be this way. As she sat with this truth, a sense of resolve began to take root.

Over the next few weeks, whenever Alana disrupted their alone time by complaining about something Kim had or hadn't done, which seemed like an attempt to pick a fight, Kim calmly disengaged. "I love you, Alana," she said one evening, her voice steady. "But it's too hard to be in a relationship with someone who can't love me in the way I need to be loved."

Despite Kim's efforts to change the dynamic, Alana's criticism and defensiveness remained unchanged. One night, after yet another argument, Kim sat in their bedroom, tears streaming down her face. She realized that no amount of love could mend their relationship without resolving Alana's discomfort with emotional intimacy. Kim knew she couldn't stay with someone who refused to accept the best parts of her.

When Kim told Alana her reasons for leaving, Alana sat in stunned silence, not knowing what to say. Then she blamed Kim for being too needy and got angry, but when Alana realized that Kim had made up her mind, Alana pleaded with her to stay and said they could work it out. But Kim remembered all the times she had tried to push for a deeper connection with Alana and had to endure her withering criticism, her attempts to change the subject, or cold silence.

In the months that followed, Kim mourned the loss of Alana and the vision she had for their relationship. Being on her own made her realize how much of herself she had sacrificed to maintain a connection with someone who couldn't accept her fully. She learned that disregarding her needs and compromising her values in the relationship would never create a close bond with Alana, and she chose herself first.

Zara
Reclaiming Equality

Zara shouldered all the responsibility for running the home she shared with her husband, Omar. She worked just as many hours as he did in her job as a community college teacher. Still, as soon as she got home, a second shift awaited her: cooking, cleaning, and caring for their two young daughters while Omar sank into a cozy armchair in the family room to text friends or watch TV. He focused on his needs, making Zara feel more like his caretaker than an equal partner. She never had time to do the things that gave her a sense of fulfillment and independence.

Zara often concealed her disappointment and frustration, believing that silence would bring peace and prevent conflict in her relationship, as her mother had with her father. Conflict felt too draining and risky. However, during her lunch break at work, Zara had been taking an online course on self-compassion, and the content resonated with her. She realized that practicing self-compassion and asking for what she needed didn't mean she was creating more conflict. Instead, it meant recognizing that her needs were just as important as Omar's.

One evening, Zara asked Omar to help her clear the dinner table so she could finish grading student papers and prepare to teach a new course the next day. "Stop nagging me about the housework! Can't you see I'm tired too?" he responded. The old Zara would have backed down and apologized, but this was a new Zara who had come to realize the importance of self-compassion. With steady resolve, she met his scowl and said, "I won't be treated this way. I'm not asking for much, just a little help so I can finish my work. We're supposed to be partners, Omar." She reminded Omar of the Islamic principles of fairness and partnership in marriage, quoting verses and hadiths that emphasized mutual respect and shared responsibility. Although she felt nervous speaking to him this way, she remained confident in her faith and in what she had asked for. Omar sighed, stood up, and brusquely moved a couple of dishes to the sink, as if her request had been unreasonable.

A few weeks passed, and Zara continued to assert herself, gently but firmly. Still, Omar resisted. He interpreted Islamic principles differently, allowing him to maintain emotional distance by making her seem less important than he was. Despite this difference, Zara stood her ground, refusing to let her needs be dismissed. She also sought support from her local mosque and joined a women's group, where she received encouragement and advice from other Muslim women facing similar struggles.

Eventually, Omar began making gradual changes. First, he began to play with the kids. Then he shopped for groceries while Zara rested.

Although there were still moments of tension and frustration, Zara felt they were making progress toward a more balanced relationship. Zara recognized that Omar was unlikely to become more comfortable revealing his deeper emotions, but she drew the line at allowing him to make her feel inferior in the relationship.

It was when she insisted on having one night a week with her girlfriends that she began to truly feel more alive. Now that she had made this meaningful change, she realized that standing up for herself not only helped her reclaim her sense of self but also honored her faith's principles and made her a better role model for her daughters.

Claire
Reaching Out for Help

Golden rays of sunlight beamed through the trees surrounding Claire's back porch as she sat cradling a cup of coffee that had gone cold. A light breeze carried the scent of damp earth and blooming jasmine, but Claire didn't notice. Her mind held a stark realization triggered by an early-morning glimpse of her faded reflection in a bedroom mirror. The day before, the latest incident with Mark had helped her see a truth obscured by false hope.

Even though it was late on a Sunday afternoon, Mark had shut himself in his office. Claire heard noises and knocked on his door to ask if he wanted a piece of the blueberry pie she had made for him. When he jerked the door open, Claire's cat ran into the room. He grabbed her cat and threw it out. "Why can't you and your cat just leave me the fuck alone!" he yelled.

As she curled deeper into the pillowed deck chair and pulled a wool throw tighter around her shoulders, the weight of Mark's words settled over her again like a damp chill. How much longer could she stay with a man who spoke to her like that? A man who interrupted her words. A man who blamed her for things that weren't her fault. Six years of her attempts to gain his love and approval had transformed her into someone she barely recognized. Where had her carefree, fun-loving spirit gone? *I want to be me again*, she thought, tears welling in her eyes.

She sat up and took a deep breath of jasmine. *Nothing will change as long as I keep reacting in the same way, hoping for a different outcome.* How many hours has she wasted replaying their disputes, searching for the perfect words that might finally make him see her, hear her, love her in the way she longs to be loved? Those thoughts only deepened her heartache. *I can't keep doing this. I need a new way, one that works for me*, she realized.

The flicker of her new thinking—steadier than hope and stronger than longing—felt right. She reached for her phone, her fingers hovering over the screen for a moment before she tapped the number. A therapist. A step forward. Not for him, but for her. A step toward reclaiming herself. For the first time in a long while, she no longer felt like Mark's echo.

Self-compassion isn't about waiting for others to recognize our worth. It's about recognizing it ourselves. It means treating ourselves with kindness instead of criticism and recognizing that we deserve love, even when our partners struggle to be vulnerable or try to diminish us, rather than summoning the courage to love us fully and freely. And let me emphasize again one of the key messages I've been sharing throughout this book: Self-love means *standing up for yourself and not backing down*. You have every right to be your unique and precious self, with all your flaws, foibles, and feelings, and don't let anyone take that away from you. Doing this reflects the unwavering belief that you are enough, just as you are.

So the next time you feel small around your partner, pause. Find your voice like David. See the raw truth like Kim. Claim your right to be an equal partner like Zara. Or reach for your phone to call a therapist like Claire. Because at the heart of every strong relationship—whether with ourselves or others—is the ability to say, "I am not an echo. I am the sound itself."

Key Points

1. Instead of viewing our mistakes and limitations as flaws, we can approach them with understanding, acceptance, and a spirit of forgiveness. This mindset helps us build resilience and cultivate self-compassion.

2. Our inner critic is a harsh, unforgiving voice in our minds that's not necessarily truthful. Instead, it reflects old, learned patterns of self-doubt and shame. Understanding that our inner critic was formed in the past helps us develop a more accurate self-image of who we are today.
3. Self-compassion reminds us that we are not responsible for someone else's judgments. It helps us to stop blaming ourselves for things beyond our control.
4. Self-compassion makes the experience of failure feel safe and more manageable. Instead of getting stuck in self-criticism, we learn from our experiences and move forward with more self-confidence.
5. Practicing self-compassion involves acknowledging our negative self-talk and replacing it with kind, understanding, and encouraging words.
6. When we let go of guilt, shame, and regret, we free ourselves to embrace new opportunities for happiness and personal growth.
7. Celebrating what makes us unique—our talents, interests, and passions—enhances our sense of self-worth. When we engage with what inspires us, we build a more fulfilling relationship with ourselves.
8. Knowing our strengths reduces the likelihood that someone else's judgment and harsh treatment will weaken our sense of self.
9. A healthy relationship with ourselves requires actively tuning in to our needs, values, and desires and committing to honoring them daily.
10. Research consistently shows that people who understand their true personalities, strengths, and weaknesses are better at managing stress and are less likely to face depression and anxiety.

Exercise: Embracing Your Worth and Self-Compassion

Give each of the following questions, meant to nurture self-compassion, thoughtful consideration. Then write the answer to each one in your journal.

1. What experiences in your relationship have helped you identify what you want in a deeply connected partnership?
2. What early life experiences have shaped your self-image? How do those experiences help you understand the emotional patterns you've been working to heal?
3. What are some ways to practice honoring your own needs and feelings, even when they're unfamiliar or challenging?
4. List some circumstances that trigger your inner critic. Describe ways to counter your inner critic by replacing harsh language with the soothing and supportive words you would say to a friend.
5. What do you think are the three most essential elements needed to build a loving and compassionate relationship with yourself going forward? These can be what we've discussed in the book or something more personal you've discovered about yourself.

Exercise: A New Perspective on Your Story

Now that you've finished reading this book, it's time to revisit the story you wrote about your relationship after reading chapter 2. Take a moment to ground yourself in the fresh perspective you've gained through the exercises, your answers to the end-of-chapter questions, the seven stages of loss of self and the seven stages of reclaiming self, and the stories and insights shared in this book. Then, reread the story you wrote. Notice the differences between your old and new perspectives. Now write a new story about your relationship and yourself, drawing from the wisdom you've learned in this book. Next, review your new story and make a list of things you'd like to work on to reclaim your sense of self, whether that's in your current relationship or after a past one.

EPILOGUE

As you close this book, my hope is that you can finally see the truth of what you've lived: How a loved one's distancing behavior and your efforts to bridge a gap you did not create have shaped your sense of self. And just as important, I want you to feel the spark of what is now possible. If you recognized yourself in these stories, you see that many others have carried the weight of a partner's fear of intimacy, endured the confusion of mixed signals, and felt the sting of defenses meant to keep closeness at bay. And many others have stepped out of that cycle, reclaimed their voices, and rebuilt their lives.

My purpose in writing this book is twofold. First, to speak aloud what so often remains unspoken and to honor the deep, disorienting pain of losing yourself in a relationship. When harm is minimized or dismissed, the wound grows deeper. But when harm is finally named and understood—when we are seen, heard, and believed—it opens the way to healing.

And second, to light a path forward from being an echo of someone else to stepping into the fullness of one's own being. This path is a process of unfolding, of falling and rising, of remembering and relearning. It asks for honesty and courage, often involving grief over unmet expectations and years that felt lost. Yet within that grief lies an invitation to step into a deeper wholeness than you may have ever known.

Coming out of the Echo complex is not only about getting through the pain. It is about embracing the freedom to be fully and unapologetically yourself. It is about rediscovering joy, cultivating meaningful connections, and learning to trust your voice again.

If these words instill hope that you, too, can find the emotional freedom to reclaim your sense of self, then this book has fulfilled its purpose.

My wish for you, dear reader, is that the insights gathered here—from my own journey and from the inspiring stories of those I have worked with—will serve as reliable companions on your path. Always remember that you are not defined by the ways you lost yourself. You are defined by the resilience that brought you here, by the courage it takes to face yourself honestly, and by the vast possibility of the life still before you. Step forward with determination, self-compassion, and knowing that you are worthy of love, belonging, and joy, exactly as you are.

APPENDIX

Helping Loved Ones

When someone you care about is losing themselves in a relationship, it can be distressing and leave you feeling helpless. However, your way of communicating with them can significantly influence the situation. Since a strong relationship between the two of you is as important to them as it is to you, thoughtful, informed communication might encourage them to open up rather than withdraw.

When I work with people facing this circumstance, I offer them the following advice, represented by the acronym SAFETY. This word choice is meaningful for two reasons. First, someone experiencing a loss of self is often reluctant to share their feelings due to fear of judgment. Your relationship with them should help them feel understood and supported. Second, the word *safety* is a reminder that your relationship with them could be fraught with the potential for arguments, hurt feelings, and resentments, even estrangement. Pointing out your concern about the alarming changes you see in them can provoke strong emotions. The goal here is to help your loved one feel safe with you.

The SAFETY approach is not intended to provide instructions on how to convince a loved one to leave their partner. That's highly unlikely to happen because, as you've seen in this book, a person's reasons for staying are complex and not easily dismissed. Instead, this approach aims to reduce the risk of further strain on your relationship and cultivate opportunities for better communication.

SAFETY

Provide a *Safe* Place:

You probably won't be able to influence change in your loved one's relationship, so focus on strengthening your own relationship with them. People experiencing the Echo complex are more likely to open up about their feelings of shame, guilt, and fear if you create a safe emotional environment for them. The challenge is to offer support and validation while managing your own feelings, like worry, hurt, or anger. Before talking with your loved one, take a moment to think about ways you might unintentionally make them less willing to share their situation and feelings with you.

For example, they might be concerned about your anger or negative opinions you have about their partner. They may also want to avoid causing you to worry or the risk that you'll share their details with others. You can let them know that your focus is on their well-being, not judging them or their partner. Reassure them that what they tell you won't be shared further unless they ask for your help, and that help involves someone else. To ease their worry about upsetting you, tell them you're already worried and only want to support them.

When you sense they are emotionally drained and need a break from talking, end the conversation by expressing gratitude for their trust and reassuring them of your love and support. Feeling safe with you will encourage them to reach out for help when they are ready. Simply knowing they have a safe place to turn may also improve their chances of leaving a toxic relationship.

Address Loss of Self:

When your loved one shows they're willing to listen to your concerns, focus on the facts without expressing your feelings or opinions. Mention the changes you see in your loved one, rather than criticizing their partner. They might see goodness in their partner that you don't see, and hearing criticism about someone they care about can make them defensive.

To help prevent them from shutting down, say, "I noticed the hurt look on your face when Steve told you to 'shut up.' How did you feel about that?" Or you can say, "It seems that something has been bothering you. Can I help in any way?" Or you could say, "You haven't been available to get together lately. Is everything okay?" As you ask these questions, don't push them to reveal their feelings when they're not ready. You can say that you're there for them whenever they want to talk about it.

***Follow* Their Lead:**

Encouraging your loved one to own their experience works better than imposing your feelings, observations, opinions, or advice. Be a good listener by carefully hearing what they share with you and asking gentle, open-ended questions instead of making statements that might be perceived as blame or accusations. You can say, "I appreciate you sharing your feelings with me." Then reassure them by saying, "I love you and I'm here for you whenever you need me."

After your loved one discloses a feeling or experience, ask whether they would like to hear your perspective before you share it. You could say, "I have some thoughts about that. Can I share them with you?" Then you might say something like, "I believe that you believe Alice's behavior is not harmful to you, but you don't talk much when you're around her anymore. Is there a reason for your silence?"

Once the trouble comes to light, both of you may feel a sense of unease in your relationship. To avoid this, focus on the positive aspects of your relationship by planning quality time to enjoy each other's company. Make sure to connect with your loved one regularly about more than just the issues in their relationship.

Don't *Enable*:

When no one else in the family is disclosing their concerns about your loved one's relationship, it's up to you to bring it up, as long as you follow SAFETY guidelines. Remaining silent about what you observe or downplaying it to avoid confrontation is never a good idea. Acting like everything is fine encourages your loved one's partner to continue bad behavior and your loved one to keep putting up with it. It's essential to maintain open and authentic communication.

Gently insist on having an open and honest conversation with your loved one. If they refuse to talk about it, the main reasons are likely their feelings of fear and shame, along with the effects of their partner's isolation tactics. You can say, "It must have been hard for you when Liam put you down last night. I noticed that he does that a lot." If your loved one is open to talking, be specific without shaming them, as their partners often do. Be careful not to focus on the negative. If they seem receptive, you can suggest books, articles, or community resources that educate them about power and control, as well as the loss of self in relationships.

Tune into Their Mental State:

Your loved one may be using defense mechanisms to rationalize, minimize, or deny the impact of their partner's actions. Fear and avoiding the truth are significant factors in controlling relationships, and defense mechanisms provide a temporary respite from those feelings. They might also have a traumatic bond with their partners due to a cycle of abuse and affection. Some signs of a trauma bond include: (1) justifying their relationship, (2) making excuses for a partner's maltreatment, (3) isolating themselves from family and friends, (4) living in a fantasy rather than facing reality, and (5) submitting with resignation.

To reclaim themselves, your loved one must work through awareness, acceptance, and action (what I call the three A's). Awareness involves recognizing that a partner is using power and control to undermine their sense of self and identity. Acceptance requires acknowledging the harmful effects of their partner's behavior, which will persist without intervention. Action means seeking help for both partners, issuing an ultimatum, or leaving the relationship. You cannot change your loved one's readiness for any of these stages. You can, however, manage your own understanding and expectations.

Yield:

One of the most challenging aspects of watching a loved one lose themselves in a relationship is knowing when to let go of your desire to change them. All your well-intentioned efforts to help won't matter if they're not willing to change, and continued attempts without seeing results may further strain your relationship. Pressuring a loved one to leave their partner can also create a power struggle, making them more likely to stay in the relationship. Remember, if your loved one has to decide between your relationship and staying with their partner, they will almost always choose their partner.

Helping a loved one with the Echo complex can greatly affect your health and well-being. If you find yourself in this situation, develop a self-care plan and nurture relationships that bring joy and fulfillment. Gently let your loved one know you care about them, but you can't continue to witness the harmful effects of their relationship. This doesn't mean you have to cut all contact with them. Maintaining regular communication may be necessary to check on their well-being. Still, recognize the limits of your relationship and let go of the expectation that your loved one's situation will improve. If they stay in a relationship that is causing them to lose a sense of self, they may stop communicating with others who are aware of what's happening. Ultimately, it is their sole decision to confront the truth, accept responsibility, hold their partner accountable for harm, or choose to leave.

GRATITUDE

The seed for this book was planted many years ago when my father, who had a passion for words and languages, showed me the importance of writing through his many editorial letters. He somehow always found just the right words to cast an honorable light on those he agreed with and to cleverly outmaneuver those he didn't. He also taught me about "indicators," referring to signs of a person's character. Although learning that lesson in real life tested me through many trials, it ultimately led me to a fulfilling career helping others learn it too.

To my therapy clients, I am deeply grateful for your trust. You allowed me into your lives and gave me the privilege of walking beside you in the work of healing. What I learned from working with you has enhanced my understanding of what it takes to recover, so I can better help others. A special tribute to those who shared their stories in this book.

To those in the world of writing and publishing, I am deeply grateful for your belief in this project. Your encouragement, thoughtful guidance, and trust in me and in the importance of this book gave it a place to grow. To George Weinstein, head of the Atlanta Writers Club, thank you for leading me to the AWC conference, where I found my exceptional literary agent, Margaret Danko, with High Line Literary Collective. Along with her significant editorial contributions, she worked tirelessly to find the right editor and publisher in Shari MacDonald Strong and Broadleaf Books. Shari combined her considerable editorial skills with deep insights into the book's message, greatly enhancing its quality. Also, thanks to my early editors, Susan Pohlman, who helped me build the framework for my book, and Emily Murdock Baker, who waded through a first draft to provide important suggestions that helped flesh out my ideas. And to writing coach Tiffany Hawk, who guided me through the development of a book proposal that caught the interest of publishers.

To my dear friends, thank you for listening to me with patience and interest as this book project wove its way into our conversations. You were my sounding boards, supporters, and companions through the highs and lows of the writing process. To writers Esther Kane and Patti Cochran, thank you for reading early drafts and offering useful insights and suggestions. My gratitude extends to therapist Phyllis Carrera, who, amazed that I would take on such a demanding project, helped fuel my determination to complete it. To interior designer Susan Rice, who provided a fun balance to hours of writing at my desk by working with me on home improvement projects. And to Francine Carlin, whom I had the good fortune to randomly sit beside at a professional meeting in New York many years ago. Her friendship and loving support have been a tremendous source of encouragement through the various challenges I've faced in my life.

To my family, I am deeply grateful to you all for believing in this work and in me. My son's fine character and faith in me are reminders of why the messages in this book are so important. He and my daughter-in-law made sure I saw my grandkids every weekend while I was writing. Along with entertaining and delighting me, the kids kept me aware of the importance of nurturing a child's emotions to help them grow into adults who are capable of loving relationships. And a very special thank you to my life partner, Jay, who has been a thoughtful editor, draft reader, and steadfast encourager. Our many discussions on ideas and points in my book, along with his keen insights and suggestions, helped shape this book. Considering we met on a blind date, I can confidently say that taking a leap of faith can be very worthwhile.

NOTES

CHAPTER ONE: THE ECHO COMPLEX

13 ***a strong sense of self requires being authentic:*** Marianne Lammers, Jane Ritchie, and Neville Robertson, "Women's Experience of Emotional Abuse in Intimate Relationships: A Qualitative Study," *Journal of Emotional Abuse* 5, no. 1 (2005): 29–64. Rollo May, *Freedom and Destiny* (Basic Books, 1981). Irvin D. Yalom, *Existential Psychotherapy* (Basic Books, 1980). D. W. Winnicott, *The Maturational Processes and the Facilitating Environment* (International Universities Press, 1965). Carol Rogers, *On Becoming a Person: A Therapist's View of Psychotherapy* (Constable, 1961). Karen Horney, *Neurosis and Human Growth* (Routledge, 1951).

15 ***an emotionally abusive dynamic:*** Marti Tamm Loring, *Emotional Abuse* (Lexington Books, 1994).

16 ***loss of self in relationships can happen to anyone:*** Aimee Jeanne Burns and Charnell Peters, "Identity Veiling: Theorizing Identity Gap Negotiation Post-intimate Partner Violence," *Journal of Social and Personal Relationships* 41, no. 6 (2024): 1324–46.

17 ***without empathy, there can be no emotional intimacy:*** Judith V. Jordan, *Relational–Cultural Therapy*, 3rd ed. (American Psychological Association, 2024).

17 ***an individual can gain confidence:*** B. C. Feeney, "A Secure Base: Responsive Support of Goal Strivings and Exploration of Adult Intimate Relationships," *Journal of Personality and Social Psychology* 87, no. 5 (2004): 631–48.

20 ***"love is the best survival mechanism there is":*** Sue Johnson, *Hold Me Tight: Seven Conversations for a Lifetime of Love* (Little, Brown Spark, 2008), 47.

21 ***our emotional health deteriorates:*** Jean Baker Miller and Irene Pierce Stiver, *The Healing Connection: How Women form Relationships in Therapy and in Life* (Beacon Press, 1997).

21 ***issues can predispose individuals to shame-driven defensive behaviors:*** Seydi Ahmet Satici, Fatma Betül Yılmaz, Zahide Gül Karaağaç, and Sinan Okur, "From Childhood Psychological Maltreatment to Fear of Happiness: Exploring the Serial Mediation of External Shame and Family Communication," *Children and Youth Services Review* 157 (February 2024): 107425.

21 ***adults are often likely to repress these childhood memories:*** Alice Miller, *The Drama of The Gifted Child*, rev. ed. (Basic Books, 1997).

22 ***sharing their inner emotional life:*** John Bradshaw, *Healing the Shame That Binds You* (HCI, 2005).

27 ***individuals may remain trapped:*** Burns and Peters, "Identity Veiling."

27 ***they regulate their emotional pain by denying or minimizing it:*** Federico Lauria, Delphine Preissmann, and Fabrice Clément, "Self-Deception as Affective Coping: An Empirical Perspective on Philosophical Issues," *Consciousness and Cognition* 41 (2016): 119–34.

28 ***focused on defending themselves:*** Bradshaw, *Healing the Shame.*

CHAPTER TWO: MY STORY

52 ***sharing stories and finding meaning in them:*** "Narrative Therapy," *Psychology Today* (blog), October 13, 2022, https://www.psychologytoday.com/us/therapy-types/narrative-therapy#when-its-used.

52 ***helping them to interpret their narratives:*** Robert H. Rice, "Narrative Therapy," in *The Sage Encyclopedia of Theory in Counseling and Psychology* 2 (2015): 695–700.

CHAPTER THREE: TWELVE HEALING TRUTHS ABOUT SELF-LOSS IN RELATIONSHIPS

57 ***a frightening and destabilizing state:*** John Bowlby, *The Making and Breaking of Affectional Bonds* (Routledge Classics, 2005).

58 ***greater level of reporting by women:*** P. W. Cook, *Abused Men: The Hidden Side of Domestic Violence* (Praeger, 1997).

58 ***creates profound stress:*** Jon Allen, *Traumatic Relationships and Serious Mental Disorders* (John Wiley & Sons, 2001).

59 ***a sense of disconnection and isolation:*** J. L. Herman, *Trauma and Recovery* (Basic Books, 1992); Miller and Stiver, *The Healing Connection.*

59 ***women in emotionally abusive relationships:*** Marianne Lammers, Jane Ritchie, and Neville Robertson, "Women's Experience of Emotional Abuse in Intimate Relationships: A Qualitative Study," *Journal of Emotional Abuse* 5, no. 1 (2005): 29–64.

59 ***they've lost their core selves:*** Deborah K. Anderson, and Daniel G. Saunders, "Leaving an Abusive Partner: An Empirical Review of Predictors, the Process of Leaving, and Psychological Well-being," *Trauma, Violence, & Abuse* 4, no. 2 (2003): 163–91.

59 ***a complete breakdown of one's sense of self:*** Valerie Nash Chang, *I Just Lost Myself: Psychological Abuse of Women in Marriage* (Praeger/Greenwood Publishing Group, 1996).

63 ***reflects their struggle for self-preservation:*** P. R. Amato and A. Booth, "The Legacy of Parents' Marital Discord: Consequences for Children's Marital Quality," *Journal of Personality and Social Psychology* 81, no. 4 (October 2001): 627–38. R. D. Conger, M. Cui, C. M. Bryant, and G. J. Elder, Jr. "Competence in Early Adult Romantic Relationships: A Developmental Perspective on Family Influences," *Journal of Personality and Social Psychology* 79 (2000): 224–37, http://dx.doi.org/10.1037//0022-3514.79.2.224.

64 ***a strategy to gain attention:*** S. Dalili and B. Zohuri, "The Dynamics of AttentionSeeking Behavior: Understanding, Manifestations, and Strategies for Change," *Journal of Clinical Case Studies, Reviews & Reports* 3, no. 1 (2025): 1–6.

66 ***they grew more dependent:*** Kerrie James and Laurie MacKinnon, "The Tip of the Iceberg: A Framework for Identifying Non-Physical Abuse in Couple and Family Relationships," *Journal of Feminist Family Therapy* 22, no. 2 (2010): 112–29.

66 ***"attribute their partners' abusive actions to typical male behavior":*** Lammers, Ritchie, and Robertson, "Women's Experience of Emotional Abuse."

66 ***blamed themselves for not being good enough:*** Chang, *I Just Lost Myself.*

66 ***cloud one's judgment:*** Helen M. Hendy, Doreen Eggen, Cheryl Gustitus, Kelli C. McLeod, and Phillip Ng, "Decision to Leave Scale: Perceived Reasons to Stay in or Leave Violent Relationships," *Psychology of Women Quarterly* 27, no. 2 (2003): 162–73.

74 ***a critical step toward their recovery:*** Lammers, Ritchie, and Robertson, "Women's Experience of Emotional Abuse."

CHAPTER FIVE: INSIDE THE ECHO MINDSET

98 ***distort our perception of reality:*** Amos Tversky and Daniel Kahneman, "Judgment Under Uncertainty: Heuristics and Biases," *Science* 185, no. 4157 (1974): 1124–31.

100 ***when we experience confirmation bias:*** Raymond S. Nickerson, "Confirmation Bias: A Ubiquitous Phenomenon in Many Guises," *Review of General Psychology* 2, no. 2 (1998): 175–220.

102 ***anchoring bias involves clinging to the first piece of information:*** Amos Tversky and Daniel Kahneman, "Judgement Under Uncertainty: Heuristics and Biases," *Knowledge: Critical Concepts* 1, no. 4157 (2005): 371. Daniel Kahneman, *Thinking Fast and Slow* (Farrar, Straus and Giroux, 2011).

104 ***faces rated as more attractive:*** Edward L. Thorndike, "A Constant Error in Psychological Ratings," *Journal of Applied Psychology* 4, no. 1 (1920): 25–29, https://doi.org/10.1037/h0071663. Richard E. Nisbett and Timothy D. Wilson, "The Halo Effect: Evidence for Unconscious Alternation of Judgments," *Journal of Personality and Social Psychology* 35 no. 4 (1977): 250–56. Carlota Batres and Victor Shiramizu, "Examining the 'Attractiveness Halo Effect' Across Cultures," *Current Psychology* 42, no. 29 (2023): 25515–19.

107 ***shared reality bias:*** C. D. Hardin and E. Tory Higgins, "Shared Reality: How Social Verification Makes the Subjective Objective," in *Handbook of Motivation and Cognition*, vol. 3, *The Interpersonal Context*, ed. Richard M. Sorrentino and E. T. Higgins (Guilford, 1996).

108 ***their world becomes your world too:*** Arthur Aron and Elaine N. Aron, *Love and the Expansion of Self: Understanding Attraction and Satisfaction* (Hemisphere Publishing/Harper & Row, 1986).

108 ***our shared realities can make us vulnerable:*** E. Tory Higgins, *Shared Reality: What Makes Us Strong and Tears Us Apart* (Oxford University Press, 2019).

110 ***feel the weight of a potential loss:*** Amos Tversky and Daniel Kahneman, "Judgment Under Uncertainty: Heuristics and Biases," *Science* 185 no. 4157 (1974): 1124–31.

115 ***more genuine repair and closeness:*** Mariagrazia Di Giuseppe, John Christopher Perry, Tracy A. Prout, and Ciro Conversano, "Recent Empirical Research and Methodologies in Defense Mechanisms: Defenses as Fundamental Contributors to Adaptation," *Frontiers in Psychology* 12 (2021): 802602.

115 ***how to directly address defense mechanisms:*** Fredric N. Busch, Marie Rudden, and Theodore Shapiro, *Psychodynamic Treatment of Depression* (American Psychiatric Association Publishing, 2016).

121 ***distorted, automatic thoughts contribute to emotional distress:*** Aaron T. Beck, *Cognitive Therapy and the Emotional Disorders* (Plume, 1979).

CHAPTER SIX: ECHO REACTIONS AND OUR BODIES

127 ***when a person endures prolonged distress:*** Bessel van der Kolk, *The Body Keeps the Score: Brain, Mind, and Body in the Healing of Trauma* (Viking, 2014).

128 ***social engagement and safety, fight-or-flight, and freeze:*** Stephen W. Porges, *The Polyvagal Theory: Neurophysiological Foundations of Emotions, Attachment, Communications, and Self-Regulation, Norton Series on Interpersonal Neurobiology* (W. W. Norton, 2011).

130 ***a fourth response to threats:*** Pete Walker, *Complex PTSD: From Surviving to Thriving: A Guide and Map for Recovering from Childhood Trauma* (Azure Coyote, 2013).

131 ***he called this neuroception:*** Stephen W. Porges, "Neuroception: A Subconscious System for Detecting Threats and Safety," *Zero to Three* 24, no. 5 (May 2004): 19–24.

142 ***regulating our breath can lower the level of the stress hormone:*** Julie Corliss, "Breathing Exercises to Lower Your Blood Pressure," *Harvard Heart Letter* 9–1 (Harvard Health Publishing, 2023), https://www.health.harvard.edu/heart-health/breathing-exercises-to-lower-your-blood-pressure.

CHAPTER SEVEN: EMOTIONS ARE INNER GUIDES

152 ***emotional awareness serves as the foundation for resilience:*** Karen S. Quigley and Lisa Feldman Barrett, "Emotional Learning and Mechanisms of Intentional Psychological Change," in *Action and Development: Theory and Research Through the Lifespan,* ed. Jochen Brandtstadter and Richard M. Lerner (Sage, 1999), 435–64.

153 ***it can even be lifesaving:*** Elaine D. Eaker, Lisa M. Sullivan, Margaret Kelly-Hayes, Ralph B. D'Agostino Sr., and Emelia J. Benjamin, "Marital Status, Marital Strain, and Risk of Coronary Heart Disease or Total Mortality: the Framingham Offspring Study," *Psychosomatic Medicine* 69, no. 6 (2007): 509–13.

154 ***the inner guide that helps us make good decisions:*** Nadine Jung, Christina Wranke, Kai Hamburger, and Markus Knauff, "How Emotions Affect Logical Reasoning: Evidence from Experiments with Mood-Manipulated Participants, Spider Phobics, and People with Exam Anxiety," *Frontiers in Psychology* 5 (2014): 570.

155 ***handle situations with greater intention:*** Barbara L. Fredrickson, "What Good are Positive Emotions?" *Review of General Psychology* 2, no. 3 (1998): 300–19.

157 ***we strengthen our ability to remain steady:*** Brett Q. Ford, Phoebe Lam, Oliver P. John, and Iris B. Mauss, "The Psychological Health Benefits of Accepting Negative Emotions and Thoughts: Laboratory, Diary, and Longitudinal Evidence," *Journal of Personality and Social Psychology* 115, no. 6 (2018): 1075.

159 ***intimacy is biologically powerful:*** J. A. Coan, "Toward a Neuroscience of Attachment," in *Handbook of Attachment: Theory, Research, and Clinical Applications* 2nd ed., ed. J. Cassidy and P. R. Shaver (Guilford, 2008), 241–65.

CHAPTER TEN: FROM SELF-LOSS TO SELF-LOVE

226 ***struggle with trauma can bring about positive psychological changes:*** Richard G. Tedeschi and Lawrence G. Calhoun, "The Posttraumatic Growth Inventory: Measuring the Positive Legacy of Trauma," *Journal of Traumatic Stress* 9, no. 3 (1996): 455–72. Richard G. Tedeschi, Jane Shakespeare-Finch, and Kanako Taku, *Posttraumatic Growth: Theory, Research, and Applications* (Routledge, 2018).

226 ***individuals with traumatic experiences reported enhanced self-awareness:*** Liliana Dell'Osso, Primo Lorenzi, Benedetta Nardi, Claudia Carmassi, and Barbara Carpita, "Post Traumatic Growth (PTG) in the Frame of Traumatic Experiences," *Clinical Neuropsychiatry* 19, no. 6 (2022): 390–93.

234 ***the importance of self-awareness and self-compassion:*** Brené Brown, *Atlas of the Heart: Mapping Meaningful Connection and the Language of Human Experience* (Random House, 2021). Brown, *The Gifts of Imperfection: Let Go of Who You Think You're Supposed to Be and Embrace Who You Are* (Hazelden, 2010).